Giving Good Weight

John McPhee

GIVING GOOD WEIGHT

Farrar · Straus · Giroux

NEW YORK

DISCARD

Library of Congress Cataloging in Publication Data
McPhee, John A. Giving good weight.
CONTENTS: Giving good weight. The keel of Lake Dickey.
The pinball philosophy. The Atlantic Generating Station.
Brigade de cuisine.
I. Title. AC8.M2658 081 79-17572

The text of this book originally appeared in The New Yorker,
*and was developed with the editorial counsel
of William Shawn, Robert Bingham,
and C. P. Crow.*

For Laura

Contents

GIVING
GOOD
WEIGHT

You PEOPLE COME into the market—the Greenmarket, in the open air under the downpouring sun—and you slit the tomatoes with your fingernails. With your thumbs, you excavate the cheese. You choose your stringbeans one at a time. You pulp the nectarines and rape the sweet corn. You are something wonderful, you are—people of the city—and we, who are almost without exception strangers here, are as absorbed with you as you seem to be with the numbers on our hanging scales.

"Does every sink grow on your farm?"

"Yes, ma'am."

"It's marvellous. Absolutely every sink?"

"Some things we get from neighbors up the road."

"You don't have no avocados, do you?"

"Avocados don't grow in New York State."

"Butter beans?"

"They're a Southern crop."

"Who baked this bread?"

"My mother. A dollar twenty-five for the cinnamon. Ninety-five cents for the rye."

(3)

"I can't eat rye bread anymore. I like it very much, but it gives me a headache."

Short, born abroad, and with dark hair and quick eyes, the woman who likes rye bread comes regularly to the Brooklyn Greenmarket, at Flatbush and Atlantic. I have seen her as well at the Fifty-ninth Street Greenmarket, in Manhattan. There is abundant evidence that she likes to eat. She must have endured some spectacular hangovers from all that rye.

Farm goods are sold off trucks, vans, and pickups that come into town in the dark of the morning. The site shifts with the day of the week: Tuesdays, black Harlem; Wednesdays, Brooklyn; Fridays, Amsterdam at 102nd. There are two on Saturdays—the one at Fifty-ninth Street and Second Avenue, the other in Union Square. Certain farms are represented everywhere, others at just one or two of the markets, which have been primed by foundation funds and developed under the eye of the city. If they are something good for the urban milieu—tumbling horns of fresh plenty at the people's feet— they are an even better deal for the farmers, whose disappearance from the metropolitan borders may be slowed a bit by the many thousands of city people who flow through streets and vacant lots and crowd up six deep at the trucks to admire the peppers, fight over the corn, and gratefully fill our money aprons with fresh green city lettuce.

"How much are the tomatoes?"

"Three pounds for a dollar."

"Peaches?"

"Three pounds for a dollar twenty-five."

"Are they freestones?"

"No charge for the pits."

"How much are the tomatoes?"

"Three pounds for a dollar. It says so there on the sign."

"Venver the eggs laid?"

"Yesterday."

"Kon you eat dum raw?"

We look up from the cartons, the cashbox, the scales, to see who will eat the eggs raw. She is a good-looking big-framed young blonde.

"You bet. You can eat them raw."

"How much are the apples?"

"Three pounds for a dollar."

Three pounds, as we weigh them out, are anywhere from forty-eight to fifty-two ounces. Rich Hodgson says not to charge for an extra quarter pound. He is from Hodgson Farms, of Newburgh, New York, and I (who come from western New Jersey) have been working for him off and on for three months, summer and fall. I thought at first that I would last only a week, but there is a mesmerism in the selling, in the coins and the bills, the all-day touching of hands. I am often in charge of the peppers, and, like everyone else behind the tables by our truck, I can look at a plastic sack of them now and tell its weight.

"How much these weigh? Have I got three pounds?"

"That's maybe two and a quarter pounds you've got there."

"Weigh them, please."

"There it is. Two and a quarter pounds."

"*Very* good."

"Fantastic! Fantastic! You see that? You see that? He knew exactly how much it weighed."

I scuff a boot, take a break for a shiver in the bones. There are unsuspected heights in this game, moments that go right off the scale.

(5)

This is the Brooklyn market, in appearance the most cornucopian of all. The trucks are drawn up in a close but ample square and spill into its center the colors of the country. Greengage plums. Ruby Red onions. Yellow crookneck squash. Sweet white Spanish onions. Starking Delicious plums.

Fall pippins ("Green as grass and curl your teeth"). McIntoshes, Cortlands, Paulareds. ("Paulareds are new and are lovely apples. I'll bet they'll be in the stores in the next few years.")

Pinkish-yellow Gravensteins. Gold Star cantaloupes. Patty Pan squash.

Burpless cucumbers.

Cranberry beans.

Silver Queen corn. Sweet Sue bicolor corn, with its concise tight kernels, its well-filled tips and butts. Boston salad lettuce. Parris Island romaine lettuce. Ithaca iceberg crunchy pale lettuce. Orange tomatoes.

Cherry Bell tomatoes.

Moreton Hybrid, Jet Star, Setmore, Supersonic, Roma, Saladette tomatoes.

Campbell 38s.

Campbell 1327s.

Big Boy, Big Girl, Redpak, Ramapo, Rutgers London-broil thick-slice tomatoes.

Clean-shouldered, supple-globed Fantastic tomatoes. Celery (Imperial 44).

Hot Portugal peppers. Four-lobed Lady Bell glossy green peppers. Aconcagua frying peppers.

Parsley, carrots, collard greens.

Stuttgarter onions, mustard greens.

Dandelions.

The people, in their throngs, are the most varied we see—or

that anyone is likely to see in one place west of Suez. This intersection is the hub if not the heart of Brooklyn, where numerous streets converge, and where Fourth Avenue comes plowing into the Flatbush-Atlantic plane. It is also a nexus of the race. "Weigh these, please." "Will you please weigh these?" Greeks. Italians. Russians. Finns. Haitians. Puerto Ricans. Nubians. Muslim women in veils of shocking pink. Sunnis in total black. Women in hiking shorts, with babies in their backpacks. Young Connecticut-looking pants-suit women. Their hair hangs long and as soft as cornsilk. There are country Jamaicans, in loose dresses, bandannas tight around their heads. "Fifty cents? Yes, dahling. Come on a sweetheart, mon." There are Jews by the minyan, Jews of all persuasions —white-bearded, black-bearded, split-bearded Jews. Down off Park Slope and Cobble Hill come the neo-bohemians, out of the money and into the arts. "Will you weigh this tomato, please?" And meantime let us discuss theatre, books, environmental impacts. Maybe half the crowd are men—men in cool Haspel cords and regimental ties, men in lipstick, men with blue eyelids. Corporate-echelon pinstripe men. Their silvered hair is perfect in coif; it appears to have been audited. Easygoing old neighborhood men with their shirts hanging open in the summer heat are walking galleries of abdominal and thoracic scars—Brooklyn Jewish Hospital's bastings and tackings. (They do good work there.) A huge clock is on a tower high above us, and as dusk comes down in the autumn months the hands glow Chinese red. The stations of the hours light up like stars. The clock is on the Williamsburgh Savings Bank building, a skyscraper full of dentists. They go down at five into the Long Island Rail Road, under us. Below us, too, are all the subways of the city, in ganglion assembled.

"How much are the cabbages?"

"Forty cents a head."

"O.K. Weigh one, please."

We look around at empty storefronts, at J. Rabinowitz & Sons' SECURITY FIREPROOF STORAGE, at three gold balls (Gem Jewelers Sales), at Martin Orlofsky's Midtown Florist Nursery. Orlofsky has successfully objected to our presence as competitors here, and we can sell neither plants nor flowers. "HAVE YOU HAD ANY LATELY? CLAMS, STEAMERS." Across Fourth Avenue from the Greenmarket is the Episcopal Church of the Redeemer, a century and a quarter old, with what seem to be, even in the brightest morning light, black saints in its stained-glass windows. Far down Fourth, as if at rest on the paved horizon, stands a tower of the Verrazano-Narrows Bridge. To the northwest rises the Empire State. Not long after dawn, as trucks arrive and farmers begin to open boxes and set up wooden tables, a miscellany of whores is calling it a day—a gradual dispersal, quitting time. Their corner is Pacific and Fourth. Now and again, a big red Cadillac pauses at the curb beside them. The car's rear window is shaped like a heart. With some frequency, a squad car will slide up to the same curb—a week-in, week-out, endless duet with the Cadillac. The women hurry away. "Here come the law." The Greenmarket space, which lies between Atlantic and Pacific, was once occupied by condemned buildings— spent bars and liquor stores. The block is fenced and gravelled now, and is leased by the Brooklyn Academy of Music, which charges the Greenmarket seventy-five dollars a Wednesday. The market does not fill the lot—the rest is concession parking. Here in the din of the city, in the rivers of moving metal, some customers drive to the Greenmarket as if it were a roadside stand in Rockland County, a mall in Valley Stream.

On a sidewalk around the corner, people with a Coleman stove under a fifty-five-gallon drum are making sauce with our tomatoes. Tall black man in a business suit now picks up a slim hot pepper. Apparently he thinks it sweet, because he takes most of it with a single bite and chews it with anticipant relish. Three . . . two . . . one. The small red grenade explodes on his tongue. His eyeballs seem to smoke. By the fistful, he grabs cool stringbeans and stuffs them into his mouth.

I forget to give change to a middle-aged woman with bitter eyes. I charged her forty-five cents for a pound and a third of apples and she gave me half a dollar. Now she is demanding her nickel, and her eyes are narrower than the sides of dimes. She is a round-shouldered person, beaky and short—shortchanged. In her stare at me, there is an entire judiciary system—accusation, trial, and conviction. "You give me my nickel, mister."

"I'm sorry. I forgot. Here is your nickel."

She does not believe my mistake a mistake. She walks away in a white huff. Now she stops, turns, glowers. She moves on. Twice more, as she departs from the market, she stops, turns, and stares angrily back. I watch her all the way to the curb. She waves at the traffic and gets into a cab.

A coin will sink faster through bell peppers than it will through water. When people lose their money they go after it like splashing bears. Peppers everywhere. Peppers two deep over the apples, three deep over the plums. Peppers all over the ground. Sooner or later, the people who finger the eggs will spill and break the eggs, and the surface they walk on becomes a gray-and-yellow slurry of parking-lot gravel and egg—a Brooklyn omelette. Woman spills a dozen now. Her purse is hanging open and a falling egg plops in. Eleven smash on the ground. She makes no offer to pay. Hodgson, who is young and whimsical, grins and shrugs. He is not upset. He is authentically amused. Always, without a sign of stress, he accepts such losses. The customer fingers another dozen eggs, and asks if we are sure they are good.

I err again, making change—count out four ones, and then a five, "and ten makes twenty."

The customer says, "I gave you a ten-dollar bill, not a twenty."

I look at her softly, and say to her, "Thanks very much. You're very nice."

"What do you mean I'm very nice? I gave you a ten-dollar bill. Why does that make me very nice?"

"I meant to say I'm glad you noticed. I'm really glad you noticed."

"How much are the tomatoes?"

"Weigh these, please."

"Three pounds for a dollar."

"How much the corn?"

"Ten cents an ear. Twelve for a dollar."

"Everything is so superior. I'd forgotten what tomatoes taste like."

"Will you weigh these, please?"

"The prices are so ridiculously cheap."

"How can you charge so little?"

"In nine years in the city, I've never seen food like this."

"How much are these?"

"Fifty-five cents."

"Wow! What a rip-off!"

"Three pounds for a dollar is too much for tomatoes. You know that, don't you? I don't care how good they are."

"How much are these?"

"A dollar-ten."

"A dollar-*ten*?"

"Three eggplants. Three and a half pounds. Three pounds for a dollar. You can have them for a dollar-ten."

"Keep them."

"In the supermarket, the vegetables are unspeakable."

"They are brought in from California."

"You can't see what you are getting."

"When the frost has come and you are gone, what will we do without you?"

Around the market square, some of the trucks have stickers on them: "NO FARMERS, NO FOOD." Alvina Frey is here, and Ronald Binaghi, from farms in Bergen County, New Jersey. John Labanowski and his uncle Andy Labanowski are from the black-dirt country, the mucklands, of Orange County, New York. Bob Engle and Jim Kent tend orchards in the Hudson Valley. Bill Merriman, the honey man, is from Canaan, Connecticut; Joan Benack and Ursula Plock, the bakers, from Milan, New York. Ed and Judy Dart grow "organic" on Long Island, Richard Finch in Frenchtown, New Jersey. John Henry. Vincent Neglia. Ilija Sekulovski. Don Keller. Cleather Slade completes the ring. Slade is young, tall, paunchy, silent, and black. His wife, Dorothy, sells with him. She has a nicely lighted smile that suggests repose. Their family farmland is in Red Springs, North Carolina, but the Slades are mainly from Brooklyn. They make occasional trips South for field peas, collards, okra, yams, and for the reddest watermelons north of Chichicastenango.

Jeffrey Mack works for Hodgson part time. He has never seen a farm. He says he has never been out of the city. He lives five blocks away. He is eight years old, black. He has a taut, hard body, and glittering eyes, a round face. He piles up empty cartons for us and sometimes weighs tomatoes. On his better days he is some help.

"Jeffrey, that's enough raisin bread."

"Jeffrey, how many times do I have to tell you: get yourself out of the way."

"What are you doing here, Jeffrey? You ought to be in school."

He is not often pensive, but he is pensive for a moment now. "If you had a kid would you put him up for adoption?" he asks.

"What is that supposed to mean, Jeffrey? Why are you asking me that?"

"My mother says she's going to put me up for adoption."

With two, three, and four people working every truck, the farmers can occasionally take breaks, walk around—eat each other's apples, nectarines, and pears. Toward the end of the day, when their displays have been bought low and the crowd is becoming thin, they move around even more, and talk in small groups.

"What always surprises me is how many people are really nice here in the city."

"I was born in New York. My roots are here, you know. I'd throw away a bad cantaloupe, anything, so the people would come back."

"We have to leave them touch tomatoes, but when they do my guts go up and down. They paw them until if you stuck a pin in them they'd explode."

"They handle the fruit as if they were getting out all their aggressions. They press on the melons until their thumbs push through. I don't know why they have to handle the fruit like that. They're brutal on the fruit."

"They inspect each egg, wiggle it, make sure it's not stuck in the carton. You'd think they were buying diamonds."

"They're bag crazy. They need a bag for everything, sometimes two."

"They're nervous. So nervous."

"Today I had my third request from someone who wanted to come stay on the farm, who was looking for peace and quiet for a couple of days. He said he had found Jesus. It was unreal."

"I had two Jews in yarmulkes fighting over a head of lettuce. One called the other a kike."

"I've had people buy peppers from me and take them to another truck to check on the weight."

"Yeah, and meanwhile they put thirteen ears of corn in a bag, hand it to you, and say it's a dozen. I let them go. I only get after them when they have sixteen."

"They think we're hicks. 'Yeah,' I say. 'We're hicks and you're hookers. You're muggers and you breathe dirty air.'"

"I hardly smoke in the city. Down home I can smoke a whole pack of cigarettes and still have energy all night. You couldn't pay me to live here. I can't breathe."

If the farmers have a lot to say about their clients, they have even more to say about each other. Friendly from the skin out, they are deep competitors, and one thing that they are (in a sense) competing for is their right to be a part of the market. A high percentage of them seems to feel that a high percentage of the others should be shut down and sent away.

The Greenmarket was started in 1976. Farmers were recruited. Word got around. A wash of applicants developed. There was no practical or absolute way to check out certain facts about them—nor is there yet. For example, if some of the goods on a truck were not grown by the farmer selling them, who did grow them, and when, and where? The Green-market quickly showed itself to be a prime outlet for the retailing of farm produce. On a good day, one truck with an eighteen-foot box could gross several thousand dollars. So every imaginable kind of seller became attracted. The ever-present problem was that anyone in jeans with a rustic address painted on his truck could load up at Hunts Point, the city's wholesale fruit-and-vegetable center, and head out at 5 A.M. for the Greenmarket—a charter purpose of which was to help the regional farmer, not the fast-moving speculator, survive. Authentic farmers, moreover, could bring a little from home and a lot from Hunts Point. Wholesale goods, having been grown on big mass-production acreages (and often shipped in underripe from distant states), could be bought at Hunts Point and retailed—in some instances—at lower prices than the custom-grown produce of a small Eastern farm. Prices, however, were an incidental issue. The customers, the people of the city, believed—and were encouraged to believe—that when they walked into a Greenmarket they were surrounded by true farmers who had grown the produce they displayed and were offering it fresh from the farm. That was the purpose and promise of the Greenmarket—if not the whole idea, an unarguably large part of it—and in the instances where whole-sale, long-distance, gassed-out goods were being presented (as some inevitably were) the principle was being subverted. In fact, the term Greenmarket had been coined—and registered in Albany—to set apart these markets in the public mind from certain "farmers' markets" around the city that are annually operated by Hunts Point hicks.

"Are you a farmer, or are you buying from an auction?" was a challenge the farmers began to fling around. Few were neighbors at home—in positions to know about each other.

They lived fifty, a hundred, a hundred and fifty miles apart, and came to the city to compete as strangers. They competed in sales, and they competed in slander. They still do. To a remarkable—and generally inaccurate—extent, they regard one another as phonies.

"He doesn't even know what shoe-peg corn is."

"Never trust a farmer who doesn't know shoe-peg corn."

"What exactly is shoe-peg corn?"

"Look at *him*. He has clean fingernails."

"I happen to know he has them manicured."

"I bust my hump seven days a week all summer long and I don't like to see people bring to market things they don't grow."

"Only farmers who are not farmers can ruin this market."

"These hustlers are going to work us off the block."

"There's farmers selling stuff they don't know what it is."

"What exactly is shoe-peg corn?"

"I like coming here. It gets me out of Vineland. Of course, you pick your ass off the night before."

"Look at Don Keller's hands. You can see the farm dirt in them."

"His nails. They'll never be clean."

"Rich Hodgson. See him over there? He has the cleanest fingernails in New York State."

"That Hodgson, he's nice enough, but he doesn't know what a weed looks like. I'll tell you this: he's never even *seen* a weed."

AROUND THE BUILDINGS of Hodgson Farms are some of the tallest volunteers in New York, topheavy plants that sway

overhead—the Eastern rampant weed. With everybody working ninety hours a week, there is not much time for cosmetics.
For the most part, the buildings are chicken houses. Rich's
father, Dick Hodgson, went into the egg business in 1946 and
now has forty thousand hens. When someone in the city cooks
a Hodgson egg, it has quite recently emerged from a chicken
in a tilted cage, rolled onto a conveyor, and gone out past a
candler and through a grader and into a waiting truck. A
possible way to taste a fresher egg would be to boil the chicken
with the egg still in it.

Dick Hodgson—prematurely white-haired, drivingly busy
—is an agrarian paterfamilias whose eighty-two-year-old
mother-in-law grades tomatoes for him. His wife, Frances, is
his secretary and bookkeeper. He branched into truck farming
some years ago specifically to keep his daughter, Judy, close to
home. Judy runs the Hodgsons' roadside stand, in Plattekill,
and her husband, Jan Krol, is the family's vegetable grower,
the field boss—more than a hundred acres now under cultivation. Rich, meanwhile, went off to college and studied
horticulture, with special emphasis on the fate of tropical
houseplants. To attract him home, his father constructed a
greenhouse, where Rich now grows wandering Jews, spider
plants, impatiens, coleus, asparagus ferns—and he takes them
with him to Harlem and wherever else he is allowed to sell
them. Rich, who likes the crowds and the stir of the city, is the
farm's marketer.

The Greenmarket, even more than the arriving Hodgson
generation, has expanded Hodgson Farms. Before 1976, the
family had scarcely twenty acres under cultivation and, even
so, had difficulty finding adequate outlets for the vegetables
Jan grew. The roadside stand moved only a minor volume.

Much of the rest was sold in New Jersey, at the Paterson Market, with discouraging results. "Paterson is semi-whole-sale," Rich says. "You have to sell in units of a peck or more. You're lucky if you get three dollars for a half bushel of tomatoes. You ask for more and all you hear all day is 'That's a too much a money. That's a too much a money.'" (A half bushel of tomatoes weighs twenty-six pounds, and brings at least eight dollars at the Greenmarket, giving good weight.) The Hodgsons tried the fruit-and-vegetable auction in Milton, New York, but the auctioneer's cut was thirteen per cent and the farmers were working for him. They also tried a farmers' market in Albany, but sold three bushels of peppers and a couple of bags of corn in one depressing day. They were more or less failing as small-scale truck farmers. Dick Hodgson's theory of family cohesion through agricultural diversification was in need of an unknown spray. NBC News presented a short item one evening covering the début of the Greenmarket. The Hodgsons happened to be watching.

"The first place we went to was Fifty-ninth Street, and the people were fifteen deep waiting to get to the eggs. I couldn't believe it. There were just masses of faces. I looked at them and felt panic and broke into a cold sweat. They went after the corn so fast I just dumped it on the ground. The people fell on it, stripped it, threw the husks around. They were fighting, grabbing, snatching at anything they could get their hands on. I had never seen people that way, never seen anything like it. We sold a full truck in five hours. It was as if there was a famine going on. The people are quieter now."

Quietly, in a single day in the Greenmarket, Rich has sold as many as fifteen hundred dozen eggs. In one day, nearly five thousand ears of corn. In one day, three-quarters of a ton of tomatoes.

"How much are the tomatoes?"

"Fifteen hundred pounds for five hundred dollars."

Rich is in his mid-twenties, has a tumbling shag of bright-red hair, a beard that comes and goes. When it is gone, as now, in the high season of 1977, he retains not only a mustache but also a pair of frontburns: a couple of pelts that descend from either end of the mustache and pass quite close to his mouth on their way to his chin. He is about six feet tall and wears glasses. Their frames are pale blue. His energy is of the steady kind, and he works hard all day with an easygoing imperturbability—always bemused; always a controlled, sly smile. Rarely, he looks tired. On market days, he gets up at four, is on the Thruway by five, is setting up tables and opening cartons at seven, has a working breakfast around nine (Egg McMuffin), and, with only a short break, sells on his feet until six or seven, when he packs up to drive home, take a shower, drop into bed, and rise again at four. His companion, Melissa Mousseau, shares his schedule and sells beside him. There is no market on Mondays, so Rich works a fourteen-hour day at home. He packs cartons at the farm—cartons of cauliflowers, cartons of tomatoes—and meanders around the county collecting a load for Harlem. The truck is, say, the six-ton International with the Fruehauf fourteen-foot box—"HODGSON FARMS, NEWBURGH, N.Y., SINCE 1946." Corn goes in the nose—corn in dilapidating lath-and-wire crates that are strewn beside the fields where Jan has been bossing the pickers. The pickers are Newburgh high-school students. The fields, for the most part, are rented from the State of New York. A few years ago, the state bought Stewart Air Force

Base, outside Newburgh, with intent to lengthen the main runway and create an immense international freightport, an all-cargo jetport. The state also bought extensive farms lying off the west end of the base. Scarcely were the farmers packed up and on the road to Tampa Bay when bulldozers flattened their ancestral homes and dump trucks took off with the debris. The big freightport is still in the future, and meanwhile the milieu of the vanished farms is ghostly with upgrowing fields and clusters of shade trees around patches of smoothed ground where families centered their lives. The Hodgsons came upon this scene as farmers moving in an unusual direction. With the number of farms and farmers in steady decline in most places on the urban fringe, the Hodgsons were looking for land on which to expand. For the time being, rented land will do, but they hope that profits will be sufficient to enable them before long to buy a farm or two—to acquire land that would otherwise, in all likelihood, be industrially or residentially developed. The Greenmarket is the outlet—the sole outlet—that has encouraged their ambition. In the penumbral world of the airport land, there are occasional breaks in the sumac where long clean lines of Hodgson peppers reach to distant hedgerows, Hodgson cantaloupes, Hodgson cucumbers, Hodgson broccoli, collards, eggplants, Hodgson tomatoes, cabbages, corn—part vegetable patch, part disenfranchised farm, with a tractor, a sprayer, and a spreader housed not in sheds and barns but under big dusty maples. The family business is integrated by the spreader, which fertilizes the Greenmarket vegetables with the manure of the forty thousand chickens.

Corn in the nose, Rich drives to the icehouse, where he operates a machine that grinds up a three-hundred-pound block and sprays granulated snow all over the corn. Corn snow. He stops, too, at local orchards for apples, Seckel pears, nectarines, peaches, and plums. The Greenmarket allows farmers to amplify their offerings by bringing the produce of neighbors. A neighbor is not a wholesale market but another farmer, whose farm is reasonably near—a rule easier made than enforced. The Hodgsons pick things up—bread included —from several other farms in the county, but two-thirds to three-quarters of any day's load for the city consists of goods they grow themselves.

In the cooler of E. Borchert & Sons, the opiate aroma of peaches is overwhelming, unquenched by the refrigerant air. When the door opens, it frames, in summer heat, hazy orchards on ground that falls away to rise again in far perspective, orchards everywhere we can see. While loading half-bushel boxes onto the truck, we stop to eat a couple of peaches and half a dozen blue free plums. Not the least of the pleasures of working with Hodgson is the bounty of provender at hand, enough to have made the most sybaritic Roman prop himself up on one elbow. I eat, most days, something like a dozen plums, four apples, seven pears, six peaches, ten nectarines, six tomatoes, and a green pepper.

Eating his peach, Rich says, "The people down there in the city can't imagine this. They don't believe that peaches come from Newburgh, New York. They say that peaches come only from Georgia. People in the city have no concept of what our farming is like. They have no idea what a tomato plant looks like, or how a tomato is picked. They can't envision a place with forty thousand chickens. They have no concept how sweet corn grows. And the people around here have a false concept of the city. Before we went down there the first time, people up here said, 'You're out of your mind. You're going to get robbed. You're going to get stabbed.' But I just don't have any fears there. People in black Harlem are just as nice as people anywhere. City people generally are a lot calmer than I expected. I thought they would be loud, pushy, aggressive, and mean. But eighty per cent of them are nice and calm. Blacks and whites get along much better there than they do in Newburgh. Newburgh Free Academy, where I went to high school, was twenty-five per cent black. We had riots every year and lots of tension. Cars were set on fire. Actually, I prefer Harlem to most of the other markets. Harlem people are not so fussy. They don't manhandle the fruit. And they buy in quantity. They'll buy two dozen ears of corn, six pounds of tomatoes, and three dozen eggs. At Fifty-ninth Street, someone will buy one ear of corn for ten cents and want it in a bag. The reason we're down there is the money, of course. But the one-to-one contact with the people is really good—especially when they come back the next week and say, 'Those peaches were really delicious.' "

IN THE MOONLESS NIGHT, with the air too heavy for much sleep anyway, we are up and on the road, four abreast: Anders Thueson, Rich Hodgson, David Hemingway . . . A door handle is cracking my fifth right rib. Melissa Mousseau is not with us today, and for Hemingway it is the first time selling. He is a Newburgh teen-ager in sneakers and a red football shirt lettered "OKLAHOMA." Hemingway is marking time. He has mentioned January half a dozen ways since we started out, in a tone that reveres the word—January, an arriving milestone in his life, with a college out there waiting for him, and, by implication, the approach of stardom. Hemingway can high-jump seven feet. He remarks that the Greenmarket will require endurance and will therefore help build his stamina for January. He is black, and says he is eager to see Harlem, to be "constantly working with different people—that's a trip in the head by itself."

When the truck lurches onto the Thruway and begins the long rollout to the city, Hodgson falls asleep. Anders Thueson is driving. He is an athlete, too, with the sort of legs that make football coaches whistle softly. Thueson has small, fine features, light-blue eyes, and short-cropped hair, Scandinavian yellow. He is our corn specialist, by predilection—would apparently prefer to count ears than to compute prices from weights. When he arrives in Harlem he will touch his toes and do deep knee bends to warm himself up for the corn.

Dawn is ruddy over Tappan Zee, the far end of the great bridge indistinct in mist. Don Keller, coming from Middle-town, broke down on the bridge not long ago, rebuilt his starter at the toll-booth apron, and rolled into market at noon. Days later, Jim Kent's truck was totalled on the way to Greenmarket—Hudson Valley grapes, apples, peaches, and corn all over the road. Gradually now, Irvington and Dobbs Ferry come into view across the water—big square houses of the riverbank, molars, packed in cloud. In towns like that, where somnolence is the main resource, this is the summit of the business day. Hodgson wakes up for the toll. For five minutes he talks sports and vegetable prices, and again he dozes away. On his lap is a carton of double-yolk eggs. His hands protect them. The fingernails are clean. Hodgson obviously sees no need to dress like Piers Plowman. He wears a yellow chemise Lacoste. The eggs are for Derryck Brooks-Smith, a

Brooklyn schoolteacher, who is a regular Hodgson city employee. Brooks-Smith is by appearances our best athlete. He runs long distances and lifts significant weights. He and Thueson have repeatedly tried to see who can be the first to throw an egg over an eight-story building on Amsterdam Avenue. To date their record of failure is one hundred per cent—although each has succeeded with a peach.

We arrive at six-fifteen, to find Van Houten, Slade, and Keller already setting up—in fact, already selling. People are awake, and much around, and Dorothy Slade is weighing yams, three pounds for a dollar. Meanwhile, it is extremely difficult to erect display tables, open boxes, and pile up peppers and tomatoes when the crowd helps take off the lids. They grab the contents.

"Weigh these, please."

"May I have a plastic bag?"

"Wait—while I get the scales off the truck." The sun has yet to show above the brownstones.

This is the corner of 137th Street and Adam Clayton Powell Jr. Boulevard, known elsewhere in the city as Seventh Avenue. The entire name—Adam Clayton Powell Jr. Boulevard—is spelled out on the street sign, which, as a result, has a tip-to-tip span so wide it seems prepared to fly. The big thoroughfare itself is of extraordinary width, and islanded, like parts of Broadway and Park Avenue. A few steps north of us are the Harlem Performance Center and the Egbe Omo Nago African Music Center, and just east along 137th Street from our trucks is the Mother A.M.E. Zion Church. For the Tuesday Greenmarket, the street has been barricaded and cars sent out, an exception being an old Plymouth without tires that rests on flaking steel. On the front wall of the church is a decorous advertisement: "Marion A. Daniels & Sons, Funeral Directors." The block has four young sycamores, and contiguous buildings in every sort of shape from the neat and trim to broken-windowed houses with basements that are open like caves. On 137th Street beyond Adam Clayton Powell are two particularly handsome facing rows of brownstones, their cornices convex and dentilled, their entrances engrandeured with high, ceremonious flights of stairs. Beyond them, our view west is abruptly shut off by the City College cliffs in St. Nicholas Park—the natural wall of Harlem.

The farm trucks are parked on the sidewalks. Displays are in the street. Broad-canopied green, orange, purple, and red umbrellas shield produce from the sun. We have an awning, bolted to the truck. Anders Thueson, with a Magic Marker, is writing our prices on brown paper bags, taping them up as signs. "Is plums spelled with a 'b'?" he asks.

Hemingway tells him no.

A tall, slim woman in a straw hat says to me, "I come down here get broke every Tuesday. Weigh these eggplants, please."

"There you are. Do you want those in a bag?"

"You gave me good weight. You don't have to give me bags."

Minerva Coleman walks by, complaining. She is short and acidulous, with graying hair and quick, sardonic eyes. She wears bluejeans and a white short-sleeved sweatshirt. She has lived in this block twenty-three years. "You farmers come in too early," she says. "Why do you have to come in so early? I have to get up at four o'clock every Tuesday, and that don't make sense. I don't get paid."

Not by the Greenmarket, at any rate. Minerva works for Harlem Teams for Self-Help, an organization that is something like a Y.M.-Y.W.C.A. It is housed, in fact, in a former Y, the entrance to which is behind our truck. Minerva is Director of Economic Development. As such, she brought the Greenmarket to 137th Street—petitioned the city for it, arranged with the precinct to close off the street. While her assistants sell Harlem Teams for Self-Help shopping bags (fifteen cents), Minerva talks tomatoes with the farmers, and monitors the passing crowd. As the neighborhood kleptos come around the corner, she is quick to point them out. When a middle-aged man in a business suit appears on the scene wearing a sandwich board, she reads the message—"HARLEM TEAM FOR DESTROYING BLACK BUSINESS"—and at once goes out of her tree. "What do you mean, 'destroying black business'? Who is destroying black business? *What* is destroying black business? Get your ass off this block. Can't you see this market is good for everybody? The quality and the price against the quality and the price at the supermarket—there's no comparison."

Exit sandwich board.

"How much are the apples?"

"Three pounds for a dollar, madam."

"Are they sweet?"

"You can eat them straight or bake them in a pie."

"Give me six pounds of apples, six pounds of tomatoes, and three dozen extra-large eggs. Here the boxes from the eggs I bought last week."

Mary Hill, Lenox Avenue. Florrie Thomas, Grand Concourse. Leroy Price, Bradhurst Avenue. Les Boyd, the Polo Grounds. Ylonia Phillips, 159th Street. Selma Williamson, 141st Street. Hattie Mack, Lenox Avenue. Ten in the morning and the crowd is thick. The sun is high and hot. People are drinking from fireplugs. A white cop goes by, the radio on his buttock small and volcanic, erupting: ". . . beating her for two hours." In the upstairs windows of the houses across the street, women sit quietly smoking.

"Are these peppers hot?"

"Those little ones? Yeah. They're hot as hell."

"How do you know how hot hell is? How do you know?"

The speaker is male and middle-aged, wears a jacket and tie, and is small, compact, peppery. He continues, "How do you know how hot hell is? You been over there? I don't think you know how hot hell is."

"Fifty cents, please."

The hundreds of people add up into thousands, and more are turning the corner—every face among them black. Rarely, a white one will come along, an oddity, a floating moon. Just as a bearded person becomes unaware of his beard and feels that he looks like everyone else, you can forget for a time that your own face is white. There are no reminders from the crowd.

Middle-aged man with a woman in blue. She reaches for the roll of thin plastic bags, tugs one off, and tries to open it. The sides are stuck together and resist coming apart. She looks up helplessly, looks at me. Like everyone else on this side of the tables, I am an expert at opening plastic bags.

"These bags are terrible," I tell her, rubbing one between my thumb and fingers. When it comes open, I hand it to her.

"Why, thank you," she says. "You're nice to do that for me. I guess that is the privilege of a lady."

Her husband looks me over, and explains to her, "He's from the old school." There is a pause, some handling of fruit. Then he adds, "But the old schools are closing these days."

"They're demolished," she says. "The building's gone."

They fill their sack with peppers (Lady Bell).

The older the men are here, the more likely it is that they are wearing suits and ties. Gray fedoras. Long cigars. The younger they are, the more likely it is that they are carrying shoulder-strapped Panasonics, turned on, turned up—blaring. Fortunately, the market seems to attract a high proportion of venerable people, dressed as if for church, exchanging news and some opinion.

Among our customers are young women in laboratory smocks with small gold rings in the sides of their noses— swinging from a pierced nostril. They work in Harlem Hospital, at the end of the block, on Lenox Avenue.

Fat man stops to assess the peppers. His T-shirt says, "I SURVIVED THE BERMUDA TRIANGLE." Little boy about a foot high. His T-shirt says, "MAN'S BEST FRIEND."

Our cabbages are in full original leaf, untrimmed, each one so broad and beautiful it appears to be a carnation from the lapel of the Jolly Green Giant. They do not fit well in collapsible shopping carts, so people often ask me to strip away the wrapper leaves. I do so, and sell the cabbage, and go back to weighing peppers, making change, more peppers, more change. Now comes a twenty-dollar bill. When I go into my money apron for some ones, a five, a ten, all I come up with is cabbage.

I prefer selling peppers. When you stay in one position long enough, a proprietary sense develops—as with Thueson and the corn. Hodgson, the true proprietor, seems to enjoy selling anything—houseplants and stringbeans, squash and pears. Derryck Brooks-Smith likes eggs and tomatoes. Hemingway is an apple man. Or seems to be. It is early to tell. He is five hours into his first day, and I ask how he is getting along. Hemingway says, "These women in Harlem are driving me nuts, but the Jews in Brooklyn will be worse." Across his dark face flies a quick, sarcastic smile. "How *you* doing?" he asks me.

"Fine. I am a pepper seller who long ago missed his calling."

"You like peppers?"

"I have come to crave them. When I go home, I take a sackful with me, and slice them, and fill a big iron skillet to the gunwales—and when they're done I eat them all myself."

"Cool."

"These tomatoes come from a remote corner of Afghanistan," Derryck Brooks-Smith is saying to some hapless client. "They will send you into ecstasy." She is young and appears to believe him, but she may be in ecstasy already. Brooks-Smith is a physical masterpiece. He wears running shorts. Under a blue T-shirt, his breasts bulge. His calves and thighs are ribbed with muscle. His biceps are smooth brown loaves. His hair is short and for the most part black, here and there brindled with gray. His face is fine-featured, smile disarming. He continues about the tomatoes: "The smaller ones are from Hunza, a little country in the Himalayas. The people of Hunza attribute their longevity to these tomatoes. Yes, three pounds for a dollar. They also attribute their longevity to yogurt and a friendly family. I like your dress. It fits you well."

Brooks-Smith teaches at John Marshall Intermediate School, in Brooklyn. "A nice white name in a black neighborhood," he once remarked. He was referring to the name of the school, but he could as well have meant his own. He was born in the British West Indies. His family moved to New York in 1950, when he was ten. He has a master's degree from City University. "It is exciting for me to be up here in Harlem, among my own people," he has told me over the scale. "Many of them are from the South. They talk about Georgia, about South Carolina. They have a feeling for the farm a lot of people in the city don't have." He quotes Rimbaud to his customers. He fills up the sky for them with the "permanganate sunsets" of Henry Miller. He instructs them in nutrition. He lectures on architecture in a manner that makes them conclude correctly that he is talking about them. They bring him things. Books, mainly. Cards of salutation and farewell, anticipating his return to the school. "Peace, brother, may you always get back the true kindness you give." The message is handwritten. The card and its envelope are four feet wide. A woman in her eighties who is a Jehovah's Witness hands him a book, her purpose to immortalize his soul. She will miss him. He has always given her a little more than good weight. "I love old people," he says when she departs. "We have a lot to learn from them."

"This is where it is, man. This is where it is!" says a basketball player, shouldering through the crowd toward the eggplants and tomatoes, onions and pears. He is well on his way to three metres in height, and his friend is taller still. They wear red shorts with blue stripes and black-and-white Adidas shoes. The one who knows where it is picks up seven or eight onions, each the size of a baseball, and holds them all in one hand. He palms an eggplant and it disappears. "Man," he goes on, "since these farmers came here I don't hardly eat meat no more."

Now comes a uniformed racing cyclist—All-Sports Day at the Greenmarket. He is slender, trained, more or less thirty, and he seems to be on furlough from the Tour de France. He looks expensive in his yellow racing gloves, his green racing shoes. Partly walking, partly gliding, he straddles his machine. He leans over and carefully chooses peppers, apparently preferring the fire-engine-red ones. Brooks-Smith whispers to me, "That bicycle frame is a Carlton, made in England. It's worth at least five hundred dollars. They're rare. They're not made much anymore."

"That will be one dollar, please," I say to the cyclist, and he pays me with a food stamp.

Woman says, "What is this stuff on these peaches?"

"It's called fuzz."

"It was on your peaches last week, too."

"We don't take it off. When you buy peaches in the store, the fuzz has been rubbed off."

"Well, I never."

"You never saw peach fuzz before? You're kidding."

"I don't like that fuzz. It makes me itchy. How much are the tomatoes?"

"Three pounds for a dollar."

"Give me three pounds. Tomatoes don't have fuzz."

"I'm a bachelor. Give me a pound of plums." The man is tall, is wearing a brown suit, and appears to be nearing seventy. "They're only for me, I don't need more," he explains. "I'm a bachelor. I don't like the word 'bachelor.' I'm really a widower. A bachelor sounds like a playboy."

"Thirty-five cents, please. Who's next?"

"Will somebody lend me a dollar so I can get some brandy and act like a civilized human for a change?" We see very few drunks. This one wears plaid trousers, a green blazer, an open-collared print shirt. He has not so much as feigned interest in the peppers but is asking directly for money. "This is my birthday," he continues. "Happy birthday, Gus. My mother and father are dead. If they were alive, I'd kick the hell out of them. They got me into this bag. For twenty years, I shined shoes outside the Empire State Building. And now I'm here, a bum. I need to borrow a dollar. Happy birthday, Gus."

SLADE, OPPOSITE, is taking a break. He sits on an upturned tall narrow basket, with his head curled into his shoulder. Like a sleeping bird, he has drifted away. I need a break, too—some relief from the computations, the chaotic pulsations of the needle on the scale.

"Two and a quarter pounds at three pounds for a dollar comes to, let's see, seventy-five cents. Five and a half pounds at three for a dollar twenty-five, call it two and a quarter. That's three dollars."

"Even?"

"Even."

"Y'all going up every week. Y'all going to be richer than hell."

"How much are the nectarines?"

"Weigh these, please."

Turn. Put the fruit in the pan. Calculate. Turn again. Spin the plastic bag. Knot the top. Hand it over. Change a bill.

"You take food stamps?"

"Yes, but I can't give you change."

"How much are the green beans pounds for a dollar and with you in a minute next one—please."

I take off my money apron, give it to Rich, and drift around the market. I compare prices with the Van Houtens. I talk cows with Joe Hlatky. We are from the same part of New Jersey, and he once worked for the Walker-Gordon dairy, in Plainsboro, with its Rotolactor merry-go-round milking platform. Hlatky is a big, stolid man with a shock of blond hair not as neatly prepared as his wife's, which has been professionally reorganized as a gold hive. They work together, selling their sweet white corn and crimson tomatoes—not for nothing is it called the Garden State. Hlatky's twenty-one-year-old daughter, Juanita, often sells with him, too. She is a large-boned, strongly built, large-busted blonde like her mother. Hlatky says that he and his family are comfortable here in Harlem, feeling always, among other things, the appreciative good will of the people. I remember Minerva Coleman telling me that when the farmers came into Harlem the first Tuesday they were "a little nervous—but after that they were O.K." She went on to say, "You can tell when people don't feel quite secure. But now they come in here and go about their business and they don't pay nobody no mind. They like the people here better than anywhere else. I don't know why. I would assume they'd get ripped off a little bit—but not too much." And now Hlatky, standing on 137th Street weighing tomatoes, says again how much he likes this market, and adds that he feels safer here than he does in other parts of the city. He says, "I'll tell you the most dangerous place we sell at. The roughest part of the city we go to is Union Square." So rough, he confides, that when he goes there, on Saturdays, he takes along an iron pipe.

Hlatky today has supplemented his homegrown New Jersey vegetables with peaches from a neighbor in California. They are wrapped in individual tissues. They are packed and presented in a fine wooden box. He bought them at a wholesale market. Robert Lewis, assistant director of the Greenmarket, happens along and sees the peaches. Lewis is a regional planner about to receive an advanced degree from the University of Pennsylvania, a gentle person, slight of build, a little round of shoulder, with a bandanna around his throat, a daypack on his back, steel-rimmed spectacles—all of which contribute to an impression of amiable, academic frailty. He says to big Joe Hlatky, "Get those peaches out of sight!"

With an iron pipe, a single tap on the forehead could send Lewis to heaven twice. Hlatky respects him, though, and is grateful to him, too, for the existence of the market. Hlatky says he will sell off these peaches, with a promise not to bring more—never again to bring to a Greenmarket so much as a single box of wholesale fruit.

"The peaches are from California," says Lewis. "They must go back on the truck."

Hlatky casts aspersions up one side of 137th Street and down the other. Has Lewis noticed Slade's beans, Hodgson's onions, Van Houten's lettuce, Sekulovski's entire load? He says he feels unfairly singled out. He knows, though, that without Lewis and Barry Benepe, who created and developed the Greenmarket, the Hlatky farm in New Jersey would be even more marginal than it is now. ("Here you can make double what you make wholesale. If I sold my stuff in a wholesale market, I couldn't begin to exist.") And while Lewis and Benepe might lack a certain shrewdness with regard to the origin of beans, they contribute an essential that no farmer could provide: a sophisticated knowledge of the city.

One does not just drive across a bridge with a load of summer squash, look around for a vacant lot, and create a farmers' market in New York. Tape of every color is in the way:

(3 3)

community boards, zoning committees, local merchants, City Hall. In order to set up even one open-air market—not to mention five or six—it was necessary to persuade, and in many cases to struggle against, nine city agencies, which Benepe describes in aggregate as "an octopus without a head; pull off one tentacle and another has a grip." Benepe is an architect who has worked as a planner not only for the city government but also in Orange County, watching the orchards disappear. When he conceived of the Greenmarket, in 1974, it seemed "a natural answer to a twofold problem": loss of farmland in the metropolitan area and a lack of "fresh, decent food" in the city. Moreover, farmers selling produce from their trucks would start conversations, help resuscitate neighborhoods, brighten the aesthetic of the troubled town. "It seemed too obvious to ignore," Benepe says. "But most obvious things do get ignored." Benepe, like Lewis, is a native of the city. Son of an importer of linen, he studied art history at Williams College (1950) and went on to M.I.T. His dress and appearance remain youthful. To the Greenmarket office, on Fortieth Street, he wears brown denim highwaters, polo shirts, and suède Wallabees. He has long sandy graying hair, a lithe frame, a flat stomach. He rides a bicycle around town. He has a steady gaze, pale-blue eyes. He knows where City Hall is. He once worked for the Housing and Redevelopment Board. To start the Greenmarket, he knew which doors to knock on, and why they would not open. He approached the Real Estate Department. "They seemed to think I wanted to rip them off." He affiliated the project with the Council on the Environment of New York City in order to be eligible to receive foundation funds. He tried the Vinmont Foundation, the Richmond Foundation, the Fund for the City of New York, the America the Beautiful Fund. Finally, the J. M. Kaplan Fund said it would match anything he raised elsewhere. He went back to the others, and enough came through. Of the Greenmarket's overall cost—forty-two thousand dollars in 1977—the farmers, renting space, pay a third.

Lewis, twenty years younger, was a colleague of Benepe in Benepe's urban-planning firm, and helped him start the market. They searched for sites where farmers would be welcome, where neighborhoods would be particularly benefitted, where local fruit-and-vegetable stores were unlikely to open fire. Lewis to a large extent recruited the farmers. He sought advice from Cornell and Rutgers, and wrote to county agents, and interviewed people whose names the agents supplied. He went to roadside-marketing conferences, to farmers' associations, to wholesale outlets. Under his generally disarranged locks, his undefeated shrug, Lewis has a deep and patient intelligence that tends to linger over any matter or problem that comes within its scrutiny. If he is ready to rebuke the farmers (for selling West Coast peaches), he is also ready to listen, without limit, to their numerous problems and even more numerous complaints. Day by day, market to market, he is a most evident link between the farmers and the city. He binds them to it, interprets it for them. Son of a New York University professor, he has no idea what shoe-peg corn is, but he was born in Brooklyn Jewish Hospital, grew up in Crown Heights, and has a sense of neighborhoods, of urban ways, that reaches from Flatbush to the hem of Yonkers. He is not much frightened by Harlem or intimidated by Fifty-ninth Street. He is a city man, and, more important, he is an emeritus city kid.

After staring up the street for a while, Hlatky puts the peaches back on the truck.

"Cigarette lighters! Cigarette lighters!"

The Zippo man did not grow his produce down home. "Cigarette lighters!" Never mind where they're from. They're fifty per cent off and selling fast. While Lewis goes after the Zippo man—effecting an at best temporary expulsion—I return to my peppers.

"Give me two, please. Just two. I ain't got nobody with me. I live by myself. I throw food in the pot. I stick a fork in it. When it gets soft, I eat it."

"Lysol! Lysol!"

A man has come along selling Lysol. He offers cans to Rich Hodgson and, at the same time, to a woman to whom Rich is selling apples. One result of the Greenmarket's considerable success is the attraction it presents to street hucksters, not the Sabrett's-hot-dog sort of street venders, who are licensed by the city, but itinerant merchants of the most mercurial kind. Some conceal things under their jackets. They are readily identifiable because their arms hang straight, as whose would not with five pounds of watches on either wrist? They sell anything—ski hats, tooled-leather belts, turquoise rings, inflatable airplanes. They spread blankets on the sidewalk and sprinkle them with jewelry. Man comes by now selling his dog. They always try to sell to the farmers, who are possibly better customers than the customers. A guy came up to me once in Brooklyn and offered me a case of hot mangoes. I assume they were hot. What other temperature could they be when the case-lot price was two dollars? Another day in Brooklyn, a man pulled up to the curb in an old Chevrolet sedan, opened the trunk, and began selling Finnish porgies. Cleaning them, he spilled their innards into a bucket and their scales fell like snow on the street.

As to nowhere else, though, such people are attracted to

137th Street. All day they come by, selling coconuts, guavas, and terminal-market cucumbers out of carts from the A. & P. "Crabs! Crabs!" The crab man has bright-red boiled blue crabs. Three for a dollar, they dangle from strings. Now a man arrives with a rolling clothes rack crammed with sweaters and pants. He wants eighteen dollars for a two-piece ensemble. "No, thanks," a woman tells him. "I don't want to go to jail." She turns to the peppers and glances up at me, saying, "If a cop came around the corner they'd drop that stuff and run." Now a young man and woman in turtlenecks and Earth shoes wheel up a grocery cart full of comic books, cotton hats, incense, and tube socks. He has a premature paunch. Her eyes are dreamy and the lids are slow. She leans on him in a noodly manner. She looks half asleep, while he looks half awake, as if they were passing each other in the middle of a long journey. "Tube socks! Incense! Tube socks!" The man fixes his attention on Rich. "It's going to get—I'm telling you—*cold* on that farm, man." The socks are still in the manufacturer's package, marked a dollar ninety-five a pair. "Cold, man, I'm telling you. Here's six pairs for five dollars." Sold.

Minerva Coleman, who has been watching, stares after the couple as they go. "That must have been a Long Island girl," she says. "A Harlem girl would know I'd break her ass."

There was a firehouse across the street once. It was razed, and a vest-pocket park is there now, smoothly paved, with a chain-link fence, three strands of barbed wire, and a fan-shaped basketball backboard that (most weeks) has a net. When I am not turned toward the scale, and while I wait for customers to fill their plastic bags, I often watch the games across the street. Some of the boys who play there move like light, their gestures rehearsed, adroit. They go both ways, hit well from the outside. The game they play, almost to the exclusion of any other game, begins from the outside.

Say five, in all, are playing. One starts things off with a set from outside.

"How much are the peppers?"

"Three pounds for a dollar."

"Pick me out three pounds. I'll be back after I get some corn."

"Where are your beans? What happened to your beans today?"

The shooter hits five straight from twenty feet. He is a pure shooter. Now he misses. He and the four others go for the rebound. The one who gets the ball is now on his own to try to score, while everyone else tries to stop him. He dribbles right, into the one-on-four. He stops. Jumps. Shoots. Misses.

"Weigh these, please."

"Weigh mine, please."

Another player grabs the ball. Now *he* makes his moves, trying to score against the four others. The ball pulsates in his hands. His legs are flexed. His feet do not stir. He picks his moment, leaps, arches his back (ball behind his head), scores. The ball is handed to him. He goes outside and shoots an unguarded set. He hits. He shoots another. He misses. Someone else gets the rebound. Now it is four against *that* player as he tries to drive and score. He misses. The player who gets the rebound now faces the four others. . . .

"Mister, will you weigh these peppers? Do you want to sell them to me or not?"

"Sorry. Three and a half pounds. Take them for a dollar."

Who wants to make change?

After a reverse pivot that is fluid beyond his years, the kid with the ball scores. He walks to the outside. He takes a free set. Swish. He hits again.

"Weigh these, please."

The shooter misses. The rebound goes high. All five are after it. The boy who grabs it turns and faces the mob.

We see the same game all over the city. Always, the player with the ball is alone, the isolated shooter, the incubating star —versus everyone else on the court. There is never a pass, a screen, a pick, a roll, a two-on-two, a two-on-three, a three-on-two, a teammate. I turn with some peppers and rattle the scale.

Bartley Bryt comes by and says a cop caught a thief who was ripping off Sekulovski. Bryt is young and white, in blue-jeans, Pumas, and a rugger shirt. He is doing a summer job, helping administer the market. He is slim, good-looking, with a shock of light-brown hair—Dalton School, 1977.

I ask him how old the thief was.

"About forty-five," says Bryt. "The only elderly person I've ever seen stealing here. When there's trouble here, it's usually from kids, but there's not much trouble, because the community feeling is so great here. People are so nice to you. Where I live, people go in and turn on their air-conditioners and that's it."

"Where do you live?"

"Seventy-fifth Street between Park and Lexington."

"HOW MUCH ARE THE CUCUMBERS?"

"Eight for a dollar."

"Give me some ham knuckles, too."

(39)

"No ham knuckles."

"I was here earlier and there was ham knuckles here."

"Not at this truck, ham knuckles."

"Bobby Van Houten has ham knuckles."

"Yeah. He's killing us."

"Look at all those people at his truck. They're ten deep."

"He'll gross five thousand dollars today if he takes home a cent."

"He buys the stuff at a slaughterhouse."

"I'd like to see those pigs he talks about."

"If he raises pigs, I raise bananas."

The Van Houtens, next to us, are working from a truck with an eighteen-foot box. There is no larger vehicle here. To secure their choice position—on the corner, at the mouth of the street—they arrived at four in the morning on the first Harlem Tuesday. Wherever you are at the start, you remain for the summer. The Van Houtens are nothing if not aggressive. With their high-piled fruit-and-vegetable displays and sixteen hundred pounds of ham hocks, hog jowls, and additional pig products coming out of a cooler on the truck, they are frenetically busy. Of the five people working there, four are named Van Houten. Like the Hodgsons', their operation is a family conglomerate. Behind the peaches and peppers is Jim Van Houten, stocky, cheerful, nervous, with a big lick of dark brown hair shading a round, thoughtful face. He is a Master of Business Administration (Cornell University). His wife, Sue Ellen, is close to the cabbage. She brings paperbacks for lulls in the glut. Kay Van Houten, Jim's mother, is dark-haired, trim, youthful, and small. Tomatoes, peppers, jowls alike, she works tirelessly at the scales, the all-day conversion of weight to cash, which she accumulates in a steel box in the cab of the truck. Her other son, Bobby, while selling at least as much as anyone else, periodically leaps onto the truck, lights his pipe, heaves out produce, jumps off the truck, builds and rebuilds high displays, lights his pipe, and moves up and down behind the tables exhorting, encouraging, assisting, scolding, spreading the contagion that seems to impel him, his need to get the best of the bazaar. Bobby has pale-blue eyes. He has patrician high cheekbones, turn-of-the-century sideburns, the heroic good looks of an archaic star. He is obviously the boss—the field boss, anyway, his father being the corporate mastermind, the absentee trucklord.

"They have a big place out in Pennsylvania."

"They *say* they have a big place out in Pennsylvania."

"Yeah. I happen to know they run a fruit stand in Rockland County."

"They buy their stuff wholesale and bring it from the stand."

"Bobby is a truck driver, not a farmer. He makes long hauls in big rigs."

"I seen him at Hunts Point."

"Look at the stuff on their truck—all those brand-new cartons of Lake Ontario celery."

"They got lettuce from upstate, too."

"Florida cabbages."

"Long Island potatoes."

"Pennsylvania my ass."

"You know the name of their place? It's called Van Houten's Hunts Point Farms."

The Van Houtens last year spent ten thousand dollars on seeds. Their place—near Orangeville, Pennsylvania—is on a tributary of the Susquehanna River, about a hundred and fifty miles west of New York. They rent a couple of hundred neighboring acres as well, so they have about five hundred under cultivation. They work not just busily but feverishly—from dawn some distance into dark—with little time and probably less inclination to contemplate the scenery they are helping to preserve. Their farm is among the intervales where the Poconos and the Alleghenies reach toward one another in the central Appalachian uplift. Their terrain is like rising bread against backdrops of long, low mountains. These Pennsylvania ridges, steep-sided and flat-topped, run on for tens and even hundreds of miles. Knob Mountain, the nearest to the Van Houtens, stands high above the farm, its slopes mainly wooded but open, too, with fairways of upland pasture. There are red covered bridges, nut-colored unpainted barns, narrow crown roads among corn shocks in the autumn—pheasant land. It is a strangely mottled country, where, not many miles to the east, you can make your way in brilliant sunshine across long vistas of standing grain—pastures full of Guernseys, barns full of milk—all the while approaching a high plateau on which there is stationary cloud. When you go up there and out of the warm countryside you enter a spitting fog and before long come into the slippery streets of a small corroding city where atmospheric acids are eating the J. C. Penney and the town common is a huge anthracitic pit. Not much seems to link these plateau towns with the needlepoint-sampler valleys that surround them—not much except, perhaps, the pheasant. The bird is curious and goes up there, too—pecks at the edges of the pit. On a coal-town street, I killed one with my car one day when I went out with Bob Lewis to visit the Van Houtens. The right front fender broke its neck and little else. I tossed it into the back seat and dressed it later at home, expecting pea coal to come out of its gizzard but discovering instead the pebbles of the valley. Stuffed with bread, raisins, and Greenmarket onions, it was as succulent a bird as ever climbed a hill.

The Van Houtens' packinghouse is a white barn in a state of picturesque dilapidation. The farmhouse is brick, square, solid, and Dutch, with a windowed cupola at the apex of a pyramidal roof. It is surrounded by heavy oaks and maples, and a hundred acres of field corn are visible from the kitchen. Bobby's parents have a place nearby, while he lives in the farmhouse with his wife, Anne, who is a schoolteacher, and their four young children, including twins. He was wearing the same threadbare jeans and faded denim shirt he wears in New York, his belt buckle roughly a pound of steel, on which raised letters said "FIELD BOSS." We cruised in his pickup, climbed steep roadless hills, and crossed bottomlands crowded with cabbage—savoy cabbage, with its spinachlike cobbled leaves. Cucumbers, broccoli, collards, cauliflower, cantaloupes, eggplant, peppers, lettuce—Van Houten's "Hunts Point" Farms. "Yeah," said Bobby. "The good Lord made twenty-four hours in a day and seven days in a week, and we work every bit of it. We spray with parathion. We spend forty thousand a year for fertilizer and chemicals, and another two thousand for the chopper that spreads the chemicals. Parathion is deadly, but in three days it's dissipated. It will never take the place of DDT. It's not as safe, either. You can drink DDT straight. It won't hurt you. During the war, Italian prisoners were sprayed with DDT. No one ever died from it. The government hurt us bad when they took away the DDT."

There was a stock pond and a fenced-in woodlot, with pigs and cows among the hemlocks, cherries, and pines. Pigs were squealing and fighting for position around an Agway feeder. We leaned on the fence and watched. "Field-corn prices are dropping every week, and the futures are worse," said Bobby, with a suck and a puff and a dash of flame. He uses a steel cylindrical lighter that shoots a foot-long tongue of gas. "So right now it pays to put the field corn through the pigs. If the price goes up, it won't pay. Pigs go well behind cows. They run together. Pigs will eat what the cows won't eat. A third of corn goes through a cow. Pigs thrive on that stuff." Burlap bags soaked in crankcase oil were wrapped around the trunks of trees. After the pigs rub up against the trees the oil that coats them discourages lice. In a lean-to deep in the woodlot rested a pig three times the size of any of the other pigs. "The truck must have missed that one," Bobby said. "And more than once. Some of them hide in the woods when the truck comes. We have up to a hundred and fifty here at any one time. We send off about twenty a week. The slaughterhouse gives us extra jowls and knuckles for the New York market. No one around here eats that stuff. You'd be surprised what they do eat, though. When the testicles are sliced off, the more farmer farmers take them in and cook them. I throw them away." Standing nearby was a Mercedes-Benz diesel fifty-ton refrigeration unit, keeping cool the knuckles, jowls, spareribs, sausage, baloney, and smoked neck bones that within a few hours would be transferred to the truck for Harlem.

Van Houten Farms is a heavy supplier for Mrs. Smith's Pies, of Pottstown, Pennsylvania, where Mrs. Smith bakes ten thousand pumpkin pies an hour and uses Van Houten Boston marrow squash. They are grown by the no-till method. Just plant the seeds and let the field go—sixty-five acres, two thousand tons of squash, big orange bombs hidden under thatches of weed.

"Did you ever see ketchup *before* it went into a bottle?" Bobby said, turning into a field of tomatoes grown for the kitchens of Chef Boy-ar-dee. They appeared to have been harvested by migrant sauropods who had ripped whole vines from the soil and thrashed the tomatoes free. Hundreds of thousands—crushed and split—were now ready for delivery. On arrival at the plant they would be unloaded with a high-pressure hose—tomato slurry. We went up on a dome of channery shale, hundreds of feet above the surrounding terrain, where tomatoes grew wider than the spread of a man's hand, almost to the size of curling stones. The ground was so steep that, to hold the soil, rows of hay and sod were interspersed with the vines. While the low-ground tomatoes were on the way to Boy-ar-dee, these would be rolling toward Harlem.

The Van Houtens sell to Boy-ar-dee for three cents a pound. The tomatoes they take to Harlem return ten times that. They sell tomatoes at Hunts Point, too—for less than half of what they get in the Greenmarket. "Lots of times we don't make money selling wholesale. When corn goes at Hunts Point for two-seventy-five a box, there's nothing left for us." From big canneries to city sidewalks, they sell at every type of outlet. They have to—to dispense their considerable production. And, as one would imagine, their roadside stand is not a card table. Rather, it is a fair-sized store. It is close to the New York-New Jersey line, less than twenty miles north of the George Washington Bridge. "It attracts the carriage trade," Bobby said. "Cadillacs, Lincolns, Jaguars. We pay a hundred and seventy dollars a week in taxes there, and the customers are bitches. One Tuesday in Harlem, we had six salespeople working the counter. *Each* of the six grossed as much as the roadside stand for that day—and four people were working the stand. I'd rather wait on those people in Harlem anyway.

I'd rather wait on them for ten hours than on our affluent trade at the stand for ten minutes. If I had my choice I'd take a market every day solid black. Second choice I'd take the Spanish, last of all the whites. They're a solid pain in the ass. They ask if something has sodium nitrite. Well, to preserve something, the only alternative is embalming fluid. Some woman gets out of a Lincoln Continental and peels back an ear of corn. 'Oooo, a worm!' she says. 'Do you use chemicals on this corn?' And I say, 'Lady, you can't have it both ways.' The people in Harlem appreciate our being there. We sell cabbage three heads for a dollar there. Three heads for a dollar is a good deal for those people and a good deal for us. They rarely complain. They tell you how nice the tomatoes are, how nice the sweet corn is. It gives you a nice feeling at the end of the day."

The Van Houtens are, as Bobby says it, "Blauvelt Holland Dutch," yielding only twenty years' seniority to Henry Hudson himself. Gerrit Hendricksen Blauvelt was their seminal patroon. His sons were part of a syndicate that bought the Tappan Patent, west of the Tappan Zee. "Oh, yeah, we're S.A.R., C.A.R., D.A.R. Both my mother and father are Blauvelts. I'm Blauvelts fourteen ways. The Van Houtens didn't come over until 1670. The house I grew up in was built in 1731." The original address was Muddy Brook, New York, a name that was changed a century ago—in an early example of suburban semantics—to Pearl River.

When Bobby was growing up, the family ran a dairy farm in Pearl River that is now three fathoms deep—a reservoir owned by the Hackensack Water Company. In 1953, when he was in kindergarten, he and Jim put up a table beside the road and sold vegetables from the family garden. With the money they took in, they bought their first TV. They planted a larger garden the next year, and bought an automatic washing machine for their mother. Four years later, they built the present stand. In the late sixties came the reservoir. "Dad and I were not going to be storekeepers. We didn't want to grow things on a few acres for window dressing and bring in all the rest—like most roadside stands." From Albany to Delaware, they searched for a farm, and, answering an ad, found the one in Pennsylvania. In the big woodlot where the pigs now hide were thirty-eight oaks, each with a girth of eight to ten feet, and coveted by cabinetmakers. These oaks were older than the nation—O.A.R. Fortunately, the previous farmer had repeatedly refused to sell them. As a result, the farm was in a position to make a payment on itself. The Van Houtens sold the trees.

Bobby, out of Pearl River High School, did not go on to college. "What could it teach me?" His extraordinarily integrated knowledge of what was coming to be called agribusiness would develop empirically on the farm, and his passion for the driving of behemoth trucks would develop on the road. Twenty-six hours here, thirty-three there, he often takes field corn from Orangeville to sell to cattlemen in Florida, and something in him lives for those journeys. "I know every route number going to and around the South, and that's worth something. It may not be worth much, but it's worth as much as Greek mythology." Once, in a big tandem-axle twin-screw sleeper-cab tractor-trailer, he started alone out of Vero Beach with twenty-five tons of Indian River oranges, and thirty-six hours and no pills later he delivered the fruit in Toronto. The air there was twenty below zero and he was still in his Florida shirtsleeves. He had supported his stamina with "sixteen gallons of coffee." He feels sheer contempt toward all the young drivers on pills.

Hanging around Hunts Point over the years, Bobby developed considerable admiration for the savoir-faire of a certain broker there. He once observed him taking on a buyer to whom he had sold rotting peppers. There had been a layer of good ones on the top. Now the buyer was back in a rage, and the broker was rising to the situation. Speaking with disarming and convincing candor, he succeeded in calming the man down. Then he sold him another load of peppers. As these, too, went out of the terminal, they were split and seamy but covered with a healthy green-pepper veneer. Bobby said, "You're crazy. You're really crazy. That guy will kill you."

"Bobby, you don't understand," said the broker. "Think about it. And tell me a better way to get that man back here tomorrow."

"Yeah, this is some business," Bobby said, finishing the story. "We have friends in New Jersey, and they hope we'll have a cyclone, or a flood. We hope they'll have a hurricane. Things like that drive the prices up for the lucky ones. Every year has its own difficulties. In 1972, we had a dry, dry summer. We irrigate from two creeks, and they were running very low. We took a bulldozer and dammed both of them—ended them right here. People downstream all said it was the driest year they'd ever seen."

We went into the farmhouse for dinner with Bobby's wife, Anne, and his father, James, who has the air of a contented President retired on a farm in Pennsylvania—a big man with a baby's grin, a tan scalp, protruding ears, a swift staccato manner of speech. Like Hodgson *père*, though, he runs the place, prepares the trucks for Bobby's trips to town. "Your market there in Harlem, now, your colored want a good heavy yellow corn," he observed, and went on to say that among the various outlets for their produce the Greenmarket, by a wide margin, is in every way the best. Anne set turkey before us and gravy, stuffing, and single tomato slices that overlapped their plates. "It's too good to be true," she said. "The Greenmarket is too good to be true." Before sitting down herself, she added a buttery-crusted peach pie that was above two inches thick. "Something will spoil it," she went on. "I know it will. It's just too good to be true."

"It's a land of plenty," Bobby said.

"It's a land of too much," said his father.

Monday evenings Bobby is loaded and away by nine. Over the mountains and through the Water Gap he runs four hours to Pearl River, where he sleeps two hours in the cab. Jim, who lives nearby, meets him at three, and they unload produce for the stand. Then they load on onions, potatoes, fruit—the things they will sell in the city that they don't grow on the farm. By four-thirty, Bobby is away for Harlem. By six he is selling hard. Now, in the afternoon, he is still unflaggingly at it—displays descending, his mother and brother beside him, scales rocking gently like boats.

Bartley Bryt brings us the news. Like the rest of us, the Van Houtens keep their cab doors locked, but this afternoon for a short time someone forgot. The door (it was not the outside one but the door on *their* side of the truck) was left unlocked for perhaps fifteen minutes. We are watched more closely than we think, for in that brief lapse someone, somehow—coming possibly from under the truck—reached into the cab and took the steel box there, which contained upward of two thousand dollars. Without detectable changes of expression, the family continues to sell.

BROOKLYN, and the pickpocket in the burgundy jacket appears just before noon. Melissa Mousseau recognizes him much as if he were an old customer and points him out to Bob Lewis, who follows him from truck to truck. Aware of Lewis, he leaves the market. By two, he will have made another run. A woman with deep-auburn hair and pale, nervous hands clumsily attracts the attention of a customer whose large white purse she is rifling. Until a moment ago, the customer was occupied with the choosing of apples and peppers, but now she shouts out, "Hey, what are you doing? Your hand is in my purse. What are you doing?" The auburn-haired woman not only has her hand in the purse but most of her arm as well. She withdraws it, and with intense absorption begins to finger the peppers. "How much are the peppers? Mister, give me some of these!" she says, looking up at me with a gypsy's dark, starburst eyes. "Three pounds for a dollar," I tell her, with a swift glance around for Lewis or a cop. When I look back, the pickpocket is gone. Other faces have filled in—people unconcernedly examining the fruit. The woman with the white purse has returned her attention to the apples. She merely seems annoyed. Lewis once sent word around from truck to truck that we should regularly announce in loud voices that pickpockets were present in the market, but none of the farmers complied. Hodgson shrugged and said, "Why distract the customers?" Possibly Fifty-ninth Street is the New York Pickpocket Academy. Half a dozen scores have been made there in a day. I once looked up and saw a well-dressed gentleman under a gray fedora being kicked and kicked again by a man in a green polo shirt. He kicked him in the calves. He kicked him in the thighs. He kicked him in the gluteal bulge. He kicked him from the middle of the market out to the edge, and he kicked him into the street. "Get your ass out of here!" shouted the booter, redundantly. Turning back toward the market, he addressed the curious. "Pickpocket," he explained. The dip did not press charges.

People switch shopping carts from time to time. They make off with a loaded one and leave an empty cart behind. Crime on such levels is a part of the background here, something in the urban air, so many parts per million. The condition is accepted with a resignation that approaches nonchalance. The Van Houtens' loss was extraordinary but theirs was by no means the only cash box that has been stolen. We lost one once in Brooklyn, with something like two hundred dollars. For various reasons, suspicion immediately attached itself to a part-time employee who was selling with us and probably handed the box in a bag to a confederate. The previous Wednesday, he had been working for another farmer, who discharged him for dishonesty. Now, just after our cash box disappeared, he began saying, and repeating, in an excited voice, "It's real, man. It's real. We don't like it but that's reality—reality, man—and there is nothing we can do." Rich felt there *was* something he could do. He said, "You're fired."

Politely, the man inquired if he could know the reason for his dismissal.

"Sure," Rich said. "I don't trust you."

"That's cool, man, cool," said our ex-employee. He took off his apron and was gone.

Most thievery is petty and is on the other side of the tables. As Rich describes it, "Brooklyn, Fifty-ninth Street, people rip off stuff everywhere. You just expect it. An old man comes along and puts a dozen eggs in a bag. Women choosing peaches steal one for every one they buy—a peach for me, a peach for you. What can you do? You stand there and watch. When they take too many, you complain. I watched a guy one day taking nectarines. He would put one in a plastic bag, then one in a pocket, then one in a pile on the ground. After he did that half a dozen times, he had me weigh the bag."

"This isn't England," Barry Benepe informed us once, "and a lot of people are pretty dishonest."

Now, in Brooklyn, a heavyset woman well past the middle of life is sobbing pitifully, flailing her arms in despair. She is sitting on a bench in the middle of the market. She is wearing a print dress, a wide-brimmed straw hat. Between sobs, she presents in a heavy Russian accent the reason for her distress. She was buying green beans from Don Keller, and when she was about to pay him she discovered that someone had opened her handbag—even while it was on her arm, she said—and had removed several books of food stamps, a telephone bill, and eighty dollars in cash. Lewis, in his daypack, stands over her and tells her he is sorry. He says, "This sort of thing will happen wherever there's a crowd."

Another customer breaks in to scold Lewis, saying, "This is the biggest rip-off place in Brooklyn. Two of my friends were pickpocketed here last week and I had to give them carfare home."

Lewis puts a hand on his forehead and, after a pensive moment, says, "That was very kind of you."

The Russian woman is shrieking now. Lewis attends her

like a working dentist. "It's all right. It will be O.K. It may not be as bad as you think." He remarks that he would call the police if he thought there was something they could do.

Jeffrey Mack, eight years old, has been listening to all this, and he now says, "I see a cop."

Jeffrey has an eye for cops that no one else seems to share. (A squad car came here for him one morning and took him off to face a truant officer. Seeing his fright, a Pacific Street prostitute got into the car and rode with him.)

"Where, Jeffrey?"

"There." Jeffrey lifts an arm and points.

"Where?"

"There." He points again—at trucks, farmers, a falafel man.

"I don't see a policeman," Lewis says to him. "If you see one, Jeffrey, go and get him."

Jeffrey goes, and comes back with an off-duty 78th Precinct cop who is wearing a white apron and has been selling fruits and vegetables in the market. The officer speaks sternly to the crying woman. "Your name?"

"Catherine Barta."

"Address?"

"Eighty-five Eastern Parkway."

Every Wednesday, she walks a mile or so to the Green-market. She has lived in Brooklyn close to half her life, the rest of it in the Ukraine. Heading back to his vegetables, the officer observes that there is nothing he can do.

Out from behind her tables comes Joan Benack, the baker, of Rocky Acres Farm, Milan, New York—a small woman with a high, thin voice. Leaving her tropical carrot bread, her zucchini bread, her anadama bread, her beer bread, she goes around with a borrowed hat collecting money from the farm-

ers for Catherine Barta. Bills stuff the hat, size 7—the money
of Alvina Frey and John Labanowski and Cleather Slade and
Rich Hodgson and Bob Engle, who has seen it come and go.
He was a broker for Merrill Lynch before the stock market
imploded, and now he is a blond-bearded farmer in a basketball shirt selling apples that he grows in Clintondale, New
York. Don Keller offers a dozen eggs, and one by one the
farmers come out from their trucks to fill Mrs. Barta's shopping cart with beans and zucchini, apples, eggplants, tomatoes, peppers, and corn. As a result, her wails and sobs grow
louder.

A man who gave Rich Hodgson a ten-dollar bill for a
ninety-five-cent box of brown eggs asks Rich to give the ten
back after Rich has handed him nine dollars and five cents,
explaining that he has some smaller bills that he wants to
exchange for a twenty. Rich hands him the ten. Into Rich's
palm he counts out five ones, a five, and the ten for a twenty
and goes away satisfied, as he has every reason to be, having
conned Rich out of nine dollars, five cents, and a box of
brown eggs. Rich smiles at his foolishness, shrugs, and sells
some cheese. If cash were equanimity, he would never lose a
cent. One day, a gang of kids began taking Don Keller's vegetables and throwing them at the Hodgson truck. Anders Thueson threw an apple at the kids, who then picked up rocks.
Thueson reached into the back of the truck and came up with
a machete. While Hodgson told him to put it away, pant legs
went up, switchblades came into view. Part of the gang bom-
barded the truck with debris from a nearby roof. Any indica-
tion of panic might have been disastrous. Hodgson packed
deliberately, and drove away.

Todd Jameson, who comes in with his brother Dan from

Farmingdale, New Jersey, weighed some squash one day, and put it in a brown bag. He set the package down while he weighed something else. Then, reaching for the squash, he picked up an identical bag that happened to contain fifty dollars in rolled coins. He handed it to the customer who had asked for the squash. Too late, Todd discovered the mistake. A couple of hours later, though, the customer—"I'll never forget him as long as I live, the white hair, the glasses, the ruddy face"—came back. He said, "Hey, this isn't squash. I didn't ask for money, I asked for squash." Whenever that man comes to market, the Jamesons give him a bag full of food. "You see, where I come from, that would never, never happen," Todd explains. "If I made a mistake like that in Farmingdale, no one—no one—would come back with fifty dollars' worth of change."

Dusk comes down without further crime in Brooklyn, and the farmers are packing to go. John Labanowski—short, compact, with a beer in his hand—is expounding on his day. "The white people are educating the colored on the use of beet greens," he reports. "A colored woman was telling me today, 'Cut the tops off,' and a white woman spoke up and said, 'Hold it,' and told the colored woman, 'You're throwing the best part away.' They go on talking, and pretty soon the colored woman is saying, 'I'm seventy-three on Monday,' and the white says, 'I don't believe a word you say.' You want to know why I come in here? I come in here for fun. For profit, of course, but for relaxation, too. I like being here with these people. They say the city is a rat race, but they've got it backwards. The farm is what gets to be a rat race. You should come out and see what I—" He is interrupted by the reappearance in the market of Catherine Barta, who went home

(55)

long ago and has now returned, her eyes hidden by her wide-brimmed hat, her shopping cart full beside her. On the kitchen table, at 85 Eastern Parkway, she found her telephone bill, her stamps, and her cash. She has come back to the farmers with their food and money.

WEST OF THE SUBURBS, thirty and more miles from Manhattan, the New Jersey–New York border terrain is precipitous and glaciated and—across a considerable area—innocent of high-speed roads. Minor roads run north and south, flanking the walls of hogback ridges—Pochuck Mountain, Bearfort Mountain, Wawayanda Mountain—but the only route that travels westward with any suggestion of efficiency is the Appalachian Trail. The landscape is remarkably similar to Vermont's: small clearings, striated outcroppings, bouldery fields; rail fences under hard maples; angular roads, not well marked, with wooden signs; wild junipers signalling, as they do, penurious soil; unfenced cemeteries on treeless hillsides; conflagrationary colors in the autumn woods. Moving among such scenes, climbing, descending, losing the way and turning back—remarking how similar to rural New England all this is—one sooner or later tops a rise where the comparison in an instant blinks out. Some distance below, and reaching as far as the eye can conveniently see, is a surface perfectly flat, and not merely flat but also level, and not only level but black as carbon. There are half a dozen such phenomena in this region, each as startling to come upon as the last. Across their smooth expanses, distant hills look like shorelines, the edges of obsidian lakes. The black surfaces were, indeed, once fluid and blue—lakes that stood for many centuries where north-flowing streams were blocked by this or that digital terminus of the retreating Laurentide glacier. Streamborne silt and black organic muck gradually replaced the water—prognosticating Lake Mead, Lake Powell, Lake Sakakawea, and the Lake of the Ozarks some years hence when they have filled in solid behind their dams. The surface of the mucklands (as they are called) is not altogether firm. It will support a five-inch globe onion. For that matter, it will support a tractor—but it is not nearly dense enough to hold up a house. There are only a few sheds on the wide flats. People live on "islands," once and present islands, knobs that break through the black surface just as they did when it was blue. Pine Island, New York, is a town in a black-dirt sea—the largest and most productive muckland of them all. Maple Island, Merritts Island, Big Island, Black Walnut Island are spaced across it as well, and their clustered houses resemble small European farming communities. The fields surrounding them seem European, too, for the acreages of black dirt are ruled off in small, familial segments, like vineyards in Valencia or the Côte d'Or. No fences, no hedgerows interrupt the vista or separate one farmer from another. Plots abut. The vegetables that come out of this rich organic soil are in their way as special as wines: tall celeries, moist beets, iceberg lettuce as crisp as new money, soft Boston salad lettuce, broccoli, cauliflower, carrots—and, above all, onions. What the beluga is to caviar the muckland is to the onion. Millions upon millions of onions are grown in the black dirt. Early flat onions. Hybrid onions. Red Globe, White Globe, Yellow Globe onions. Buccaneer, Bronze Age, Benny's Red Onions. Tokyo Long White Bunching Onions. Harvestmore, Ebenezer, Nutmeg Onions. Yellow sweet Spanish late mild onions. Everywhere you go and everywhere you look are bags and boxes and bushels of onions. Pine Island, where the crop is warehoused, is Onionapolis. The hot days are dry on the muckland. After leaving it, in the evening, farmers sometimes go hopping from island to island, have a beer or two at the Meadow Tavern, and two to four at Mike's Tavern, and four to eight at Leo's Tavern in order to be ready for the Red Onion, a sort of staging area, or base camp, as good a place as any to prepare an all-out assault on the Jolly Onion.

Onion boxes, in this early-autumn harvest season, are in random stacks across the level plain. All day long, harvesting rigs move slowly among them like floating dredges, scooping the powdery soil, "pulling onions." John Labanowski has been pulling onions for twenty days now, stirred toward delirium by the fine black dust, the hammering sun, the asynchronous cacophony of his odd machine. The lower end of a steel conveyor belt, which is angled toward the ground like a stairway, moves forward through the soft earth and nuzzles under the onions. The conveyor consists of runglike rods set apart so that dirt can fall through, but not as far apart as the diameter of an onion. Tops and all, the onions ride uphill. The tops are brittle and dry. Bolted to the rig is a fan that could fly a Jenny. It blows off the tops and scatters them downwind. Clean now, appearing just as they will in a market, the onions reach the top of the conveyor, turn a corner, and roll down a chute. Andy Labanowski, John's uncle, is sitting on a cantilevered seat shoving crates into place beneath the downpour of onions. Roughly four hundred and fifty will fill a crate—in nine seconds. The crates are wooden and heavy. Their loaded weight is eighty pounds apiece. With his left hand, Andy begins to ease one (on rollers) off the harvester, and with his right hand he moves another one below the falling onions. Empty crates are piled on the harvester almost to the point of toppling, and John feeds them down to Andy while the whole grotesque contrivance is kept in motion by John's father, John Labanowski, who sits out in front on a steel-padded tractor—taciturn, enigmatic, in his visored cap and tinted glasses—and advances the enterprise at ten to the minus seven miles per hour. There are thunderheads along the border of the sky, but even if they were directly above us we could not hear the rumbling. Three separate engines power the rig. We are well into the afternoon now, four of us working this Orange County clipper ship. Our skins are as black as the four of spades. There are white doughnuts around the eyes. Old John has the look of a coal miner moments out of the shaft. His brother, Andy—spare, dark-eyed, gregarious—is courting sunstroke under a Budweiser hat that has turned black. Young John, also called Yash, came to work in high-top leather boots, gray twill trousers, monkey-fist gloves, a blue porkpie hat, and a pink T-shirt—all of which now are solid black. He turns away from a gust of dirt. "You can get blowed out," he says. "Winds blow fine dirt so hard it sometimes cuts the tops. But don't worry. This dirt will never kill you. My father's sixty-three and he's still going."

A stone jams the conveyor, and John the elder stops the tractor, gets off, picks up a wrench, and crushes the stone. When Polish farmers first cleared the muckland, stones were hauled in and dumped on the soil to help it support the weight of horses. There are fifty Labanowskis in the valley now. Their cousins the Osczepinskis—who also go to Greenmarket—farm here, too. The harvester moves on. Its weight shakes the earth. The tenth part of an acre vibrates around us like a quaking bog. There are cracks in the dry muck—crevasses of a sort—that will go as much as six feet deep. Onions by the hundred are lost in the cracks. The soil is so rich it will burn. Now and then a farmer flicks a cigarette off his rig and starts a ground fire. Old John, who smokes, has put out three such fires on his fifty acres this summer. Blazing black dirt is not easily controlled. In 1964, there was a fire in which a couple of thousand acres of soil burned. The fire crossed many property lines. It was harvest time, and crated onions were stacked across the plain. Fifteen million onions roasted. The fallout quickened appetites in Greece. "There were big winds. You couldn't go nowheres evenings. The air was too thick to see." A tractor blew up. The fire engines of many towns and a firefighting helicopter converged upon the muckland without significant effect. The fire lasted more than a week, and went out under long heavy rains.

John's father, John, flies in chartered aircraft to spy on onions elsewhere in the state. He is the Francis Gary Powers of the Labanowskis. If black-dirt farmers know the stages of the harvest in competitive counties, they can decide whether to wait or pull. Labanowski and his wife and two neighbors hire a twin-engine plane at the airfield that was Stewart Air Force Base, and, taking off over Hodgson's Brussels sprouts, head north by northwest—to Canandaigua, Canastota, Batavia, Elba, Fulton, Oswego. They land in some places and snoop by car. They fly low over other checkpoints and bulbous destinations.

Lurching onward. It is now my turn to align the boxes under the thundering onionfall. One small timing error and two hundred onions crash in your lap, spew out over the ground. I somehow lose a foot between two rollers, and nearly crack an ankle. "I guess that's dangerous," I remark, recovering the foot.

"On a farm, everything is dangerous," says Yash.

After thirty minutes of filling boxes, my arms feel as if they have gone eighteen innings each. I scarcely notice, though, under the dictates of the action, the complete concentration on the shifting of the crates, the hypnotic effect—veiling everything else in this black-surfaced hill-bordered surreally level world—of the cascade of golden onions. Onions. Onions. Multilayered, multilevelled, ovate, imbricated, white-fleshed, orange-scaled onions. Native to Asia. Aromatic when bruised. When my turn is over and a break comes for me, I am so crazed with lust for these bulbous herbs—these enlarged, compressed buds—that I run to an unharvested row and pull from the earth a one-pound onion, rip off the membranous bulb coat, bare the flesh, and sink my teeth through leaf after leaf after savory mouth-needling sweet-sharp water-bearing leaf to the flowering stalk that is the center and the secret of the onion. Yash at the end of the day will give me three hundred pounds of onions to take home, and well past the fall they will stand in their sacks in a corner of the kitchen—the pluperfect preservers of sweet, fresh moisture—holding in winter the rains of summer.

We quit in early evening, having filled two thousand crates with a hundred and fifty thousand pounds of onions, which would bring thirty thousand dollars at Greenmarket prices if only so many could move there. They will bring about eight thousand dollars at the current (and not attractive) wholesale price. They are five per cent of the Labanowski harvest. In the family's packinghouse on Big Island is a tall refrigerator filled to capacity with beer and surrounded by onion crates full of empty cans. We open sixteen cans to smooth off the day. Beer running down our arms streaks them white. We sit on onion crates with the building between us and the falling sun, and we look out over the black lake to forested hills called Mount Adam and Mount Eve. "Yeah, it gets to be a rat race here," says Yash. "In the city, sometimes, I slam things and screech at the customers. I don't know why. We've made a lot of friends there, you know. I sort of favor Brooklyn. The colored go for the big beets there. The whites go for the small beets. I don't know why. Everybody wants the Boston lettuce. I say, 'If I'd known you wanted to buy it this bad, I'd of grew a whole acre for you.' They like to bargain in Brooklyn. My cabbage is fifty cents a head, and they say they want three for a dollar. Tomatoes they watch the scale. I give them two pounds always for a pound and a half. Fifty-ninth Street? That's like high class. At Fifty-ninth Street, I get people with gloves."

FIFTY-NINTH STREET in the rain, and—despite the awning—the apples and peppers are wet.

"Is there a towel?" a customer asks. She wears a white hat, no gloves.

"Excuse me?"

"A towel. Water weighs something, you know."

I give her three and a third pounds for three. "There you are, madam. I weighed your water."

I remember asking Derryck Brooks-Smith, before I'd ever been here, to describe the Fifty-ninth Street Greenmarket for me, and he said, "White people. *Mucho* white people—or ones passing for white. Be careful with nickels and dimes. People are more careful there than in any other market. Sixty per cent of them are richies, and people who are really making it, and upper middle class, but when you weigh something you have to defend what you say. They'll ask you, 'Why is this a dollar-ten, and not a dollar-five?' They are—shall we say?—a little tight."

Brown bags are breaking open, corn and potatoes spilling into mud. Nonetheless, as midday approaches, the crowd becomes ever more dense and compressed, moving between parallel rows of farmers in complex slow currents.

"Amazing!" I remark across the table. "So many people out in the rain."

"It's this or the supermarket," says a tall woman in a transparent coat, handing me a sack of pears.

"Two pounds even, at three for a dollar twenty-five—that's eighty-five cents, please."

"Twice forty-two is eighty-four."

"Eighty-four, then." Out of one wet dollar. My apron is filled with wet bills. When a twenty comes along, five minutes are required to change it.

"How much are the tomatoes?"

"Three pounds for a dollar."

"How much are the apples?"

"Three pounds for a dollar. It says so there on the sign."

"They are McIntoshes, are they not?"

"Yes, they are."

"Why are they called McIntoshes?"

"After Charles Macintosh (1766–1843), who invented their waterproof skin."

(63)

"I'm finally discovering what real vegetables smell like."

"I never knew lima beans came in a pod."

"These beans, they don't snap."

"My bean hasn't snapped in years."

"Where is your lettuce? I'll take a head of lettuce."

"We don't have any lettuce. Try the Labanowskis, across the way."

The rain is not hurting their beautiful lettuce, and Yash is soaked to the skin. In salute, he lifts a Budweiser. People are formed around his truck in scrums. They press in from all sides, bent over, pushing hard, and now and again a head of lettuce flies out to the side. Between beers, the Labanowskis munch carrots. They pick up heads of lettuce and bite into them as if they were large green apples.

"If I had to stay on the farm seven days a week I'd go crazy!" shouts Yash, over the crowd.

"I'd say he went some time ago," mutters a man choosing peppers in a London Fog.

Across the sky immediately to the north of us run the improbable cables of the Roosevelt Island tramway, and from time to time a gondola appears, floating up and eastward, or slowly descending, suspended, increasing the sense of carnival in the scene that lies below. The Greenmarket occupies a quarter of an acre running from Fifty-ninth Street to Fifty-eighth along Second Avenue, bordered with fence-climbing vines and trees of heaven. The lot is rented from the city for a dollar a year. Not long ago it contained a row of shops and restaurants, and upstairs apartments—all of which were wiped out in the name of a fresh approach to the Queensboro Bridge. The approach road has not been built, but tall cooperatives have risen overhead—thirty-six floors and upward, with balconies sprocketing their sides and swimming pools deep in their kidneys. One building has a Rolls-Royce agency on the ground floor. The Greenmarket's obvious popularity at this address is not altogether welcomed by the people of the big co-ops, and through their community board they and others of the upper East Side have imposed some severe if not Draconian rules. No cider by the glass. No brownies by the square. No bread. No jam. No jelly. No houseplants. No balloons. No banners. No music (the market attracts enough riffraff as it is). No market, in fact, in the early or late season —an articulated suspicion that everything ever sold here has not been grown, as claimed, on regional farms.

"How many acres do you have up there?"

"A hundred and twenty."

"And how many chickens?"

"Forty thousand."

"*Forty thousand chickens?*"

"Four times ten to the fourth."

"Are they running loose?"

"They are not running anywhere."

"What do you feed them?"

"Grain products, plant-protein products, animal-protein products, processed grain by-products, dehydrated alfalfa meal with Ethoxyquin added as a preservative, ground limestone, salt, calcium iodate . . ." Prepared for the question, I am reading from a card. "Cobalt carbonate, copper oxide, copper sulfate, iron sulfate, manganous oxide, zinc oxide, methionine hydroxy analogue calcium, Vitamin A supplement, D-activated animal sterol, niacin, calcium pantothenate, riboflavin supplement, Vitamin B-12 supplement, menadione dimethylpyrimidinol bisulfite, Vitamin E supplement, and folic acid."

"Just as I suspected. And how fresh are the eggs?"

Derryck Brooks-Smith—working Saturday, off from school —speaks up to answer. "They were laid, to be perfectly frank, two days ago or one day ago but not this morning."

"Oh. You call yourself a farmer. The eggs should be fresh."

"They *are* fresh. The yolks will stand up and yell at you. The average egg in a supermarket is three weeks away from the hen."

Brooks-Smith sells two dozen jumbos to a black man with seven bracelets on each wrist, hair in ringlets, and what appears to be about six pounds of tin around his neck. An occasional star comes in here, a face shot out of the midnight tube, and people also arrive in Lincolns, which they park in the Kinney next door. For the most part, though, they are everyday eye-shadowed urban Americans. A dog is in the market. Male. He is not loose. He is leashed. He is, nonetheless, in the market, and a woman makes strong complaint. "Put up a sign! Keep them out! A person's legs are too precious!" she screams.

She has gained the attention of Bob Lewis. "This woman is referring to the fact that we don't really allow dogs in here," Lewis says quietly to the dog's owner.

"She is crazy, too," says the owner, whose dog is six inches high.

The rain has ended and shafts of bright sun have broken through, with the result that mists are rising. An elderly woman tells me she walked a mile to be here. A big bald man in a button-down shirt is drinking beer from a one-quart can. The can is in a brown bag. "The heaviest consumption of beer in the world is in Belgium," he informs us. "Belgium is one place where I believe I could get in trouble." He buys six pounds of apples and an ear of corn. There is a short man before us now in lemon-lime-cherry-and-grape striped trousers and a shirt in bourbon, burgundy, and crème-de-menthe squares. He explains to a neighbor how to bake an eggplant. "Insert holes in it," he tells her, "or the thing will explode."

Man in a Harley-Davidson T-shirt over a gravid half-mast paunch. He wants the telephone number of the community board so he can call and complain that the farmers here are not permitted to sell plants. The number is 679-2287, and Bob Lewis writes it, crossing the stems of the sevens.

Harley-Davidson: "That's a *seven?*"

"That's the way they write sevens in Europe."

"This isn't Europe. This is America. We've got too many Europeans here. And Spanish. What we need is more Americans, not Spanish. They came here—these animals—and won't learn English."

"Honey! Honey here!" shouts Brooks-Smith. (We have no honey. We never sell honey.)

"Eggs! Eggs! Get your eggs here!" shouts the honey man, across the way.

There is a rhythm in the movement of the crowd, in the stopping, the selecting, the moving on—the time unconsciously budgeted to assess one farm against another, to convict a tomato, to choose a peach. The seller comes to feel the rate of flow, and—for all the small remarks, the meeting of eyes—to feel as well the seclusion of anonymity that comes with the money aprons and the hanging scales. Rich Hodgson —handing them their blue free plums. They don't know he skis in Utah. Melissa Mousseau—changing a twenty for a bag of pears. They don't know that she goes, too. Hemingway and Thueson, the athletes, have heard more encouraging sounds from other crowds. "If you charge for three pounds, give me three full pounds and not two pounds and fifteen ounces, boy."

By a blue Chevrolet panel truck, opposite us, the crowd's rate of flow is perceptibly arrested. The displays there are smaller than most, the list of items shorter. Some of the prices are higher. The zucchini is fifty cents a pound. The corn, the tomatoes, the green beans, the squash are not *all* superior to their counterparts around the market, and certainly not to ours. So why, then, does the crowd almost crystallize when they come to Alvina Frey? They don't know anything about her except her address (Chad's Farm, Mahwah, New Jersey), if they happen to notice it on the truck, but they can easily sense a consistent standard, a kind of personal signature, in the colors and textures before her.

"What the small farmer offers is fresher, more selected material," Alvina has said. "The small farmer throws away the bad stuff. If my produce is better than some people's, I'll charge more for it. Some of the other guys say I'm Fifth Avenue. I don't care."

She is trim and attractive, petite, with intensity in her narrow, gentle face, and gold earrings that swing and flash. Her hair is short and has flecks of gray in it. Her skin is richly tan, her eyes a bright pale blue. She wears tennis shoes and light-blue denims with bell bottoms and a striped cardigan that looks soft and expensive. At first glance she seems so Short Hills that one wonders whether she is playing, and whether she, as some others have done, starts from home empty and collects her goods on the way to market—hand-me-down potatoes, Hunts Point pears. From years in the sun, though, there are deep radial lines around her eyes. And now, toward the end of the season, her hands are rough, callused, cracked, her fingers like small bananas. Her nails are split, and the skin that surrounds them is dark with terrarian stains.

She is very busy, and pressed for time, selling. But she takes time to educate, too. She tells people not to be impressed by fat cucumbers. The long thin ones have fewer seeds. To the universal question "Is the corn fresh?" she says, "You can tell for yourself." She reaches for an ear and holds it upside down. If the stem at the break is a damp, pale green, the corn has been off the stalk less than a day. After about twenty-four hours, the stem turns white and chalky, opaque. With more time, it turns various shades of brown. The stem at the break of the ear in her hand is damp, pale green.

"Are the beans fresh?"

"Eat one. If you can eat it and it's juicy and not stringy, it's fresh."

People may also sense when they linger close around Alvina Frey that she is—perhaps a little more than anyone else here—what the Greenmarket is about. Not far from the city, she works a long-established farm that, before the Greenmarket, was on its way to being cut up and sold. While the Hodgsons look for new ground and the Van Houtens have found it, Alvina is all but desperate to hold the farm she has, which her grandmother farmed before her. Her grandmother, in fact, cleared the land. The grandmother's name was Alwine Pelz, and she was born on a farm in Saxony in the eighteen-sixties, emigrating as an adult to New Jersey. Her husband was a loom mechanic, and he found a job in a Paterson mill while she looked through the country for a farm. Fifteen miles northeast of Paterson, in the township of Ho-Ho-Kus, she bought fifty-five acres, close by the New York State line. To irrigate her crops, she dug a well, and walled it with fieldstone, topped by four stone columns and a pagoda roof. With her husband's help, she then constructed a fieldstone barn. "She did what she knew how to do, my grandmother—she farmed.

When my grandfather went to the mills in Paterson, he took her tomatoes, corn, beans, potatoes, beets—you name it—to the Island Market and sold them there. He went down with his horse and wagon. He didn't have a truck until the late twenties. My grandmother grew strawberries, too—two or three acres of them—and she had apples. She made cider, and I know damned well that during Prohibition she made hooch. She worked every day out in the fields until six months before she died. She was ninety-one years old. She farmed with horses. She never went in for anything mechanized. Neither did I, at first. Toward the end, when stuff grows high, you can't get in with a tractor. I had horses until fifteen years ago. About the only mechanical thing my grandmother ever had was the cider mill. It was steam-driven and made an awful racket. The ones that lived over the hill, they used to complain."

Her nearest neighbors are no longer over the hill. They are on the hill, around the hill, in the hill. The farm is on an old, blacktopped crown road that has become a suburban street, with a Little League field, swimming pools, trim lawns, and mini-wheelbarrows a foot high that have house numbers on their sides. The well is still there, however—its masonry tight, its water serving the farm. The stone barn is a high and beautiful structure that is now covered, like a superannuated college, with ivy. The countryside Alvina remembers from her girlhood had many truck farms, dairy farms, separating what have become contiguous towns: a future that the New Jersey State Highway Department began to sketch in the nineteen-thirties, when it created what is now Route 17, a north-south bifurcation of Bergen County, its purpose being to bring the Catskills closer to the city. Alvina remembers the new road running through garden country with rich dark earth full of carrots, radishes, and beets. All of what is now Paramus—of what is now a levitated Levittown with houses checkered to the curve of the earth—was celeryland and lettuceland. Where Okonite and Minolta are now, Alvina's father, Frank Pelz, had a farm of his own. The day the new road opened he went down it with a load of cabbages. The truck body was not bolted on well, and the load shook loose—heads all over the road. Route 17 has come to be called a "butcher boulevard," and when heads roll on it now they are more likely to be human. Alvina is safe enough at six in the morning as the Chad's Farm truck moves south toward the city past the Olds-Toyota and the Swiss Chalet, past the Tiffany Diner and Pay Less Building Supply, past steak houses the size of high schools. Castle Auto Truck Parts (turrets, battlements). Car Crazy Eddie. The Value House. The Cottage Beautiful. Mc-Donald's, Burger King, Shatzi's Hofbrauhaus (Bavarian half-timber). John Barleycorn's Restaurant. The Golden Plough (a barn full of steak and lobsters). The Jade Fountain ("Chinese-Polynesian"). Nasser Aftab's House of Carpets. When Route 17 opened, New Jersey had twenty-nine thousand farms. Today there are seventy-nine hundred. Only forty-eight are left in all of Bergen County, and one is Alvina Frey's.

After her grandmother was gone and her father, too, Alvina worked the place with her first husband, Chad Chodorowski, and for some years they sold all their produce wholesale, mainly in Paterson. Eventually they built a roadside stand. The day it opened, in 1968, Chad suffered a heart attack. A year later, he died. Alvina's grandmother had had ten children, most of whom helped her with the farm. Alvina has no children. She has reduced the acreage under cultivation to

(71)

thirty-eight, and works it generally alone, with part-time help in the fields and in the stand. Her husband, Ed Frey, assists to some extent, but he is an excavator with a full-time business of his own, and while she is digging furrows he digs sewers and graves. "I love to see stuff grow. When it doesn't do well I could cry," she says. "But I don't like herbicide. The last time I used it was in tomatoes. I use as little chemical as I possibly can."

People who come regularly to the Greenmarket often bring things to Alvina. At Fifty-ninth Street, an elderly woman appears weekly with a container of orange juice for her. When there is no juice, Alvina sucks on the ice with which John Labanowski chills his beer. People take pictures of her. They invite her up for coffee. "I got one customer here at Fifty-ninth Street who's a drinker, male—a damned good-looking distinguished man, even if he drinks. He once brought me a hard-boiled egg in clear gelatin. Some kind of French dish. You don't like it, but you have to eat it." She receives weekly reports from a man who once bought a gourd. Following her directions, he cut holes in it and hung it out a twentieth-story window. A bird came to live in his gourd.

"I love the city—meeting different people, learning that all the things you learn about the city are not true. I see more people in the two markets I come to—Brooklyn and Fifty-ninth Street—than I do in several weeks in Mahwah at the stand. I wouldn't quit this for nothing in the world. The people are wonderful, and the market means a lot to them. They don't want anything to screw it up so we won't come in anymore."

A short time ago, Chad's Farm was drifting down a long and steady economic decline. In the wholesale markets, the middleman, in her opinion, wanted too much. A couple of years ago, a half bushel of tomatoes brought as much as four dollars and fifty cents. Now it brings five dollars, a difference that fails to compensate for the inflating costs of gasoline, fertilizer, utilities, containers, and dust. "I'm too small for Hunts Point and too big to make a living only out of a roadside stand. There was four of us—farmers—on my road once. When Johnny Werling went out of business he was forty. He finally had to get a job. That's rough—to farm all your life and then have to get a job. That's where I was headed when the Greenmarket came along. The Greenmarket is a godsend. Next year, I'd like to do different. I'd like to rent out my stand and come into the city every day."

THE
ATLANTIC
GENERATING
STATION

THE ATLANTIC GENERATING STATION was first imagined early one morning in 1969 by a man in Westfield, New Jersey, who happened at the moment to be taking a shower before dressing and going to work. His name was Richard Eckert. He was a Public Service Electric & Gas Company engineer, fairly high in the corporate tree. A large part of his job was to seek out new sites for power plants—an assignment that had once, in a less complicated era, called for a person who could look at a map and find a river. Now difficulties had thickened to a point near desperation, and plant siting required scientific and diplomatic talents undreamed of in the age of the pluming smokestack and the good five-cent cigar. Apparently needed as well, by now, was a leap of the imagination, for New Jersey was not only among the smallest of the fifty states, it was also the most densely populated, and nearly all appropriate sites for any kind of power plant, fossil or nuclear, had been chosen and used. Environmentalists and intervenors were phalanxed upon the sites that remained, and the environmentalists and intervenors seemed to be multiplying even more rapidly than the population at large. In the absence of new plants, demand for power would before long exceed supply. Then, when New Jersey went brown, New Jersey would serve as an indicator to the rest of the country that the rest of the country was going to go brown, too, because the problem was a universal one and was only somewhat more immediate in the superconcentrated, megalopolitan, residential-industrial-transportational corridor between Philadelphia and New York. If New Jersey's problem was to be solved, Public Service would have to solve it, for the company's territory included eighty per cent of the state's people. A power plant needed plenty of space and plenty of cooling water—five hundred acres of ground and a million gallons a minute. The state's interior rivers were small. The utility had nowhere to go. The compact human warren it served—containing, in some places, forty-five thousand people per square mile—was hemmed in between Pennsylvania and the open Atlantic.

Those were the terms of the dilemma constantly on Eckert's mind, and it was the last part—the Atlantic—that became arrested there for a moment that morning in 1969, opening to him a form of solution. Standing wet, naked, and soapy in his shower, he envisioned a huge nuclear-power plant, as prodigious as any yet built on land, mounted on an immense hull, floating on the sea. There was certainly enough room on the ocean, and, heaven knew, enough water. Other advantages suggested themselves as well. To construct a nuclear-power plant at a specific site on land, something like thirty-five hundred skilled workers had to be sought out, hired, and assembled. They had become nomads of the times, moving from state to state, reactor to reactor—stainless-steel welders, for the most part, of a class so high that they were hard to find.

With the proliferation of the nuclear-power industry, they would become scarcer still, as would nuclear engineers and designers, of whom there might soon not be enough to go on making unique designs to fit the conditions of new sites. If all these people were to build floating power plants, however, the situation would reverse itself. The personnel would stay in one place, and the plants would travel. An assembly line could be set up somewhere, and a permanent work force could settle in around it, to manufacture plants and ship them out. With standardization, the cost of making a nuclear-power plant would decline, and the margin for errors of all kinds would narrow. Start to finish, the amount of time required to build a nuclear plant might be reduced by several years. Moreover, a floating plant would go up and down with the tides. Its water-sucking orifices would remain in a constant position with respect to the surface of the sea and not have to adjust to sudden and sometimes considerable changes in the water level—a problem inevitable at river sites. Eckert ate his breakfast and told his wife, Joan, that he wanted to launch nuclear-power plants as, in effect, ships on the ocean.

"There you go again," she said.

Eckert was not quite forty at the time. A lean man, amiable, slightly bald, he did not by appearance in any way suggest the fearsome, two-dimensional, fictive American businessman with reinforcing rods in his jaws, emerging from some dark, polluted labyrinth to hand out the wages of fear. Eckert was a man given to gray suits, gray socks, black shoes, white shirts, and Paisley ties. He commuted to Newark and liked to sail with his children on New Jersey estuaries and bays. He was a New Jersey native, a lifelong resident, born and raised in Plainfield, with a boyhood behind him of New

Jersey saltwater vacations. In an anonymous way, he would soon be the Antichrist to several hundred thousand people along the barrier beaches of the state. Yet he was one of them. And he had not invented the electric toothpick or the electric scalpel or the aluminum beer can or central air-conditioning or the six-thousand-watt sauna, or any of the other hardware, large and small, vital or vulgar, that had helped to make a necessity of something that had not existed—not in commercial form—a century before. All those people on the beach had, in a sense, given Eckert his job, and his job was to find sites and then build nuclear-power plants, and now he was imagining one in the ocean, for the plain reason that there was nowhere else to build it.

In Newark, at the Public Service Company's principal office, Eckert's idea readily acquired buoyancy of its own. Utilities are renowned for their conservatism, but this one was not in a position to watch and wait. In Eckert's words, it had to "keep searching for any exotic idea that would improve and sustain the breed." Public Service was already giving large annual sums to support university research in the control of thermonuclear fusion. And now it unblinkingly agreed that Eckert and his staff should explore the concept of the oceanborne nuclear plant, and spend enough time and money to answer the primary question: Is there any reason, technically, that it won't work?

There were fragments of precedent. In 1929, when Tacoma, Washington, temporarily ran out of power, the aircraft carrier Lexington went down Puget Sound, hove to, and fed electric current to the stricken city. Ships were used as power plants during the Second World War, when they were sometimes equipped as mobile, diesel-fuelled generating stations. By

1969, of course, submarines and certain surface vessels had for some years been using nuclear reactors to make the heat to make the steam to drive them, and there was even one example of a ship that contained a nuclear reactor intended primarily for the production of electricity. Operated by the United States Army, it had been anchored since October of 1968 in Gatun Lake, there to cope with a bizarre situation in the Panama Canal. The lake supplied water both to the locks of the canal and to the hydroelectric plant that made the power that enabled the locks to operate. Every time a ship went through the locks, fifty-two million gallons of water irretrievably left the lake, and millions more fell to the hydroelectric plant. The lake, as an integral segment of the canal system, also had to float ships, and during the dry season the surface often went down to a critical level at which there might be water enough to bring ships in but not enough to float them once they got there. The result was a heavy curtailment of traffic in the canal—until the Sturgis, a Liberty ship with a new pressurized-water reactor in it, came into the lake and began to supplement the Panama Canal power system with enough electricity to save, for use in the locks, twenty-three billion gallons of water a month, an amount sufficient for the transit of four hundred and forty ships.

Compared with the watt resource that Public Service was about to develop, though, the stories of the Lexington and the Sturgis would be mere curiosities in the history of electrical power on the sea. The Sturgis's reactor was rated at ten megawatts of electricity. The Atlantic Generating Station would send ashore, through cables buried in the seabed, a net electrical output of twenty-three hundred megawatts. As discussion and research went forward, it was decided that the power would come from two plants, identical, floating side by side—so that, for refuelling and other purposes, half the generating station could go on operating while the other half was shut down.

Eckert and others—notably Muzaffer Kehnemuyi, a Turk who had received a master's degree in civil engineering from the University of Illinois in 1948 and would eventually, under Eckert, be the project manager—travelled the United States in search of answers to basic questions. They never encountered the irrefutable negative that would have ended the project for technical reasons, and meanwhile, in their gropings, they gradually discovered the dimensions and characteristics of what they planned to build. For example, they learned that no shipyard in the United States had a slipway wider than a hundred and forty feet, so a floating nuclear plant would either have to be very long, like the Cunard Queens, or have to be built in components, on several separate hulls—a reactor here, a turbine there. Public Service at first considered the component way but later decided that a new shipyard would have to be built to construct hulls that were nearly square—four hundred feet long and three hundred and seventy-eight feet wide. A breakwater would be needed to protect the hulls from the assaults of waves, which could come from any direction, so the breakwater should surround the floating plants. For its shape, a rectangle was considered first, but, as Eckert put it, "a square corner in the ocean doesn't last," and the shape that evolved was penannular—a kind of atoll, with a great curve convex to the east and the open sea, a straight wall on the landward side, and openings for the passage of boats that would bring, among other things, assemblies of fresh nuclear fuel. The curved segment alone would be from end to end three thousand feet, and it would be built in sloping form, like an earthfill dam, the whole structure rising from the seafloor like a pyramid.

WHEN CHEOPS undertook to build the Great Pyramid, nearly thirty centuries before Christ, he brought into being, where nothing had been but sands of the desert, a labor market, of sorts, that lasted thirty years, employing, on the average, a hundred thousand people. In 1971, within the halls of Public Service, the Atlantic Generating Station was pronounced feasible. From segments of the nuclear, industrial, consultative, and academic worlds, people in expanding numbers began to be drawn into a project still so nebulous that not even a specific site had been chosen—beyond the understanding that it would be some miles off the Jersey coast, in the undeveloped sea. Costs were underwritten on the immediate level by Public Service, of course, but eventually they were absorbed by the pharaoh himself—a collective name for people in New Jersey who pay electricity bills. Construction of the breakwater alone would take four years and four million manhours, but numerous endeavors of far-reaching complexity had to be initiated first. Westinghouse had put several dozen people to work on the concept; General Electric had a team, too—preparing to make eventual bids for the reactor contract. Public Service had also tried to arouse the interest of Babcock & Wilcox and Combustion Engineering, the two other makers of conventional light-water reactors, but they had said, in effect, "Nothing doing. We are too small for this one. We'll have to stand by and let someone else do it first." Shipyards

(83)

from Massachusetts to Texas were approached, and presentations were made in Washington to some thirty-five federal agencies, among them the National Oceanic and Atmospheric Administration, the Federal Aviation Administration, the Federal Power Commission, the Coast Guard, the Army Corps of Engineers, the Environmental Protection Agency, and, of course, the Atomic Energy Commission—any of which, having licensing power over one or another aspect of the project, could kill it. Reaction in Washington was favorable. The agencies, in their turn, and a whole list of analogous units of the state government set people to work preparing to contribute their part when the time came for hearings.

Most remarkable, though, was the kind of money that came spilling out of the pharaoh as a result of the environmental movement. Where once someone might have sized up the wind drift and then sited the plant, it was now necessary for scientists of multiple and overlapping disciplines to describe the New Jersey coast and adjacent seas probably in more detail than had ever been contemplated by anyone. It was a bonanza for the scientific community. Research grants that had once been copious from the federal government had dwindled considerably, causing panics in universities, and now, thanks to the friends of the earth, money was flowing from the corporate world for everything from core-borings in the bed of the ocean to exhaustive studies of pelagic life. Ichthyological Associates, a group formed at Cornell, was engaged by Public Service, and set up a branch laboratory in Absecon, near Atlantic City, to study all species of regional marine life, to establish a baseline description of the ecological environment, and to keep on gathering data for many years—all through construction and into the era of electrical pro-

(84)

duction—in order to record the effects of such things as the breakwater, the cooling system, and the thermal-discharge plume on every form of life from phytoplankton to the biggest of fish, and to suggest to the plant's designers modifications that might reduce detrimental effects. Similarly, a group of physical oceanographers was brought to New Jersey to establish a baseline on tides, waves, currents, wind. A group of seismologists and geologists was commissioned to study, among other things, foundation conditions of the ocean floor, geological structures, regional earthquake history. An earthquake broke windows in Asbury Park on June 1, 1927. The earthquake of October 9, 1871, whose epicenter was near Wilmington, Delaware, delivered what for this area was the most intense earth shock in historical times. The New York City earthquakes of 1884 and 1737 were less intense but on the same order of magnitude. With a proton magnetometer, the geologists began aeromagnetic surveys to develop a general view of the region's geological structure. To profile the seabed, they cruised around in boats using seismic instruments —high-resolution boomers, high-resolution sparkers. Deep borings into the bottom showed almost a mile of miscellaneous clays and sands resting on rock that had been where it was for at least two hundred million years. Earthquake risk, small as it was, would affect only the breakwater anyway, because the generating station, being afloat, would be decoupled from the earth. The only seismic effect that could reach the floating hulls would be a tsunami. The largest tsunami ever recorded locally had been originated by an earthquake off the Iberian coast and had been less than a foot high when it reached New Jersey.

Analyses of seventy-nine constituents of New Jersey ocean

water were done by chemists from Rutgers. Meteorologists were commissioned to make detailed portraits of New Jersey's coastal temperatures, humidity, precipitation, fogs, thunderstorms, tornado potentialities, and "probable maximum hurricanes." Hydrologists were brought in to make thermal studies to establish isotherms for varying tide and current conditions. Because cables would someday have to come out of the water and traverse land in order to bring power from the ocean to the people, general ecologists were commissioned to begin field studies that would eventually consider every tree, every bird, every animal—literally, every mouse—that might in any way be disturbed: white-footed mouse, meadow jumping mouse, house mouse, pine vole, Norway rat, short-tailed shrew, least shrew, semipalmated sandpiper, American widgeon, horned grebe, Atlantic white cedar, pitch pine, rabbit-foot clover, many hundreds of other species.

As more and more people became involved and information grew like dunes, the prime movers back in the Electric Engineering Department, in Newark, were increasingly encouraged. The ocean now seemed to be not just the only remaining place to go but in some respects the best place to be. To dissipate the plant's waste heat, the ocean, technically, was the world's best heat sink. Floating nuclear plants could be moved from place to place, if desired, to meet immediate needs. Engineering uniformity would bring such rewards that one day it would make sense to float plants even to sites on rivers. This, of course, could be done with any sort of power station—nuclear or fossil—but one advantage in choosing fission reactors as the heat source was that each one of them would eliminate the need to burn twelve million barrels of oil a year. "Others are waiting and watching," Kehnemuyi said.

(86)

"Once everyone is assured that we are going to get licensed, they are all going to come and jump into the water with us."

Two or three miles from land, rising and falling with the swells, the Atlantic Generating Station could be the first tentative step toward the submarine countries imagined by Glenn Seaborg, who, when he was chairman of the Atomic Energy Commission, published a book called *Man and Atom*, in which were described whole colonies of people, utterly disjunct from the rest of the race, living under vast plastic domes on the floor of the deep ocean. Each colony was built around a reactor doing the work of the sun.

A schedule was eventually framed whereby the first nuclear unit of the Atlantic Generating Station would be floated into place in the spring of 1985, the second in 1987. Construction of the breakwater would begin at least four years earlier. As seen even from conflicting points of view, the floating nuclear plant could make a considerable contribution to the developing fate of mankind. The Great Pyramid, for its part, had been built in order to contain through the ages nothing more important than Cheops the Builder.

ECKERT, KEHNEMUYI, and the others would have liked to choose a site as far away from shore as possible in order to use the horizon as an aesthetic screen between the floating power plant and the people of the beach communities. There would be value in the precedent, for when substantial parts of continents were necklaced with nuclear plants, it would clearly be preferable that the plants be as inconspicuous as possible. "Out of sight, out of mind," Eckert said. There were difficulties, though, in going out of sight. For one thing, the highest parts of the Atlantic Generating Station's two plants—the summits of the containment domes over the reactors—would be a hundred and ninety feet above the water. The rough formula for the relationship between sight lines and the curve of the earth is that the square root of the observer's altitude in feet will equal the number of miles over flat land or water between the observer and the horizon. A person lying on a beach nine feet above sea level can see three miles across the water before hulls begin to be lost to view. The Atlantic Generating Station, to be out of sight from the beach, would have to be some fourteen miles at sea.

The calculated maximum practical depth for normal seas around a floating nuclear plant proved to be about seventy feet—a purely economic limitation, imposed by the great size and cost of the necessary breakwater. Off the East Coast of the United States, the continental shelf is broad, reaching out seventy or eighty miles, sloping gently. And off much of New Jersey it is possible to go out fourteen miles and still be in seventy feet of water or less. The water is international, though, and murky with maritime law. The mere suggestion of such a site was enough to make tremors under the State Department. Governments were trying to reach new understandings in this field, but for the time being no distance would be secure that was greater than the traditional and conservative three miles. The minimum depth required was forty feet, because the big hulls would draw thirty-two. The site also had to be reasonably near an inlet, so that vessels ferrying people and supplies from a shore facility could dock in calm water. The site had to be away from established shipping lanes. The breakwater, of course, had to have something geologically firm to rest on. And there had to be a right-of-way on shore where the transmission line, after emerging from the seabed, could continue inland.

Nine possible sites were chosen. The northernmost was off Long Branch—less than twenty miles from New York. The southernmost was off the Cape May peninsula. All were suitable, and nine generating stations might one day float at them, but now the utility had much room in which to be particularly selective. Cape May—a hundred and forty miles from Newark —seemed a little too far away. On the other hand, waters three miles offshore gradually deepen toward the New York Bight, not prohibitively but enough to add to the cost of the breakwater. A very good site off Forked River was somewhat incommoded by a nuclear-power plant that already happened to be in operation on the mainland there. Choices soon diminished to two. One was off Harvey Cedars, on Long Beach Island, a resort that attracts, among other people, basketball coaches with loud voices, and they may have got up from the bench and shouted the utility away. Public Service, in any case, decided that it preferred not to choose a site directly in the view of summer homes, so Harvey Cedars was crossed off, and what remained as the final choice was a position eleven miles northeast of Atlantic City and two and eight-tenths miles from Little Egg Inlet and Great Bay—thirty-nine degrees, twenty-eight minutes north latitude; seventy-four degrees, fifteen minutes west longitude. Seven fathoms was the depth of the ocean there. Just seaward of the site was an extensive sand hill whose summit was less than thirty feet below the ocean's surface. Geologists quickly acupunctured the hill with stakes to see if, over time, it was moving. A couple of miles away, toward shore, there had once been an island that had

(89)

supported houses, stores, streets, and picket fences, and was now visible only at low tide. The submarine sand ridge appeared to be stable, however, for it had been recorded on charts a century old. The ridge would serve in big storms as a kind of breakwater for the breakwater—redundant engineering through the cooperative efforts of man and God.

In time, there would appear on a table in Eckert's office a triptych photograph of broad white sands and blue sea—a panorama that had been shot from the shore, looking toward the site. The foreground was patterned with wind ripples, bird tracks, and waving grass. In the middle distance was a thin white line of breaking waves. Beyond them was the sea. Given one glance, that was about all the picture included, but close observation would reveal on the horizon what appeared to be a pair of distant buttes, nearly lost under the sky. The work of an artist, of an architect, of an airbrush, this was the Atlantic Generating Station, *in situ*, veiled in summer haze.

PUBLIC SERVICE felt that it was doing quite enough pioneering in the marine aspects of the project and did not wish to be in any sense experimental with the nuclear components. The company wanted "state-of-the-art" reactors. Westinghouse was chosen to supply them, and Westinghouse, which had never been asked to build a ship before, sought help from Tenneco, an industrial conglomerate that owned the Newport News Shipbuilding & Dry Dock Company, the largest shipyard in the United States. Westinghouse and Tenneco (which has since dropped out of the partnership) formed a third company, naming it Offshore Power Systems, and bought an estuarine island near Jacksonville, there to manufacture floating nuclear plants at the eventual rate of—it was hoped—four a year. The Florida Audubon Society tried to go to court in defense of the island but was rebuffed. Offshore Power Systems then began to dig an assembly line—a broad canal, about four hundred and fifty feet wide, penetrating the center of the island and ending in a slipway that would release new hulls to the water. In shops on the surrounding acreage, the nuclear and turbine-generator components would be built in very large segments, then crane-lifted to the assembly line and set in place. The crane alone would cost thirteen million dollars. A whole nuclear plant—to go—would cost about three hundred and seventy-five million. It would displace a hundred and fifty thousand deadweight tons. Richard Eckert and Muzaffer Kehnemuyi vowed that when Atlantic Generating Station Unit 1 finally travelled up the coast they would be aboard. The trip would take about ten days, passing Georgia's Golden Isles and the island Kuwait has bought off South Carolina, rounding Cape Hatteras, traversing the wrecks of a thousand ships. An insurance syndicate would underwrite the trip. Setting a premium for such a voyage calls for, if nothing else, wit. The premium would be somewhere between five and ten million dollars. "When that first unit leaves Jacksonville, I'm going to be on it," Eckert said. "Because if it goes down at sea I'm going down with it."

A HARBOR BREAKWATER at East London, on the Wild Coast of South Africa, was rendered ineffective by a storm in 1963. The armor, as the outer layer of a breakwater's material is called, consisted of blocks of solid concrete, each weighing forty tons. East London's breakwater had been weakened by rough seas some years earlier, and now the storm of 1963 tore off sixty per cent of the armor. Eric M. Merrifield, East London's harbor engineer, wondered whether that would have happened if the armor had not been solid—had not been designed to accept on one plane in one moment the great force of the ocean. He decided to reconstruct the breakwater with porous armor, and in doing so he invented a momentous novelty in harbor engineering.

The idea was to cover the breakwater with objects of branching shape—like children's jacks—that would engage with one another, clinging together while absorbing and dissipating the power of waves. There had been similar attempts. The French had tried a four-legged concrete form, a tetrapod, and it had worked well enough but had required an expensive preciseness in construction, because each one had to be carefully set in place in relation to others. Merrifield wanted something that could almost literally be sprinkled on the breakwater core. Eventually, he thought of *dolosse*.

Dolosse—the singular is *dolos*—were crude toys that had been used by South African white children since the eighteen-thirties, when they acquired them from tribal children in the course of the eponymous trek, the overland march of the *voortrekkers* from the Cape Colony to the Transvaal. A *dolos* was the knucklebone of a goat or a sheep, and might be described as a corruption of the letter "H" with one leg turned ninety degrees. The game that had been played with *dolosse* by *voortrekker* children, and by South African children ever since, was called knucklebone. As crude toys, *dolosse* were also thought of as imaginary oxen. Witch doctors had used them as instruments of magic power. Merrifield replicated them on a grand scale in concrete, making *dolosse* that weighed twenty tons apiece, and with these he armored his breakwater. When high seas hit them, the water all but disappeared—no slaps like thunder, no geysers in the air. The revised breakwater seemed to blot up the waves after breaking them into thousands of pieces.

According to plan, the ocean floor at the site of the Atlantic Generating Station would be dredged—graded, more or less —and then huge concrete caissons would be floated to the site, lined up like boxcars going around a curve, and sunk to the bottom. The caissons would be filled with sand and gravel, and then, both above the caissons and seaward of them, a hill of rock would be built that would emerge sixty-four feet into the air above mean low water and slope on down into the sea to toe the bottom three hundred feet from the inner perimeter. Many thousands of *dolosse*—in varying sizes, but typically weighing forty tons apiece—would be used as armor. On the landward side and parallel to the coast, the straight breakwater would consist of filled caissons, armored with *dolosse* only at the ends. The straight section would complete the atoll. Caissons could be removed in order to float nuclear plants in or out.

Like the plants themselves, the breakwater was truly, as the Atomic Energy Commission described it, a "unique and first-of-its-kind" undertaking. A list was made of all hard-rock quarries from western Pennsylvania to northern Maine. Big pieces of hills would be cracked apart. Some of the rocks of the inner armor would be so large that each would ride alone, under chains, on a big flatbed truck from quarry to seaport. Then—Egyptian journey—it would ride in a barge down the coast. Meanwhile, in southern New Jersey, on Delaware Bay, a concrete yard would cast *dolosse* with armspreads of twenty feet and place them a few at a time on barges, to be tugged slowly around the Cape May peninsula and up the long fetch to the site—eighteen thousand *dolosse*. In all, more than five million tons of material would be compiled over an area of a hundred acres. The Dravo Corporation, of Pittsburgh, bid two hundred million dollars and got the job.

ON THE SAND PLAINS of the continental shelf, a foreign object that comes to rest, even if it is as small as an automobile tire, will tend to concentrate fish. Automobiles themselves have been dumped into the sea by commercial and charter fishermen as points to return to for future good days. First attracted to such objects are the organisms on which fish feed. Then come the fish. In the ocean off Murrells Inlet, South Carolina, a great mass of rock was piled up some years ago, and it attracted various fish species in concentrations ranging from three hundred times to eighteen hundred times their frequency in nearby waters. The spot was named Paradise Artificial Reef. If an entrepreneur building such a place were to contrive to warm some of the adjacent water, many more fish would be attracted. Some would stay longer in the autumn before heading south. Some would not bother to migrate at all. Bluefishing and bass fishing might become winter sports. Small boats by the hundred would converge the year round.

The Public Service Electric & Gas Company's breakwater atoll off New Jersey would become a stupendous artificial fishing reef—its armoring *dolosse* an ichthyological magnet, with warmth guaranteed to the adjacent water by two nuclear re-actors creating a thermal plume. The *dolosse* would grow lush with algae, invertebrates, barnacles, mussels. Sea bass would establish residence, and so would sculpin, skates, porgies, flukes, whitings, hakes, rock crabs, starfish, blackfish, lobsters. Lobsters are numerous in New Jersey but have to hunt around for places to hide, and for that purpose the labyrinthine hol-lows among the *dolosse* would outdo the granites of Maine. Lobsters would come to live there by the tens of thousands. In the words of David Thomas, the project director of Ichthyo-logical Associates' New Jersey Marine Ecological Study, "There would be more fish and shellfish in that area than in any other square mile in the Atlantic Ocean."

Certain questions had to be considered, though. While cool-ing themselves, the floating nuclear plants would suck in more than two million gallons of seawater per minute. Screens would cover the ingress. What would happen to fish drawn toward the screens? What kinds of fish would they be? At what speed should the water be sucked in? What should be the size of the mesh? Phytoplankton, zooplankton, larval fish, and other small creatures would go through the screens and through the plant. What percentage would die? The water would increase in temperature seventeen degrees. Biocides would be injected into it to keep the plumbing clean. After four minutes, the water would be returned to the ocean. At discharge, how fast should it come out, and at what level? Would fish die in the thermal plume?

In 1972, when the final site selection was made, the marine biologists of Ichthyological Associates, who had long since become part of the project in a more general way, marked off a grid of sixty square miles and began what their founder,

Edward Raney, described as "the best-financed, the most intense study that's ever been done of a limited area in the ocean." Raney, emeritus professor of zoology at Cornell and an authority on the striped bass, the bluefish, and the American shad, had previously set up other studies attempting to counsel the designers of nuclear plants and to save the lives of fish. Very few fish have actually been killed by the heated water emerging from power plants. They die instead from the lack of it—as they have, for example, at Forked River, in New Jersey, when, in winter, the nuclear plant there temporarily shut down. Many thousands of fish that would have been farther south but had been attracted to the warm effluent of the power plant died in the suddenly cold water. Such an event would be most unlikely at the Atlantic Generating Station, since one reactor would always be kept running. The tons of fish that died a few years ago at the nuclear station at Indian Point, New York, were attracted into channels that had been built to conduct water from the edge of the Hudson River to the Consolidated Edison Company's intake screens. The fish went into the channels, apparently, because they liked the shelter and they liked the feel of the flow of the indrawn water. They would turn and face it, and swim against it, and keep on swimming in place until they were so tired they could not swim out. They then went up against the screens and died. Consolidated Edison moved the screens out to the river. The fish kill would not have happened if the behavior of fish had been taken into account in the initial design.

Raney and his ichthyologists significantly influenced certain basic design choices for the Atlantic Generating Station, and refinements would no doubt come along with the continuing study. In tanks, they tested the swimming speed and swimming strength of various species. They recommended that the water-intake velocity be kept below a foot per second. This would require six screens per plant, each fourteen feet wide and twenty-seven feet deep. The ichthyologists also recommended that the heated water be discharged rapidly, since a jet of water would repel fish. Such a jet—sent out through pipes in the breakwater—would create a mixing area of about two acres, in which temperatures would range from seventeen to five degrees above the temperature of the surrounding seas before the water spread out as a thermal plume. Experiments with fish of varying species had shown that a rise of five degrees, in any season, would be well below "the thermal point at which the locomotory activity becomes disorganized and the animals lose their ability to escape from conditions that will cause their deaths." Because currents of the littoral drift, whether they were moving northeast or southwest, almost always ran parallel to the coast, Ichthyological Associates suggested that there be two openings in the breakwater atoll, that they be lined up with the currents, and that no obstructions float between. It was this suggestion that resulted in the penannular shape of the breakwater. Fish having a difficult time at one opening could slide back with the current and go out the other. On the rare occasions when no current was moving and the sea was calm, water would be sucked in toward the plants from both openings in the atoll, but at less than a foot per second—not enough to trap a fish. Gossip went around the nuclear-safety circuit that in the design of the Atlantic Generating Station fish were getting even more consideration than human beings.

Meanwhile, the two or three dozen people in the employ of Ichthyological Associates who were conducting the New Jersey Marine Ecological Study continued to scrape the bottom for benthic samples, to trawl systematically for demersal fishes, and to compile intricate records of species by age, by season caught, by temperature, by weather, and by hour of the day. Early one morning, Valiant II, a chartered fishing boat out of Leeds Point, traversed the plant site dragging a twenty-five-foot semi-balloon trawl. Four miles or so to the northwest, on the lower stretches of Long Beach Island, stood the water towers of Holgate and Beach Haven. The one tower was green, the other orange, and from the perspective of the site they looked like loaded golf tees. Eleven miles to the southwest was the skyline of Atlantic City, rising tall, suggesting Manhattan to an eye that moved no closer. On a summer day at the site, many dozens of small fishing boats would have crowded the foreground, but now, in winter, three clam dredges were the only neighbors the ichthyologists had. Scooping tons of big surf clams—some for Snow's, some for Howard Johnson's—the clammers moved slowly. Thick smoke from their exhausts braided above them and formed a black plume that reached from the three-mile limit to the Holgate tower. For fifteen minutes, Valiant II, moving at two knots, had been collecting a benthic sample, beginning the trawl just to landward of the submarine sand hill. (On Valiant II's Simrad depth recorder, graphite tracings showed the position of the ridge, rising from minus forty feet to minus twenty-eight and descending again to minus forty-three at the site.) A winch turned, and long ropes that trailed behind the ship were hauled in. Trawl doors came aboard first—their purpose was to keep the mouth of the net seventeen feet wide—and then the net itself. It had a fine-mesh inner liner for stopping larvae and post-larval fishes. Young men wearing rubber gloves, rubber boots, and rubber overalls lifted the net and spilled hundreds of creatures into a galvanized tub and onto the deck around it. A surf clam. Moon snails. Pipefish. Little skates. Sand shrimp. Winter flounder. Longhorn sculpin. Eelpout. Atlantic herring. Spotted hake. Red hake. A five-pound cod. In a couple of years of such hauls, this was the first cod. New Jersey cod are usually associated with wrecks. They prefer, in any case, to stay a good many miles offshore. This one was dropped into a large jar that contained ten per cent formalin and ninety per cent seawater, slits having been made in its skin so the formalin could get into the flesh beneath.

Kneeling on the deck, griping, the young men began a meticulous count of specimens and species—and now and again offered comments.

"Jesus, what a big haul."

" 'Jesus' is right."

"Yeah."

"Look at all that hake."

Red hake, when small, live inside scallop shells with scallops, they said. The scallops somehow know that their shellmates are red hake. If fish of another species try to get in, the scallops kick them out.

The teeth of the eelpout were green.

"From eating sand dollars, which are covered with algae."

Codium, a grasslike material, was copious on the deck.

"It's only been around here ten or fifteen years. It has air pockets in it. It grows on clams, rocks them loose, and floats them to the surface."

The bodies of conger-eel larvae were transparent, with eyes —black dots—bulging at one end. Through the young windowpane flounders one could see the grain of the wood of the deck.

"Windowpane flounders eat a lot of mysid shrimp."

(99)

"Summer flounders are left-eyed. Winter flounders are right-eyed."

"We look at their scales—see how fast they're growing. Look at their stomachs—see what they've been eating."

"Look. A god-damned anchovy."

"They're important in the diets of weakfish and bluefish."

"Herring time. Four. Eight. Twelve . . ."

"My grandfather smokes them."

There were forty-two herring, each about fourteen inches long.

"Butterfish. Silversides. Sand lances."

The sand lances had both the length and the diameter of standard pencils.

"We once brought in a twenty-two-pound striped bass and found a quart of sand lances in its stomach."

Don Danila was working on a master's degree there on the deck with Rich Smith and Gerry Miller. As they sorted and counted, they spoke data to Chuck Milstein, the assistant project leader. A trim and light-figured man with a blue knitted cap, blue-tinted glasses, rubber overalls, and a clipboard, Milstein recorded numbers of specimens, numbers of species, the total weight of each species, along with the depth, temperature, salinity, and dissolved-oxygen content of the water the fish had come from. The day was calm, partly cloudy, under a cool sun. The air temperature was forty-seven degrees. The sea's temperature was forty, and it varied only half a degree throughout the water column, from the surface to the bottom.

Seven stations were a day's trawling. Between counts, while the net was in the water, the ichthyologists sat in the Valiant II's cabin and read the newspaper—the National Fisherman.

Or they checked instruments. Or they threw a secchi disc into the ocean to measure turbidity. White, heavy, attached to a line knotted at one-foot intervals, it sank, and when it disappeared from view its depth in feet was recorded.

"Ten feet."

"Not very clear."

"It's getting ready for a plankton bloom, that's why."

"When phytoplankton is blooming, you can smell it. The ocean smells dank."

"When plankton is concentrated in the net, it smells sweet, like cucumbers."

"A thousand pounds of phytoplankton can support a hundred pounds of zooplankton. A hundred pounds of zooplankton can support ten pounds of small predators. Ten pounds of small predators can support one pound of large predator—in other words, a striped bass."

On other trips, on other days, they would tend their lobster pots; they would tag striped bass; they would make gillnetting runs and pelagic trawls. They once caught so many lion's-mane jellyfish they could not haul the net in. Jellyfish might be something of a problem going up against the screens, for jellyfish cannot fight a foot-per-second current.

Summer trawls had yielded, typically, sea robins, dogfish and other sharks, scup, perch, menhaden. Menhaden were the most numerous fish of the region. A school of them might weigh sixteen tons. Sixteen tons of menhaden could be a problem against the screens. A massive impingement of menhaden could shut the plant down.

Over the years, about a hundred and fifty fish species had been collected. Sturgeon. Goosefish. Fluke. Squid. Rays— including a twenty-five-pound spiny butterfly ray, out of its place, which is the deep ocean. Sea snails—a rare fish in this area. All were kept in jars on the shelves of a fish library behind the group's lab, which had once been a private home, in Absecon. When a count was finished on the deck of Valiant II, only a certain number of fish were kept for the library. The others were thrown back over the side.

Northern fish and tropical fish were migrants to the area—for example, barracuda. The summer of 1973 had brought warm seas and the highest temperature ever recorded in the surf at Atlantic City—eighty-three degrees. Tropical fish rarely seen in New Jersey waters came into the trawling nets: bigeyes, lookdowns, goatfish, pompano.

Jay Chamblin, a medical parasitologist who was now doing zooplankton studies for Ichthyological Associates, was aboard. "In one haul of the net, eighty thousand gallons are filtered," he observed. "More than two million gallons per minute are supposed to go through the cooling system of each reactor. You can begin to see the problem." Through the cooling system would go the eggs and larvae of many fish, and the phytoplankton they feed on. The plant might kill millions of organisms, but it was hard to say what the impact would be on the total population, because populations explode.

Chamblin, pleasant and subtle, had a lean and ecological look. He lived in Beach Haven, the nearest community to the site. He saw a fly, caught it in one hand, and stared at it in fascination. "I think this may be the first fly of the spring," he said. Mischievously, he added, "Look at its small abdomen. At first, I thought it was one of those radioactive flies with abnormally small abdomens they find around nuclear plants and don't talk about very much."

As a group, Ichthyological Associates prefer to stay out of

discussions about radiation. All nuclear plants emit certain radioactive isotopes—such as iodine 131 and tritium—both in gases that go into the air and in discharged cooling water. In the Atomic Energy Commission's *Survey of Unique Technical Features of the Floating Nuclear Power Plant Concept*, it had been noted that "individuals who fish near the plant and its breakwater may be exposed both to the radiation from the liquid effluent and to the accumulated radioactivity in the fish that they catch." The survey continued, "The potentially significant radiation dose from fish ingestion and from fishing and boating near the plant will have to be evaluated at each proposed site. The problem could be similar to that at a lakeside nuclear power plant, although it may be more severe if the breakwater becomes a site for accumulation of radionuclides that can be taken up by edible marine organisms." The amount of radiation, in any case, would be small, the A.E.C. said. As around any land-based plant, it would be "a small fraction of the population dose attributable to the natural radiation background." Or, as one Public Service consultant later put it, "the radiation content of the plant's discharge water will actually be less per unit volume than that present in an ordinary can of beer." Ichthyological Associates' director, Edward Raney, testifying before the New Jersey State Assembly's Committee on Air, Water Pollution, and Public Health, had forthrightly said, "Radioactivity has nothing to do with fish. This is not in my field of expertise, but . . . I can assure you that the fish you eat from out there will be no different than the fish you get anywhere else."

Now, on Valiant II, Chamblin said, "No one in the lab is a proponent of nuclear energy. The staff is wary of fission."

It was marine biology, in the context of what Milstein

called a "wide-scale ecological project," that had attracted
them to the job—a chance to advance their knowledge and
their degrees with what amounted to a grant from Public Service.

"We have no constraints on what we do," Milstein said.

Chamblin said, "We know more and more about what we
are destroying."

Milstein said, "Some companies would insist that all findings be kept in-house. Public Service actually disseminates the
information. And our reports are not sanitized before they are
published. To do the job adequately, we try to avoid getting
into the nuclear-safety discussion generally. Let me say this,
though: if this were an oil rig going in, we wouldn't want to
work here."

On another winter day, more raw and windy, a research
vessel called Sea Quest went out through the inlet and on into
confused and choppy water to tend what the Atlantic Generating Station's full-time oceanographers referred to as "the
farm." In the immediate acreage of the site they had planted
some hundreds of instruments at varying depths. Wave riders
rested on the sea. Spherical, tied to long lines, they could ride
any wave from trough to crest. They knew where they were in
feet from the bottom, and they broadcast their movements to
recorders ashore, which, in turn, provided numbers to com-
puters. Wind instruments were bolted to a toroidal buoy.
Dominating the farm was a tower that rose sixteen to twenty
feet above the ocean surface and stood on a tripod of heavy
steel pipes. It stood in thirty-eight feet of water, and its pilings

went down fifty-five feet into the seabed. A few months before, a once-in-forty-years wave had completely overtopped the tower, causing damage but not destruction. Instruments excluded, the tower had cost more than a hundred thousand dollars. It had been put there by the Environmental Equipment Division of E.G.&G. International, Public Service's oceanographic consultants. Instruments clung to it like mollusks—an anemometer, a bubbler tide gauge, a barnacle collector, an orthogonal current meter, a tank for red dye.

The purpose was to construct a hydrographic profile through many seasons over a broad ocean grid—to predict the effect that the sea would have on the generating station and to predict the effect that the generating station would have on the sea, most notably in the outspreading thermal plume. Many of the instruments were powered with batteries. Some contained 16-mm. cameras. All needed regular attention on a rotating schedule. Divers in wet suits stood prepared on Sea Quest's deck, their legs braced against pitch and roll—bare flesh showing between their rubber pants and rubber shirts.

"Is it cold in those things?"

"You're damned right it's cold."

Green spray came across the cockpit coaming. The divers jumped into the ocean. Treading water, they inspected wave riders. Going below, they brought up a nine-hundred-pound railroad wheel with current meters and temperature recorders strung along a chain behind it. Remaining on deck were John Cooper, the chief oceanographer on the project, and his boss, Ralph Eldridge, the program manager for E.G.&G. Eldridge —partly bald, middle-aged, quick with words—was by training a meteorologist. He described Cooper as a wet oceanographer, explaining that a wet oceanographer works in literal touch with the sea, while a dry one sits at a desk and uses data. Cooper was a heavyset man, still youthful, with tortoiseshell glasses, which were now flaky with salt. His hair was stringy, brine-soaked. He had a warm, disarming smile. He said he had been at the Woods Hole Oceanographic Institution, on Cape Cod, for nine years before signing on for this project. At Woods Hole, when he was there, no one had been doing shallow-water oceanography. "After the Second World War, they all went into deep water," he said. "It was easier. Now, with the environmental movement, they have been coming inshore. It's good. People are very much interested in what we are doing here, just from the oceanographic point of view."

They were finding out where the water came from, he said. Water from the New York Bight, for example, apparently moved south in gyres—great vortices ten miles in diameter, rolling down the coast. They mixed, gradually, with waters of the continental shelf. One could tell where water had come from by its temperature and salinity. Mediterranean water, for instance, is thirteen degrees centigrade, and its salinity is thirty-seven parts per thousand. Moving into the Atlantic, it sinks. Wherever it goes, it keeps its Mediterranean characteristics for years. Look deep enough and you can find it in the Caribbean. Typical ocean salinity is thirty-five parts per thousand. The water from the New York Bight can be as low as twenty-nine. On this part of the continental shelf, Cooper said, the characteristic salinity was thirty-two. Using such facts, one could determine where water had come from and pretty much where it was going. Oceanographers used to think that when water had settled somewhere it would stay down and old for centuries. That was not necessarily true. The Atomic Energy Commission, making such an assumption, had once dumped radioactive wastes in the Gulf of Mexico, only to discover that the water was much younger than people had thought.

These were boundary conditions here—two and eight-tenths miles offshore, near an inlet, near the surface, near the bottom. It was neither deep nor estuarine water. It was "a never-never region," Cooper said, where some waves were feeling the bottom and others were not. Winds, predominantly, were what created the local currents. Years ago, Vagn Walfrid Ekman, the great Swedish oceanographer, had written a book on wind-drift currents, and that was about all that E.G.&G. had to refer to beyond its own accumulating data. The prevailing current here ran southwest. About a fifth of the time, it turned around and flowed northeast. When it did, considerable upwelling occurred just seaward of the site, and that, said Cooper, contradicted everything he had previously learned. ("Classically, you learn that upwelling takes place in deep water and is then advected in.") Taking all things together—wind stresses, shallow-water waves, upwelling, the variability of current systems, interreaction of air and sea—the oceanographers had as their goal to reach an understanding of mixing processes in near-coastal areas, this one in particular. Water masses were being created here which would then flow somewhere else. In a decade or so, they were to begin to carry the effluent of a Westinghouse reactor.

When the oceanographers were not checking fixed instruments, Eldridge put in, they sometimes chased drogues for as much as ten hours, simulating a tracking of the thermal plume. Drogues were floats that consisted of intersecting planes designed to be equally affected from any direction by the push of current. Often, here, it was a two-layer ocean. While the littoral drift moved southwest in the lower fathoms, wind-drift currents made tangents above. So E.G.&G. had developed two kinds of drogue—surface and subsurface—and the oceanographers often chased sixteen at a time.

Or they might drop five hundred cc.s of rhodomine-B into the sea at the site and watch as a plume the color of Mercurochrome began to drift. As the plume matured, it would turn into what Cooper described as a "rotating swastika"—spinning along the coast, or toward land, or toward the open sea. As the dye diffused, the eye could continue to see it until the solution was as weak as two parts per billion. A fluorometer on Sea Quest could see four times as well as that.

To an extent much greater than had been true with the ichthyologists, the oceanographic people seemed dedicated to the success of the utility's project. They said that indeed they were. "We try to keep our thinking reasonably germane to what we're trying to do out here," Eldridge said. "We feel no conflict with the interests of Public Service Electric & Gas." Cooper, for his part, said he felt that his commitment was fifty per cent to oceanographic study and fifty per cent to the utility. Cooper and Eldridge both said they thought the concept of ocean-floating nuclear plants was sound and sensible. Eldridge said, "My first reactions were 'What a hell of a place to put a plant! Can't they think of a better place than the ocean? Why put a nuclear plant in such a hostile environment?' But after I got into it I changed my mind. We all did. And everyone in my group here is a professional environmentalist—not a cocktail environmentalist, self-appointed. Regulations are nebulous for this site and this concept. The work we do will help establish regulations for future floating plants."

More spray had dried on Cooper's glasses, but he did not seem to notice. "Seventy million cubic metres per second goes by in the Gulf Stream," he said. "To me, the real brass ring is trying to figure out how to grab it. Take one per cent of the energy of the Gulf Stream and you've done it. That's it. All you'll ever need. The problem is solved. Of course, I don't know how you'd do it."

THE DESIGN LIFE of the floating nuclear plants would be forty years. What if a storm so great that it would happen only once in a million years should come along during that time? The million-year storm would be a hurricane about eighty miles in diameter, moving with an advance speed of fifty knots, with sustained winds blowing at something like a hundred and fifty miles an hour, and with gusts far higher than that. Such a hurricane coming into the vicinity of the plant site would surge the surface of the ocean to a point beyond which it could be surged no more. The level of the sea would be lifted there about nineteen feet—a figure governed by the bathymetry, or depth and configuration, of the bottom. And what if the million-year storm should happen to come at a time of highest astronomical tide, which would be six feet—twice the normal daily variation? Now the water depth—forty plus nineteen plus six—would be up to sixty-five feet, the most prodigious water column that could ever stand at the selected site, two and eight-tenths miles off Little Egg Inlet. Never mind that a large percentage of southern New Jersey would now be under water. Atlantic City would be drowned outright. Vineland would be Venice. The hills of the Pine Barrens would be islands in the flood. What would happen to the floating nuclear plants? And what would happen if at the height of such a storm a three-hundred-thousand-ton supertanker—the largest that could float in these waters with its tanks discharged—were to stray off course and at sixteen knots crash head on into the breakwater? What if the supertanker rammed its prow into one of the gaps left open for the benefit of fish?

The Atomic Energy Commission wished to know the answers to these questions. For that matter, the A.E.C. wished to know what would happen if a supertanker hit the breakwater on a dead-calm day. Intentions were that the floating nuclear plants would be in "safe shut-down condition" during the "probable maximum hurricane" (the once-in-a-million-years storm), but what about the once-in-a-hundred-years storm, when the ocean surface was up sixteen feet and forty-foot waves were breaking? Could the plants continue to make fissions, steam, and electricity safely under such conditions? Could the hundred-year storm be the maximum "operating-basis storm"? The A.E.C. required that information, too.

At the Stevens Institute of Technology, in Hoboken, in 1972, a crude model breakwater made of wood, chicken wire, and pebbles was put in a tank and hit with the scaled equivalent of fifty-foot waves. The idea was that green water should never overtop the breakwater, and thus, for twenty-five thousand dollars or so, Public Service learned how high to build it. More advanced tests of model nuclear plants and a model breakwater were made at the Army Corps of Engineers Waterways Experiment Station, in Vicksburg, Mississippi. Certain basics about the configuration of the breakwater were determined there—the angles of its slopes, the appropriate weight for the armoring *dolosse*. (In an early test, the million-year storm knocked a few *dolosse* off the breakwater.) Such tests gave answers only for components, though, and ultimately nothing less than a total model would do—a model of the bathymetry of the entire region of the chosen site, with a model ocean upon it, and a model nuclear generating station floating there, surrounded by a breakwater made of stone and sand and *dolosse*. A suitable scale would be one to sixty-four. Within two thousand miles of Newark, there was only one test basin large enough to contain such a design. Europeans were far ahead of Americans in such coastal-engineering facilities. The Dutch, for example, could have placed a suitable piece of New Jersey's ocean in a corner of their laboratory at Delft. The one sufficiently ample facility in the United States was at the University of Florida, in Gainesville, where a coastal-and-oceanographic-engineering laboratory had been built to house extensive working models of Florida bays, inlets, estuaries, and beaches—whose erosion was worth preventing, because it could produce concomitant erosion in the treasuries of the state.

Kehnemuyi took me there one day in 1975. As we approached the building, on the edge of the university campus, he commented that the European, particularly Dutch, laboratories of this type were more numerous because "in this world we do what we need to do, and they live with water." And now, he said, New Jersey was in a predicament analogous to Holland's. The structure we entered was steel-walled and might have been a gymnasium. Its "model slab" was close to twelve thousand square feet in size (roughly four basketball courts), and had been molded to the bathymetry of the New Jersey seabed. Almost a foot of water covered the entire basin—a level scaled to the water column as it would be during a once-in-a-hundred-years storm. Floating in the center of the room were two squarish hulls supporting scaled nuclear-power plants, and these were surrounded by an atoll breakwater complete from caissons to *dolosse*. Eighteen thousand *dolosse* would be required for the breakwater in the sea, so eighteen thousand *dolosse*—precisely configured, made to scale—covered the breakwater here. Electrical wires from the model power plants went up to a central ganglion suspended from the ceiling and then ran over to a control room, where electronic equipment could absorb the findings of a hundred and twenty instruments that profiled, among other things, hull pressures, mooring forces, and six degrees of freedom of motion: pitch, yaw, roll, heave, surge, and sway. Afloat in a sheltered corner of the basin was a supertanker about eighteen feet long. "All that is missing are fish," Kehnemuyi said. "We don't know how to one-sixty-fourth a fish." Across one end of the basin was a wave generator—a set of a hundred paddles on a cam—repetitively shoving toward the breakwater waves of the once-in-a-hundred-years storm. The waves were seven or eight inches high. Scaled up, they would have been forty-footers—great, booming rollers—and they simply went into the *dolosse* like ripples licking the edge of a pond, while the nuclear plants themselves, steady in the atoll, pitched and rolled to a degree imperceptible to the eye. The degree was less than one. The generating station could operate with impunity in the midst of tremendous seas, Kehnemuyi observed. "I'm sure you could design a floating nuclear plant that would take ten or fifteen degrees of roll and pitch, but you would have to change systems inside them. Our design maximum is three degrees, and at three degrees everything that would be in a land-based plant would operate O.K. on the sea."

Stone beaches absorbed the waves at the far end. There was no apparent backwash, or "reflection." A desk and a chair stood surreally in the ocean, landward of the plant, the better for the test director to make notes in proximity to the model. His name was Robert Dean, and he was a University of Florida professor, physical oceanographer, civil engineer—a tall, slender man with dark-rimmed glasses, a black mustache, and an extraordinary affection for water. On his days off, he liked nothing more than to dive into one or another of Florida's limestone sinks, scuba gear on his back, and swim upstream into the total darkness of an underground river, carrying a light and seeing albino crayfish that had no functioning eyes. He had found stone knives from the Ice Age, when the water table was lower and such caverns were dry. He had to watch his oxygen supply closely, and turn back when it was not quite half gone. And now he strode through the ocean in long rubber boots, and pointed to other boots for us to put on, but said to be careful, because not long ago a visitor from the Atomic Energy Commission had pulled on one of those boots and there had been a snake in it.

We walked through the ocean to the plants and the breakwater. They were built on a turntable, so that waves could approach from any angle. In a typical winter storm, Dean said, when eighteen-foot waves would be hitting the breakwater, they would merely ripple around its base and look like swells. So the tests had indicated. In a two- or three-year storm —the biggest storm to come along in such a period—the plants would pitch and roll about a quarter of one degree.

The model ocean was fresh water, but the density difference—salt water is two and a half per cent denser than fresh water—had been calculated into every part of the model. The plants themselves were just platforms of wood and steel covered with calibrated weights and plumbed to deliver thermal discharge. A large boiler on one side of the room provided the "nuclear" heat. Also off to one side were two glistening white Styrofoam shells that had been sculptured in the shape of the ultimate power plants. Purely cosmetic, they could be placed over the weighted platforms to impress a camera.

Certain harbors sometimes have problems with a phenomenon known as resonance, wherein waves that might be, say, two feet high on the outside build up energy within the harbor until waves in there stand ten feet high or higher. The harbor at Marina del Rey, in California, has this problem, and so does Los Angeles-Long Beach. Such harbors are energy traps. The most notable one in the world is Capetown. Under certain conditions of incoming wind and wave, resonance builds up there to such an extent that ships snap their hawsers. Resonance seems to be a function of, more than anything else, the periods of the waves. Various A.E.C. consultants, including one from Capetown, had worried about resonance within the New Jersey atoll, so the Gainesville lab had created waves of widely differing size and periodicity in an attempt to get a real chop going within the breakwater. The biggest stir they could create was one-quarter the size of the waves outside, and they concluded that the Atlantic Generating Station would have no difficulty with resonance.

The formula for the tallest wave that can stand in a given swatch of relatively shallow sea is seventy-eight hundredths of the depth of the water it moves through. If the ocean is sixty-five feet deep, as it would be during a superhurricane at the site off New Jersey, the largest wave that could stand there would be a forty-eight-footer. Anything larger would have broken before it got there. "So we are not interested in the hundred-foot wave," Kehnemuyi said. "It would never get to us. A wave feels the bottom, feels any object. The bathymetry is not an absolute ramp. When the wave feels that there is an object in front of it, it breaks. A forty-eight-foot wave would be almost impossible, but we test for it. We also feel that the storm that would produce it is not credible, but we make the storm."

The most punishing of waves come at fifteen-second intervals. To imitate such waves on a one-to-sixty-four scale, it is necessary—according to the laws of hydraulic modelling—to divide the desired interval between the waves by the square root of the scale, which in this case is eight. So the waves in Gainesville generally pound the breakwater eight times as fast as they would in the ocean. Cameras film them at eight times normal film speed. When the pictures are projected on a screen at normal speed, the waves fragment and shoot spray in the air exactly as they would in the ocean. Public Service's films are something to see, with probable-maximum-hurricane waves, in Ektachrome, sending white water over the top of the breakwater, but never a sheet of green. The supertanker has been filmed, too, hitting the breakwater from every angle at sixteen knots, with the ocean surface up to the big-hurricane levels. A supertanker crash is anticlimactic. After a minor crunch, the ship stops dead. The bows do not buckle. Instead, they form a nest in the *dolosse*. When the ship is removed, the breakwater heals itself, as *dolosse* fall into the nest.

Peter C. H. Pritchard, vice-president of the Florida Audubon Society, appeared unexpectedly in the model basin, waded out from shore, and began to beard Kehnemuyi about the safety of nuclear-power plants, floating or otherwise. He said he wanted to make clear, first, that he had no patience with people who deplore power plants while freehandedly consuming the power they produce. He said he recognized the complexity of the utilities' problem. But still he was worried about loss-of-coolant accidents, core meltdowns, and breaches of containment walls—accidents that could release to the air and the sea much more radioactivity than there was in the bombs of Hiroshima and Nagasaki.

Kehnemuyi said that the company was doing tests for core meltdowns—seeing, by computer more than by tank testing, what might happen if a core got into the water. "But we categorically and very emphatically feel that this is a paper exercise," he said. "Such a thing will never happen. Studies are showing that the chances of a reactor's having a major accident are one in a billion years—reactors are that carefully and that redundantly designed. Let me assure you, our company would not put a penny into this sort of project if we thought such a thing could happen."

Pritchard—young, handsome, tall—stood there towering above the floating nuclear plants and looking doubtful. As it happened, he had been born in Belfast and educated at Oxford. He was the author of a book called *Turtles of the World.* Kehnemuyi—stocky, with short-cropped graying hair and shining brown eyes—had grown up in Istanbul, where his father was an importer of fine stationery. And now here they were, paths crossed, a Turk educated in Illinois and an Irishman from Oxford, standing in an artificial ocean in Florida and joining the issue of a floating nuclear plant off the coast of New Jersey and aspects of it that conceivably could concern the world.

The power station floating beside them was still the only thing of its kind, of any size, anywhere—and would be for some time to come. Years had passed since it had been conceived. Not so much as a pail of gravel had yet been placed in the authentic ocean.

Public Service and Offshore Power Systems would first have to obtain construction and operating permits. From the A.E.C.—now split into two government agencies—they had received only "generic approval." Opposition had formed among the beach communities ("S.O.S., Save Our Seas"), and the Atlantic County Citizens' Council on the Environment had petitioned to intervene. Hearings would be held at every level, and the fate of the project depended on the outcome of each hearing. Public Service had already put tens of millions of dollars into the project. Opponents complained that so much committed money might serve unfairly as leverage toward the granting of permits. The company, for its part, complained that the United States was "approaching an unworkable system" when so much had to be spent on a concept merely to prepare it for the hearing stage.

The company people were, if nothing else, prepared. They knew how many planes flew over the site—two hundred and fifty a day. They had mapped the location of every major well within a twenty-mile radius. They knew how many people were likely to be living within fifty miles of the site in the year 2020. They knew the exact distance—eleven and two-tenths miles—from the site to the nearest dairy cow. They had published an *Environmental Report—Construction Permit Stage*, which weighed twenty-two pounds and contained fifteen hundred pages. And now—roughly halfway toward their goal—they had come to the isthmus of the hourglass, where everything could, quite conceivably, stop.

Like bulbs around a mirror, floating nuclear plants might one day edge the seas. People who thought the concept was madness still had much time in which to say so. People who thought the concept was among the best of possible alternatives could present their case as well. More than fifty construction and operating permits were absolutely required. So far, not one had been issued.

In December 1978, Public Service put off its order for the two Atlantic power plants, explaining that rising rates and conservation of electricity had reduced the annual increase in demand for the company's product, with the result that new generating sites would not be needed, after all, for the remainder of this century. To float large-scale nuclear-power plants on the surface of the sea was apparently an idea whose time had not yet come—at any rate, in New Jersey. One might think that the idea would be more remote than ever in the aftermath of Three Mile Island, the nuclear plant on the Susquehanna that in the early spring of 1979 seemed to be preparing to relocate itself on the banks of the Yangtze River. But Offshore Power Systems, the manufacturer, continues to advance the licensing process, and hopes to put eight floating nuclear plants into production as soon as a license is granted by the Nuclear Regulatory Commission.

THE
PINBALL
PHILOSOPHY

New York City, March 1975

J. Anthony Lukas is a world-class pinball player who, between tilts, does some free-lance writing. In our city, he is No. ½. That is to say, he is one of two players who share pinball preeminence—two players whose special skills within the sport are so multiple and varied that they defy comparative analysis. The other star is Tom Buckley, of the *Times*. Pinball people tend to gravitate toward Lukas or Buckley. Lukas is a Lukasite. He respects Buckley, but he sees himself as the whole figure, the number "1." His machine is a Bally. Public pinball has been illegal in New York for many decades, but private ownership is permitted, and Lukas plays, for the most part, at home.

Lukas lives in an old mansion, a city landmark, on West Seventy-sixth Street. The machine is in his living room, under a high, elegant ceiling, near an archway to rooms beyond. Bally is the Rolls-Royce of pinball, he explains as he snaps a ball into action. It rockets into the ellipse at the top of the playfield. It ricochets four times before beginning its descent. Lukas likes a four-bounce hold in the ellipse—to set things up for a long ball. There is something faintly, and perhaps consciously, nefarious about Lukas, who is an aristocratic, olive-skinned, Andalusian sort of man, with deep eyes in dark wells. As the butts of his hands pound the corners of his machine, one can imagine him cheating at polo. "It's a wrist game," he says, tremoring the Bally, helping the steel ball to bounce six times off the top thumper-bumper and, each time, go back up a slot to the ellipse—an awesome economy of fresh beginnings. "Strong wrists are really all you want to use. The term for what I am doing is 'reinforcing.'" His voice, rich and dense, pours out like cigarette smoke filtered through a New England prep school. "There are certain basics to remember," he says. "Above all, don't flail with the flipper. You *carry* the ball in the direction you want it to go. You can almost cradle the ball on the flipper. And always hit the slingshot hard. That's the slingshot there—where the rubber is stretched between bumpers. Reinforce it hard. And never—never—drift toward the free-ball gate." Lukas reinforces the machine just as the ball hits the slingshot. The rebound comes off with blurring speed, striking bumpers, causing gongs to ring and lights to flash. Under his hands, the chrome on the frame has long since worn away.

Lukas points out that one of the beauties of his Bally is that it is asymmetrical. Early pinball machines had symmetrical playfields—symmetrical thumper-bumpers—but in time they became free-form, such as this one, with its field laid out not just for structure but also for surprise. Lukas works in this room—stacks of manuscript on shelves and tables. He has been working for many months on a book that will weigh five pounds. It will be called *Nightmare: The Dark Side of the Nixon Years*—a congenially chosen title, implying that there was a bright side.* The pinball machine is Lukas's collaborator. "When a paragraph just won't go," he says, "and I begin to say to myself, 'I can't make this work,' I get up and play the machine. I score in a high range. Then I go back to the typewriter a new man. I have beat the machine. Therefore I can beat the paragraph." He once won a Pulitzer Prize.

The steel ball rolls into the "death channel"—Lukas's term for a long alley down the left side—and drops out of sight off the low end of the playfield, finished.

"I have thought of analogies between Watergate and pinball. Everything is connected. Bumpers. Rebounds. You light lights and score. Chuck Colson is involved in almost every aspect of the Watergate story: the dirty tricks, the coverup, the laundered money—all connected. How hard you hit off the thumper-bumper depends on how hard you hit off the slingshot depends on how well you work the corners. In a sense, pinball is a reflection of the complexity of the subject I am writing about. Bear in mind, I take this with considerable tongue-in-cheek."

With another ball, he ignites an aurora on the scoreboard. During the ball's complex, prolonged descent, he continues to set forth the pinball philosophy. "More seriously, the game does give you a sense of controlling things in a way that in life you can't do. And there is risk in it, too. The ball flies into the ellipse, into the playfield—full of opportunities. But there's

* Lukas ultimately decided to be less congenial, and changed the title to *Nightmare: The Underside of the Nixon Years* (Viking Press, 1976).

always the death channel—the run-out slot. There are rewards, prizes, coming off the thumper-bumper. The ball crazily bounces from danger to opportunity and back to danger. You need reassurance in life that in taking risks you will triumph, and pinball gives you that reaffirmation. Life is a risky game, but you can beat it."

Unfortunately, Lukas has a sick flipper. At the low end of the playfield, two flippers guard the run-out slot, but one waggles like a broken wing, pathetic, unable to function, to fling the ball uphill for renewed rewards. The ball, instead, slides by the crippled flipper and drops from view.

Lukas opens the machine. He lifts the entire playfield, which is hinged at the back, and props it up on a steel arm, like the lid of a grand piano. Revealed below is a neat, arresting world that includes spring-loaded hole kickers, contact switches, target switches, slingshot assemblies, the score-motor unit, the electric anti-cheat, three thumper-bumper relays, the top rebound relay, the key-gate assembly ("the key gate will keep you out of the death channel"), the free-ball-gate assembly, and—not least—the one-and-a-quarter-amp slo-blo. To one side, something that resembles a plumb bob hangs suspended within a metal ring. If the bob moves too far out of plumb, it touches the ring. Tilt. The game is dead.

Lukas is not an electrician. All he can do is massage the flipper's switch assembly, which does not respond—not even with a shock. He has about had it with this machine. One cannot collaborate with a sick flipper. The queasy truth comes over him: no pinball, no paragraphs. So he hurries downstairs and into a taxi, telling the driver to go to Tenth

Avenue in the low Forties—a pocket of the city known as Coin Row.

EN ROUTE, Lukas reflects on his long history in the game—New York, Cambridge, Paris—and his relationships with specific machines ("they're like wives"). When he was the *Times'* man in the Congo, in the early sixties, the post was considered a position of hardship, so he was periodically sent to Paris for rest and rehabilitation, which he got playing pinball in a Left Ban brasserie. He had perfected his style as an undergraduate at Harvard, sharing a machine at the *Crimson* with David Halberstam ("Halberstam is aggressive at everything he does, and he was very good"). Lukas's father was a Manhattan attorney. Lukas's mother died when he was eight. He grew up, for the most part, in a New England community—Putney, Vermont—where he went to pre-prep and prep school. Putney was "straitlaced," "very high-minded," "a life away from the maelstrom"—potters' wheels, no pinball. Lukas craved "liberation," and developed a yearning for what he imagined as low life, and so did his schoolmate Christopher Lehmann-Haupt. Together, one weekend, they dipped as low as they knew how. They went to New York. And they went to two movies! They went to shooting galleries! They went to a flea circus! They played every coin-operated machine they could find—and they stayed up until after dawn! All this was pretty low, but not low enough, for that was the spring of 1951, and still beyond reach—out there past the fingertips of Tantalus—was pinball, the ban on which had been emphatically reinforced a few years earlier by Fiorello H. LaGuardia, who saw pinball as a gambling device corruptive of the city's youth. To Lukas, pinball symbolized all the time-wasting and ne'er-do-welling that puritan Putney did not. In result, he mastered the game. He says, "It puts me in touch with a world in which I never lived. I am attracted to pinball for its seediness, its slightly disreputable reputation."

On Coin Row, Lukas knows just where he is going, and without a sidewise glance passes storefronts bearing names like The World of Pinball Amusement ("SALES—REPAIR") and Manhattan Coin Machine ("PARTS—SUPPLIES"). He heads directly for the Mike Munves Corporation, 577 Tenth Avenue, the New York pinball exchange, oldest house (1912) on the row. Inside is Ralph Hotkins, in double-breasted blazer—broker in pinball machines. The place is more warehouse than store, and around Hotkins, and upstairs above him, are rank upon rank of Gottliebs, Williamses, Ballys, Playmatics—every name in the game, including forty-year-old antique completely mechanical machines, ten balls for a nickel, the type that Mayor LaGuardia himself destroyed with an axe. Hotkins—a prosperous man, touched with humor, not hurting for girth—got his start in cigarette machines in the thirties, moved up to jukeboxes, and then, in 1945, while LaGuardia was still mayor, to game machines. He had two daughters, and he brought them up on pinball. They were in the shop almost every afternoon after school, and all day Saturday. One daughter now has a Ph.D. in English literature and the other a Ph.D. in political science. So much for the Little Flower. In this era of open massage and off-track betting, Hotkins has expected the ban to lift, but the courts, strangely, continue to uphold it.* Meanwhile, his customers —most of whom are technically "private"—include Wall Street brokerage houses where investors shoot free pinball under the ticker, Seventh Avenue dress houses that wish to keep their buyers amused, the Circus Circus peepshow emporium on West Forty-second Street, many salesrooms, many showrooms, and J. Anthony Lukas.

"Yes, Mr. Lukas. What can we do for you?"

Lukas greets Hotkins and then runs balls through a few selected machines. Lukas attempts to deal with Hotkins, but Hotkins wants Lukas's machine and a hundred and fifty dollars. Lukas would rather fix his flipper. He asks for George Cedeño, master technician, who makes house calls and often travels as far as Massachusetts to fix a pinball machine. Cedeño—blue work smock, white shoes, burgundy trousers, silver hair—makes a date with Lukas.

LUKAS STARTS FOR HOME but, crossing Forty-second Street, decides on pure whim to have a look at Circus Circus, where he has never been. Circus Circus is, after all, just four blocks away. The stroll is pleasant in the afternoon sunlight, to and through Times Square, under the marquees of pornographic movies—*Valley of the Nymphs, The Danish Sandwich, The Organ Trail.* Circus Circus ("GIRLS! GIRLS! GIRLS! LIVE EXOTIC MODELS") is close to Sixth Avenue and consists, principally, of a front room and a back room. Prices are a quarter a peep in the back room and a quarter to play (two games) in the

* And they did so until 1976, when pinball at last became legal.

(127)

front. The game room is dim, and Lukas, entering, sees little at first but the flashing scoreboards of five machines. Four of them—a Bally, a Williams, two Gottliebs—flash slowly, reporting inexperienced play, but the fifth, the one in the middle, is exploding with light and sound. The player causing all this is hunched over, concentrating—in his arms and his hands a choreography of talent. Lukas's eyes adjust to the light. Then he reaches for his holster. The man on the hot machine, busy keeping statistics of his practice, is Tom Buckley.

"Tom."

"Tone."

"How is the machine?"

"Better than yours, Tone. You don't realize what a lemon you have."

"I love my Bally."

"The Bally is the Corvair of pinball machines. I don't even care for the art on the back-glass. Williams and Gottlieb are the best. Bally is nowhere."

Buckley, slightly older than Lukas, has a spectacled and professorial look. He wears a double-breasted blazer, a buff turtleneck. He lives on York Avenue now. He came out of Beechhurst, Queens, and learned his pinball in the Army—in Wrightstown, New Jersey; in Kansas City. He was stationed in an office building in Kansas City, and he moved up through the pinball ranks from beginner to virtuoso on a machine in a Katz drugstore.

Lukas and Buckley begin to play. Best of five games. Five balls a game. Alternate shots. The machine is a Williams Fun-Fest, and Buckley points out that it is "classic," because it is symmetrical. Each kick-out well and thumper-bumper is a mirror of another. The slingshots are dual. On this machine, a level of forty thousand points is where the sun sets and the stars come out. Buckley, describing his own style as "guts pinball," has a first-game score of forty-four thousand three hundred and ten. While Lukas plays his fifth ball, Buckley becomes avuncular. "Careful, Tony. You might think you're in an up-post position, but if you let it slide a little you're in a down-post position and you're finished." Buckley's advice is generous indeed. Lukas—forty-eight thousand eight hundred and seventy—wins the first game.

It is Buckley's manner to lean into the machine from three feet out. His whole body, steeply inclined, tics as he reinforces. In the second game, he scores fifty thousand one hundred and sixty. Lukas's address is like a fencer's *en garde*. He stands close to the machine, with one foot projecting under it. His chin is high. Buckley tells him, "You're playing nice, average pinball, Tony." And Lukas's response is fifty-seven thousand nine hundred and fifty points. He leads Buckley, two games to none.

"I'm ashamed," Buckley confesses. And as he leans—palms pounding—into the third game, he reminds himself, "Concentration, Tom. Concentration is everything."

Lukas notes aloud that Buckley is "full of empty rhetoric." But Lukas, in Game 3, fires one ball straight into the death channel and can deliver only thirty-five thousand points. Buckley wins with forty. Perhaps Lukas feels rushed. He prefers to play a more deliberate, cogitative game. At home, between shots, in the middle of a game, he will go to the kitchen for a beer and return to study the situation. Buckley, for his part, seems anxious, and with good reason: one mistake now and it's all over. In the fourth game, Lukas lights up forty-three thousand and fifty points; but Buckley's fifth ball, just before it dies, hits forty-four thousand two hundred and sixty. Games are two all, with one to go. Buckley takes a deep breath, and says, "You're a competitor, Tony. Your flipper action is bad, but you're a real competitor."

Game 5 under way. They are pummelling the machine. They are heavy on the corners but light on the flippers, and the scoreboard is reacting like a storm at sea. With three balls down, both are in the thirty-thousand range. Buckley, going unorthodox, plays his fourth ball with one foot off the floor, and raises his score to forty-five thousand points—more than he scored in winning the two previous games. He smiles. He is on his way in, flaring, with still another ball to play. Now Lukas snaps his fourth ball into the ellipse. It moves down and around the board, hitting slingshots and flippers and rising again and again to high ground to begin additional scoring runs. It hits sunburst caps and hole kickers, swinging targets and bonus gates. Minute upon minute, it stays in play. It will not die.

When the ball finally slips between flippers and off the playfield, Lukas has registered eighty-three thousand two hundred points. And he still has one ball to go.

Buckley turns into a Lukasite. As Lukas plays his fifth ball, Buckley cheers. "Atta way! Atta way, babes!" He goes on cheering until Lukas peaks out at ninety-four thousand one hundred and seventy.

"That was superb. And there's no luck in it," Buckley says. "It's as good a score as I've seen."

Lukas takes a cool final look around Circus Circus. "Buckley has a way of tracking down the secret joys of the city," he says, and then he is gone.

Still shaking his head in wonder, Buckley starts a last, solo game. His arms move mechanically, groovedly, reinforcing. His flipper timing is offhandedly flawless. He scores a hundred thousand two hundred points. But Lukas is out of sight.

THE
KEEL OF
LAKE
DICKEY

WE HAVE BEEN out here four days now and rain has been falling three. The rain appears to be ending. Breaks of blue are opening in the sky. Sunlight is coming through, and a wind is rising.

I was not prepared for the St. John River, did not anticipate its size. I saw it as a narrow trail flowing north, twisting through balsam and spruce—a small and intimate forest river, something like the Allagash, which is not many miles away. The river I imagined would have been river enough, but the real one, the actual St. John, is awesome and surprising. How could it, unaltered, be here still in the northeastern United States? There is nothing intimate about it. Cities could be standing beside it. It's a big river.

I call to the next canoe. "How wide is it now, Sam?" I asked him that yesterday, and he said it was eight chains, he guessed, there, approaching Seven Islands. Sam—Sam Warren—is a timber cruiser up here, and when he looks through the woods or across the river he thinks in chains. When he is cruising—walking by compass through the forest—he never wears raingear, and he wears none now. He has been paddling three days soaking wet, and he doesn't seem to mind. The air temperature is fifty degrees. He has cruised the woods at minus thirty. He says he thinks the river is ten chains wide now—six hundred and sixty feet.

We are a bend or two below the Priestly Rapid, and we can see more than a mile ahead before the river turns from view. Bank to bank, the current is running fast. It is May 28th. The ice went out about a month ago. We have seen remnant snow in shadowed places on the edges of the river. The hardwoods are just budding, and they are scattered among the conifers, so the riverine hills are bright and dark green, streaked with the white stems of canoe birch. The river is potable, God knows, for it rises here in the Maine woods, and almost nothing stands near it except hundreds of millions of trees. The only structures we have seen were three logging bridges and a few cabins—one in use by a game warden, another the fishing camp of a timber-management company, the others, for the most part, roofless and moldering.

John Kauffmann, in the stern of a red Royalex canoe, has come from Alaska to go down the St. John. We are four canoes and eight people. Kauffmann has been here before. He is the author of a book on Eastern rivers and, in part of his time, is a professional canoe traveller—a planner with the National Park Service, going out from his office, in Anchorage, to study, from water level, wilderness rivers that might one day be part of the national-park system. A big man, tall, he has finished pushing fifty. He wears a dark, broad-brimmed hat. Twenty years in the National Park Service—he looks like a smoked bear. Here, there, he has seen a lot of rivers.

"What rivers remind you of this one, John?"

Kauffmann thinks awhile, paddling. "Oh, I don't know. I guess there's some flavor of it in the upper Androscoggin," he says, and he lets it go at that for a hundred yards. "It has more presence than the Penobscot," he adds. "It's not a second-string, minor waterway—and it's not another Allagash, close as it is. Its dimensions are so much grander. Just look at it. It has stature, character. It's a majestic, noble river. It's something like the upper Hudson, but not much. I am groping for comparisons, but I can't think of a river like this one—not in the United States. It's a wild river, not a scenic river in the Shenandoah sense. Or the Connecticut or Housatonic Valleys. You have reminiscences of it in the Delaware, high up, and even, in a way, in the Kobuk—but you can't compare a taiga river to a Maine river. This one is unique. It's like some rivers in eastern Canada, but of our rivers it is unto itself. It's the St. John."

Time soon to put things away and look over the Big Black Rapid. Ahead we hear the coal-chute white-water sound, even though the wind is blowing stiffly behind us in squalls. Running before them, we fairly scud downriver. We pull over and, from the left bank, study the rapid. It is not a particularly long one. In on the left, out on the right appears to be the driest way to do it. One does not have to be a limnologist to see that.

One does not have to be cocky, either. Any rapid can be trouble—bad luck, bad guesses—and, looking at this one, I feel adrenalin run. Twenty years ago, on a fairly cold October day, Kauffmann and I turned over in a gorge of the upper Delaware, having gone there in a time of near flood, and we washed down at least a mile before we were able to get the canoe out of the big, chocolate river. I'm sure we will never be fools enough to do that again, but, together and separately, we

(1 3 5)

have had canoes capsize under us in less dangerous places. So a little adrenalin runs. The rapid is beautiful, bouldery, and bending—the forest rising steeply from the two sides. It is called the Big Black Rapid because it is near the mouth of the Big Black River, which flows into the St. John a mile downstream. There is nothing black about the rapid. It is blue and mostly white, running over big rocks and ledges, with standing waves on long diagonals, like ranges of hills. The wind is so stiff now it is tearing spray off the tops of the waves. The rapid curves left, then right. If I thought I had one chance in ten of going into the river, I wouldn't run the rapid. I would line it—let the canoe down slowly on ropes—or carry around it. If I do get a thrill out of missing a rock and flying along on racing water, that is not what I came for. The rapid is only a part of the river—of a hundred and some miles of this trip and this part of the St. John—and the highest pleasure I can derive from running it is to get from the beginning to the end of the stretch of white water with canoe and cargo sound and, if possible, dry. This is a canoe trip, not a rodeo. When the Canadian *voyageurs*, in the eighteenth and nineteenth centuries, came to rapids in their bark canoes, they did not seek out the deepest souse holes and the highest standing waves. With their four-ton cargoes of furs, they looked for the *fil d'eau* —the safest, surest route through the rapid. For us, just being out here—in this country, on this river—is the purpose of the journey, and not shooting like spears to hit God knows what and where. A test of courage is not the point—not my point, anyway. I have too little courage to waste any on a test. In our own fashion, with our own bulging gear lashed into the four canoes, we had better think like the *voyageurs*.

The plan is that I will lead (paddling an eighteen-foot

Grumman), with Mike Moody. John Kauffmann will follow, with Tom Cabot. Lev and Dick Byrd, in their fifteen-foot Grumman, will go next. And Dick Saltonstall, with Sam Warren, in a big E. M. White canoe with mahogany gunwales, will sweep.

We shove off. One by one, the four canoes describe an easygoing, bobbing S down the rapid. The Byrds hit a rock and add a deep, tympanic bass to the contralto of the rapid, but they do not stick (as aluminum canoes too often will). No one else comes even close to buying the river. At the foot of the rapid, the aggregate water in all the canoes is maybe five or ten quarts.

"I've poled up worse rapids than that one," says Tom Cabot.

No one doubts him. Tom wrote the first of the Appalachian Mountain Club's New England canoeing guides. Also, with others, he designed the Grumman canoe.

I have been remembering all day that less than two weeks ago a canoer died in the river—in, as I thought I had understood it, the Big Black Rapid. Looking back up the steps of white water, ordered and unmenacing, I mention it. "I just don't see how anyone could have died here—could have had such an accident in this place. What do you suppose happened?"

"It didn't happen here," Saltonstall says. "This is the Big *Black* Rapid. It happened forty miles below here, just above Dickey, in the Big Rapid."

LAST NIGHT, I slept nine hours, rain thunking on the tent. Each night out here has been much the same. At home, I am lucky if I get five. Preoccupations there chase each other around and around, the strong ones fighting for the lead; and at three-thirty or four I get up and read, preferring the single track in the book to the whirling dozens in the brain. It's a chronic—or, at least, consistent—annoyance, and nights almost without exception are the same for me until I come to the woods, stretch out on the ground, and sleep nine hours.

We were brought in by air—in three float planes from Greenville, at the foot of Moosehead Lake. I was in the third plane. In the air, the two in front seemed to hang without motion, pontoons pendent—canoes tied to the pontoons. In the shallows of Moosehead we could see clearly the rocks of the bottom. There were whitecaps over the deeps. Off to the right, with more altitude, we saw Allagash Mountain, Caucomgomoc Lake, Chesuncook Lake, the West Branch of the Penobscot River, and, beyond all, the Katahdin massif, aglint with ice and snow. Moving north-northwest, we flew about sixty miles over streams and forest, and set down at the south end of Baker Lake, downstream a few miles from the string of ponds that are the headwaters of the St. John River.

I had never before taxied in an airplane up to a campsite, and when the last plane was gone I felt as if the towns and cities behind were somehow just over the trees, and I felt, too, a certain dismay with myself for not having worked my way out here with a paddle in my hands. Given all that, I thought it would take at least a day for things to simplify, for the checklist of current concerns to reduce itself sufficiently to lengthen sleep—but it took less time than the sun used going down. None of this is a matter of exercise. I get almost as much of that at home as here. Physical labor as a bringer of sleep doesn't seem to do much for me. But the woods do, where

(1 3 8)

thoughts of weather, of food, and of the day's journey so dominate the mind that everything else subsides. The rise and fall of temperature and of wind, the beginning and the end of rain matter here in a way that is irrelevant elsewhere. With the right gear, it is a pleasure to live with the weather, to wait for sun and feel the cool of rain, to watch the sky with absorption and speculation, to guess at the meaning of succeeding events. I hate feeling miserably wet and cold. But with boots, heavy wool socks, rain pants, rain parka, and a wide-brimmed hat I have been dry and warm through all the downpours, on and off the river.

Saltonstall calls himself "a mail-order freak." He says I am one, too. His desk at home is piled deep with catalogues from the premier woods-equipment houses of the land: L. L. Bean, of Freeport, Maine; Eddie Bauer, of Seattle; Recreational Equipment, of Seattle; Synergy Works and Sierra Designs, of Berkeley and Oakland; Moor & Mountain, of Andover, Massachusetts; Eastern Mountain Sports, of Peterborough, New Hampshire; Herter's, of Mitchell, South Dakota; Kirkham's AAA Tent & Awning, Salt Lake City; the Great World of Ecology Sports, West Simsbury, Connecticut—and on down to the surface of the desk, a foot below. We had scarcely hit the beach at Baker Lake when he and I had an equipment shootout, which he seemed to think he was winning. He put up his new tent, an ice-blue JanSport with glass wands and a three-quarter-length fly, the whole affair a subtle compromise —in breathing and impermeable nylons—between the statistical probabilities of incoming water and air. Round, repulsive, mycophane, it appeared to be a model of the Houston Astrodome, its ceiling four feet high. I put up my tent, a tall pavilion in traditional canvas, by Eureka, of Binghamton,

New York, with a six-foot-six-inch ceiling—instant Camelot. (John Kauffmann meanwhile removed from his pack two small bags that contained enough onionskin nylon to cover an Alp. On a framework of slender aluminum rods he then constructed a villa. He offhandedly mentioned that his architect had been Barry Bishop, of the south col of Mt. Everest, and that Bishop's name for the tent was Bishop's Ultimate. Lighting his pipe, Kauffmann sat down in his foyer and watched Saltonstall and me with apparent amusement.) Saltonstall got out his Uncle Sam's Canoe Bags, sold by Moor & Mountain—rubber, government surplus, and supposedly waterproof. He handed one to me, saying he was sure I would need it, less for the rain than for the river. He also got out his new twenty-five-cup, porcelain-enamelled Old-Fashioned Coffee Pot, dark blue with white spatters, and his new wide-mesh Allagash Dishwasher's Bag—both from the Great World of Ecology Sports. In the logging camps of the Maine woods, utensils were put in bags and shaken dry. I flicked chips into the fire with my Buck knife, an instrument of such hard steel that the manufacturer agrees to have it back for sharpening whenever necessary throughout the owner's life. Saltonstall drew attention to the sewn-in tumpline on his new Duluth pack, from Gokey, of St. Paul. I then took from a canvas bag my new thirteen-inch reflector oven, from L. L. Bean, and set it, shining, at his feet.

Saltonstall has a minor speech impediment. He cannot say "L. L. Bean." Nor can he say the variants "Bean" and "Bean's." Instead, he refers to the place as "Leon's." Saltonstall, in Maine, is more seasoned than seasonal. He is not a native, but neither is he—and this is the point—a summer parvenu. He grew up near Boston and now lives in Virginia, but he owns a house and several hundred acres on a lake in Lincoln County, Maine, and he intends to settle there before long for the rest of his life. He is a sailor and has cruised the Maine Coast since his youth. He is a writer, and the title of his most recent book is *Maine Pilgrimage*. People of his ilk—old Maine hands from other states—seek ways of distinguishing themselves from run-of-the-summer tourists, and one curious way is not to admit to patronizing L. L. Bean.

Among outdoor-equipment suppliers in the United States, Bean's is more or less the source pond—a business begun in 1912, when the Maine Hunting Shoe was developed by a noted woodsman, Leon Leonwood Bean. Boots with leather tops and rubber bottoms, they are of considerable utility in the quagmires of the north woods, and Bean's still sells them—eighty-eight thousand pairs a year. Bean's-boots simulacra are in the mail-order catalogues of nearly all the other outdoor suppliers in the country. Adding item after item over the years, Bean, who died in 1967, built a national reputation. In recent times, the company has further expanded, somewhat disturbingly, to become a kind of balsam-scented department store, but, for all its Japanese pot holders and Seventh Avenue jumpers, it still has truly serviceable woods equipment in sufficient variety to hold position in the field. If you travel in bush Alaska, you find Bean's catalogues in cabin after cabin there, and Bean's boots and garments on the people. Most transactions are by mail, but the home store, in Freeport, in Cumberland County, is open twenty-four hours a day seven days a week. I know people who have gone shopping at Bean's at four o'clock in the morning and have reported themselves to have been by no means the only customers there. The store is a rampant mutation of New England connective architecture—

an awkward, naïve building, seeming to consist of many wooden boxes stacked atop one another and held together by steel exterior trusses. There is nothing naïve about the cash register. Sometimes it is necessary to go off to the woods for indefinite periods to recover from a visit to Bean's. John Kauffmann and I have stopped there at nine in the morning, fanned out for boots, mink oil, monoculars, folding scissors, Sven saws, fishing gear, wool shirts, met at noon by the windproof-match bin, gone out to lunch (lobsters—four—on the wharf at South Freeport), and returned to Bean's for a good part of the afternoon. Saltonstall, in his travels, makes regular visits to Bean's and, among trusted friends, is not too shy to admit it.

"Dick, where did you get that canoe-repair kit?"

"Leon's."

"What do you think of this Sierra Designs jacket?"

"I guess I like Leon's a little better."

Going to Leon's, though, is second-best to buying from Leon by mail, for a mail-order freak on the Saltonstall level needs to savor merchandise in his imagination in a way that is impossible in a store. Mailorderphrenia will not happen to just anyone. It requires a yeasty imagination. Long zip gaiters, bacon ironers, folding buckets seem more magical to Saltonstall on the printed page than ever they could in a store. The mail-order freak also prefers not to deal with hortatory clerks and the pressures of commercial time. He wants his decision to arrive at leisure. He does not want to cave in before a sales pad. So he hits the mails.

Tom Cabot, of Boston, is, in Maine, more seasoned by far than Saltonstall. On the way into Maine for this trip, Cabot's car broke down in Freeport, and he called to tell Saltonstall that he would be a little late. Saltonstall understood, and told the rest of us that Cabot had stopped at Leon's. Cabot, when he arrived, emphatically denied the charge.

Now, in that first campsite, on Baker Lake, Saltonstall opened one of three pack baskets and removed a jug of wine, a ten-pound slab of steak, and an earthenware crock full of perking sourdough, its lid secured in a web of cord. He had organized the trip—done all the planning, and the chartering of planes—and now he was laying out his credentials as guide. Professional guides still work in Maine, but the day has passed when canoers, by custom, would not go into the woods without them. The guides of old did all the cooking and, often, all the paddling. Their customers were known as "sports." Saltonstall was hardly going to be paddling us down the river, but around the fire from the start we have been his sports. He is a skillful cook and a master builder of fireplaces, not to mention fires, and he seems by inclination to want to take charge of things over the heat. He is a tall man, thirty-eight, with a handsome, round, ceramic face, and curly hair and Wedgwood-blue eyes—a bit of a woods dude, with his straw hat, his Glen-plaid shirt, and his Sierra Club cup hooked onto his belt. He once worked as a reporter in the Pacific Northwest and Alaska, and he once taught sailing at the United States Naval Academy. One can do worse than be a Saltonstall sport. He is surely as hardworking as any guide the woods have known. He has also dedicated himself to the interests of this terrain, and he has put this trip together to expand his knowledge of it, and ours. The St. John is Maine's remotest river, and it is essentially unknown, somewhat mysterious, even to the people of Maine. In Congress each year, a debate takes place about the fate of the St. John, and whether the Army

Corps of Engineers can or cannot have another year's funds for the advancement of a project that would backflood the river from a dam at Dickey, the first village one encounters after going downriver through the woods. Almost no one in Congress has ever seen the St. John—least of all from water level, in the woods. Only two people in the Corps of Engineers have canoed the river. There is a conservationist coalition called the Friends of the St. John, few of whose members have seen the river, either.

Wine, steak, and to bed at nine. At midnight, some of us got up for a while and got out of our tents to stare at the full moon. The night was cold for this time in spring. No clouds. No wind. Millions of stars spread over the sky. We could blow our breath at them and cloud them for an instant before they came back bright as before. Slowly, the shadow of the earth began to move across the moon. We watched the shadow grow, and sipped bourbon or drank chocolate. The temperature fell to the high thirties. Lev Byrd had on nothing but a cotton sweatshirt that said "Property of D H A" (Harvard Department of Athletics). He had played hockey there (1972-73-74) and was a star at it, and between practices he must have slept on the ice. At any rate, while I was shivering in a down jacket and a Scottish sweater he seemed unaffected—as well might a grandson of Richard E. Byrd. The shadow continued to cover the moon until just a small brightness, like a spot of yolk, remained; and then that, too, was gone. In the crystal sky, the moon was totally eclipsed, and appeared to be hanging there in parchment. When the last of its bright light was cut off, millions and millions of additional stars seemed to come falling into the sky. The Milky Way became as white as a river. Sam Warren said skies were like that up here on clear, moonless nights in winter. With the passing of the shadow and the return of the light, the stars of lesser magnitude evanesced as quickly as they had come into view. The air was down to freezing now. In the morning, there was frost over the ground, mist curling up from the lake, and ice solid in our cups.

SPILLING OUT OF BAKER LAKE, the St. John runs white for five miles in light and uncomplicated rapids, for the most part unobstructed by protruding rock: regular waves, gentle bends. Most rivers are toughest near the source, but the St. John, as it gathers itself together and develops from a forest stream into a big river, presents a kind of introductory course in white-water canoeing, beginning with easy runs, then featuring long days of well-spaced scholastic examples (a rock here with a good practice eddy, a chute there well illustrating the forma-tion and nature of the standing wave), and then offering two or three days of assembled and more difficult rapids that cul-minate with the Big Rapid itself, the final exam. The first five miles out of Baker Lake were gone too quickly—the canoes flying along.

The river grew strikingly as tributaries came in—Turner Brook, Brailey Brook—and was a ten-lane turnpike by the end of the day, just below the confluence of its Baker and Southwest branches. The upper St. John drains an immense watershed—more than two thousand square miles—with a high proportion of streams to ponds. Water drains quickly here after it falls or ice melts. A day comes in the spring when the river's frozen surface, which has been solid four or five months, breaks into giant floes, and they begin to move downstream. Weighing many tons, they grind and screech and, in bends of the river, jam up until backrising water explodes them free. Downriver move hills of avalanchine ice, pale green, crashing, tumbling, tearing the banks, splitting the sunlight into rainbows. Great pieces skid off the edges and come to rest on the forest floor. All the way down, we have seen trees, high above the river, with sapwood glistening, big blazes of bark having been torn away by the ice. The temperature of the river now is forty-six degrees—cold still, but on the way to summer. Cold enough to hold down the catch of trout, which do not really get with it until the water warms to fifty-five degrees. Two-thirds of the St. John's annual runoff occurs in April and May. In summer, the rapids are bony, and the water is so shallow over some stretches of rock and gravel that canoers have to frog their canoes—walk in the water beside them. The St. John is hardly an intermittent stream, but it is more like one than any other river in Maine. After its high season, it is a small river in a large bed. Such is the natural year of a river—an unusual pattern now, because there are so few natural rivers. The St. John is the only Maine river of any size that has not been dammed. From its highest source—First St. John Pond, above Baker Lake—the St. John goes free for two hundred miles, until it breaks out into Canada, where it has been both dammed and, in places, polluted on its way through New Brunswick to the sea. It ends, incidentally, with a flourish, a remembrance of its upper waters—a phenomenal rapid. The phenomenon is that the rapid turns around and thunders back toward the source. The white water flows alternately in two directions—down with the river and up with the tide. In June of 1604, on the day of the feast of John the Baptist, Samuel de Champlain and the Sieur de Monts sailed into the river mouth on the voyage of discovery. They could have named it the Reversible River. Instead, they called it St. John.

We are sharing the St. John with many other canoes, and the river, to say the least, can accommodate them—ample campsites all the way. At first in a hot and blistering sun and then in the cool, steady rain, we have done as little as nine miles in a day and as much as twenty-seven. We have been eating even faster than we have been paddling—M&M's, cashews, raisins, peanuts, prunes, apricots, soybeans, sunflower seeds, hardtack, peanut butter, devilled ham, strawberry jam, and, in the campsites, sourdough pancakes, biscuits, raisin bread, gingerbread, eggs, bacon, and six or seven varieties of freeze-dried cud. Getting out of the rain, we had lunch one day (near the Ledge Rapid) on the porch of an old ranger cabin that, while still standing, was gradually settling into the forest in an attractive way. Its walls—peeled logs, notched and overlapping—were covered with a thin green film of moss. The roof, dark brown, was of arm-length cedar splits, and now, in its last seasons, had become a garden, with moss growing on it, and British soldiers (bright-red tiny lichens), and, most prominently, a sapling birch. The tree had somehow established roots in the cedar splits, and it had a trunk two inches thick reaching up to a parasol of new green leaves. It was a lovely scene—the old, long-abandoned cabin, with its colors of Harris tweed, melting into the forest on that damp day. I looked at some notes in a register there. "Liked the blackflies, gnats, and three bull moose. J. P. Hemmings, C. B. Metzler, New York, N.Y. 8-24-72." (The flies and gnats drive the moose to the river; in our cool May weather, no insects have hatched.) "Beautiful water and rain. One cow moose and two calves. Some deer and plenty of rocks. Ber-

(1 4 7)

nard Prue. 6 17-74." There were no winter notes, but Saltonstall said that people do sometimes make their way to the St. John River in winter—in snowmobiles, God apparently willing. Saltonstall refers to such people as "toads" and gives their home town as "Toadville." He says he knows one toad who bought an antique sleigh so he could haul it behind his snowmobile.

We rotate from canoe to canoe, and I moved on from the ranger cabin with Dick Byrd. He told me that he was still a small child in 1957 when his grandfather the Admiral died but that he remembered him as a great old guy who supplied him with penny candy—and demanded the pennies in return. Once a year, Admiral Byrd dressed up as a spook and tried, without much success, to scare the hell out of Dickie. Now twenty-five, Dick is red-headed and strongly built, and has a quick sense of humor. Like his brother Lev, he is recently out of Harvard, and he is enrolled in the forestry school of the University of Maine. He told me that his father and mother had long ago been divorced, and that as a result he had been particularly close through his youth to his other grandfather, Leverett Saltonstall, who is Dick Saltonstall's uncle. Sam Warren, as it happens, is Saltonstall's brother-in-law. When Saltonstall goes on a canoe trip, he likes to load it up with clan.

We camped that night at Nine Mile Bridge, so named because it is nine miles above Seven Islands, so named by someone who may not have been able to count the thirteen islands in the river there. Our tents at Nine Mile were strung out like a tribal parliament on smooth grass under big birches and white pines—all on a bluff near a spring. The grass had once been the lawn of a young warden, Curly Hamlin, and his wife, Helen, who lived at Nine Mile, winter and summer, in the nineteen-thirties, soon after the logging bridge was constructed. In *Nine Mile Bridge,* a book published in 1945, Helen left behind her a rich and simple record of life in isolation in the woods. Their cabin was made of unsplit logs, and its door was scarcely five feet high. There was plenty of room inside, though—a big kitchen, a big living room with a bulldog stove—and they passed the long winter belting each other with pillows and eating four meals a day. Their only companions were a team of huskies and other dogs that Curly used on his forays against crime, covering many hundreds of square miles of deep snow and forest in his twelve-foot racing sled. Illegal trappers were his quarry, and he arrested few, but he made his presence known—tossed traps away and left a calling card, of all things, where trappers would return. Just by being there in the woods, he kept the number of poachers down. On his days off, he fixed his equipment or stretched out on his back and studied the rafters for traversing mice. He had a gun in his hand. When a mouse put its nose out, he fired. In summer, he specialized in houseflies, giving them rides through the roof on bullets. The Hamlins' furniture was laced with rawhide, and they made incense of the bark of quaking aspen. They also used aspen bark to worm the dogs. Trout swarmed the river and its tributary streams. To fish for togue, the Hamlins went up to Chemquassabamticook Lake. They were careful to keep fish out of contact with their canoe, because a bear that smells fish on a canoe will destroy it, imagining that fish are somehow inside. The Nine Mile Bridge was part steel, and in deep cold it hummed—set up a mournful wailing in the winter night, interfering with sleep at forty below.

There would be half an inch of beautiful, lacy frost on the windowpanes, and a red-hot fire had to be kept burning all night. Forty degrees below zero sounds cold. It is cold—a dry suffocating cold. The coldest I ever experienced was fifty-four below, when I had to breathe through a woolen scarf. But I would rather see forty below in Aroostook County than ten below near the seacoast where a damp wind cuts through woolen clothes as though they were gauze.

Helen Hamlin remembered the ice going out as early as March and as late as the tenth of May. After ice-out, the Hamlins travelled the rivers, shot the rapids, went down the St. John, and—once—went up the Allagash in the middle of the night. ("It's a funny sensation not to see the rough places until you're in them and feel the canoe rocking in the swells.")

The Allagash River—Allagash means hemlock bark—is tranquil and quiet compared to the St. John River. The land is flat, and there are channels through rocky and rough places. The river is so controlled by logging dams that it no longer pounds furiously down the waterways, a characteristic that gave it its reputation.

Each quarter mile of the upper St. John River produces whitewater, and few men have run Big Black Rapids at its highest pitch. The river is wild and rocky, practically untouched by the hand of man, and still in its natural, boisterous state. It is unhampered by logging dams, and the water level rises and falls with every slight rainfall or spell of dry weather.

Life in the woods was eventful enough, and seldom drove them "woods queer." When they did go out—to the border and across to Québecois towns or down the big river to the village of Allagash and the town of Fort Kent—their sudden immersion in society was not wholly agreeable. "I could never shake off the feeling," Helen wrote, "that the world was crowded and that people were odd."

The big wall of ice in 1970 was too much for Nine Mile Bridge, and only its piers stand in the river now. The Hamlins' cabin is a heap of splintered, twisted logs and rubble, behind where it once stood. A ponderous machine has come along and crushed it, ramming it as debris into a small ravine.

We were up at six in the morning at Nine Mile Bridge, and were soon eating trout for breakfast—trout and freeze-dried eggs, mixing in our stomachs the sublime and the ridiculous. The flesh of the trout was firm and as pink as salmon's. Every hatchery trout I've ever eaten was as white as halibut. These, through their lifetimes, had fed on nymphs in the river. The rain was light, after falling heavily through the night. The Uncle Sam's Canoe Bag that Saltonstall gave me is authentically waterproof. I keep in it my change of clothes—the things I care most to keep dry—and in the night, in the interest of sleeping space, I toss it out in the rain, because not a drop will penetrate the bag. The morning temperature was fifty-three, the sky was gray, and the air felt raw. We had come into Sam's terrain now—the one million seven hundred thousand acres managed by the Seven Islands Land Company, his employer. Somewhere in the distance we heard an engine, and we looked questioningly at Sam.

"Skidder," he said.

The skidder, which vaguely resembles a pair of tractors coupled together and is flexible in its motions through the forest, replaced the horse not long ago as the means of "twitching" a tree (lugging it through the woods) from the cutter to the truck. Skidders do the job remarkably well, but they have an unsavory reputation for tearing up the ground and beginning an all too swift process of erosion.

"How far away, Sam?"

"It's hard to tell. On a clear day, you can hear a skidder for sixty miles." Sam is dark-haired and ruddy, and heavyset, like a football lineman, which he once was, and he has a sober manner that is belied by his quickness to laugh. With his shirt soaking wet, as always, and rain pebbling his glasses, he went on, "The forest industry is slow to catch on to things. The chain saw, for example, was invented in the late nineteenth century. It got into general use in the north Maine woods in the late nineteen-forties. We are already thinking, though, of getting new machinery to replace the skidder. Small tractors, maybe. Or we may try aerial logging."

The company virtually never clear-cuts land, he said—only in strips, occasionally, to remove "decaying old stuff." On the whole, it takes trees selectively—about three hundred and fifty thousand cords a year—cutting annually on about thirty thousand of its million seven hundred thousand acres. The logging crews, who are independent contractors, go where the timber manager tells them to, and the timber manager is Sam, cruising the woods with his prisms and his angle gauges, pausing in selected spots to do variable plot samplings, boring into trees for core samples, and emerging with a sense of just how much wood is where and how ready it is for the saw. Yanked from the woods of late and set at a desk in Bangor, he has been trying to put into a computer a total inventory of Seven Islands' land, including not only the timber but the ponds, lakes, streams, and rivers, too, because hunters, fishermen, and canoe people will come whether the company likes it or not, so they have to be "managed" along with the trees.

All this has given Sam a perspective of his own in the group in which he is now travelling. The rest of us, to one extent or another, are wilderness romantics—tipsy on the drafts of Mudjekeewis, the West Wind. "I don't want to take anything from the feeling you may have," Sam has said. "But this is not wilderness. Every square foot of this country is managed land."

"Yes," I said, "but what you are managing is wilderness."

Sam said that could be, but he had trouble seeing things that way when the forest was his place of work. He said, moreover, that he thought it a shame that the law setting up the Allagash Wilderness Waterway had specified that a strip of woods reaching four hundred to eight hundred feet back from the water must be left permanently uncut. "The wood there is like pick-up-sticks," he told me. "It's just rotting timber, and in its decay it is using oxygen at the same rate oxygen is being produced. The wood should be cut. The way Seven Islands handles streams, ponds, and lakes—we leave plenty of standing trees; we don't cut steep banks; we make it a point to be careful. If you cut too heavily, you slow down your total rate of growth. A tree is unique in that it is the machine as well as the product. The tree makes the fibre. So you want to cut it when the machine becomes inefficient, and have it replaced by a faster-growing or younger tree. You get the tree when it slows down. Trees that we're not cutting are *dying*. You want to get the fibre as it grows."

The St. John in Maine is a wild river because timber companies have owned its surroundings for upward of a hundred and fifty years—a fact that can be taken, or not, as ironic.

(153)

I asked Sam how he felt about the Dickey dam.

He shook his head in dismay. "Trees renew themselves," he said. "Destroying something forever is unnerving."

NINE MILES FROM NINE MILE, we moved out of a corridor of confining, high-wall, riverine forest and into a great range of open space, with long river views, and big islands, and long lateral views across fields of grass to hills distant from the river. This was Seven Islands—sweeping, isolated, abandoned. Far up a slope beyond the left bank stood five log cabins, roofless but with walls intact. We walked up there to those dark cabins, elevated and sombre on the plains of grass, and I almost expected to walk through a door and see dead soldiers, their rifles awry, their necks bent as if, in vigil, they had fallen asleep. No soldiers. Only porcupine skeletons inside the cabins, and the drumming, like distant artillery, of grouse in the near woods. The horses that once worked the forest with the loggers were fed from these fields and others like them, dispersed along the rivers—the Penobscot, the Kennebec, the Allagash, the St. John. More or less by squatters' rights, Seven Islands was a French settlement. Québecois farmers came and cleared the land, and, in their custom, piled all the rocks in the center of the fields, not building walls of them, as New Englanders would do. There were, in any case, no neighbors to fence out. The rocks, of course, remain—a great loaf of them, six feet high and sixty feet long, a memorial to Seven Islands' vanished lumberjacks and a cairn to French Canada.

We spent the rest of the day at Seven Islands, fishing, looking around—in light rain that stopped and started all afternoon. We joined a couple of other campers there—Richard Barringer and Herbert Hartman, who, together, happened to be Maine's Bureau of Public Lands. They had a big twenty-foot, exquisite, forty-year-old wood-and-canvas E. M. White canoe, and in it they were looking over terrain to which they might lay claim. They shared their lunch with us—a bit of cheese, some cucumbers, raw potatoes, a bowl of fiddleheads, an expansive drop of wine.

Maine is half of New England, and half of Maine is un-organized. The state is completely divided into something like a thousand townships, and only four hundred and forty of them have—so far in history—been settled and incorporated as towns. Almost all the others are nameless—carry only numbers and letters in squares that dominate the official map. T 16 R 9. T 16 R 10. Township Sixteen, Range Nine. Township Sixteen, Range Ten. There are as many of these as there are Kennebunks and Arundels. And most of the unorganized townships are in the north woods. A township is twenty-two thousand acres, and by constitutional provision a thousand acres of each township is public land, reserved for parsonages, churches, and schools in the nonexistent towns. Land and timber companies own the woods, own hundreds of unorganized townships, but what about the so-called public lots? In aggregate, the state has claim to some four hundred thousand acres in the unorganized townships. In recent times, the state legislature passed a bill that (never mind the parsonages in Maine's unborn cities) allowed the public lots to "float"—by decreeing, in effect, that it would be all right if deals were made whereby any number of public lots could be assembled in one place, creating a large hunk of permanent public land. Hartman and Barringer had been dubbed the Bureau of Public Lands and were sent out to scout the best places to be claimed for the state. Trading off with the timber people, they had already acquired half a dozen swatches of terrain, including Gero Island, on Chesuncook Lake; Little Squaw Mountain, on Moosehead Lake; and the margins of Holeb Pond, on the Moose River. Inevitably, they were contemplating Seven Islands and other sections of the banks of the St. John.

Barringer—wiry, athletic, in a wool shirt and a battered red hat—appeared to have been left over from a log drive that had long since gone down the river. Before taking his job in Augusta, though, he had taught economics at Harvard. Hartman, son and grandson of Bowdoin professors, was an emeritus grad student who had spent many summers and autumns as a full-time north-woods guide. He said that when he gave up trying to write his doctoral thesis—on pre-Islamic Bedouin poetry—he had become for a time a beaver trapper near Jackman (one of the few organized townships in the north Maine woods). Like Barringer, Hartman was in his thirties. He was a tall man with narrowly set, quizzical eyes behind steel-rimmed glasses, and he had a lot of talent around a canoe. He had a black-spruce setting pole, full of spring and glistening with boiled linseed oil, and with it he could move his big twenty-footer at a handsome clip upstream, even against a stiff current. Standing in the stern, the twelve-foot pole in his hands, he looked like a gondolier, with the difference that he was jabbing his pole against the bottom of the pure St. John and not sculling the cess of Venice. To move the canoe, he reached forward, set the pole (point on the bottom), and then seemed to climb it like a gymnast on a rope. Sometimes—waxing fancy—he twirled it, end over end, on the recovery. To correct his course, he now and again poled behind his back. He said that when searching the woods for a new pole it was important always to cut a dead one, because green wood will dry out and check. In his guiding days, he used to tell his sports that he would never cut a pole on which a moose had not urinated.

"Why?"

"Because you have to tell people stories to keep them amused."

Poking around the six plus seven islands (I went with them as they explored), Hartman dropped anchor occasionally, picked up a bamboo rod with an English reel, and began to massage the air with sixty feet of line. From either bank, everywhere on the river, small brooks spit nutrients into the St. John, and trout will wait there like bums for a handout. Hartman drew streamers across the mouths of these brooks and provoked strikes despite the cold.

Hartman said there was among guides an age-old practice that would always help a sport feel better about his fishing. Sooner or later, inept as he may be, the sport will catch a fish. The guide nets the fish. Placing a shoulder between the fish and the sport, the guide works studiously, apparently to extricate the hook. What he is really doing is stuffing buckshot down the trout's throat. The guide, all the while, much admires the fish. "Yes, sir, that's a fish, that is *quite* a fish." The fish, ultimately, is weighed. Three pounds. "Ay-uh, well, I guess so, quite a fish." When it's time for the guide to clean the fish, he slips the shot back into his pocket.

"Did *you* ever know anybody who did that, Herb?"

"Oh, well, I guess so."

Hartman said that guides liked to coat the bottom of a canoe with dark shellac, so it would look to a fish like a floating log. He said, too, that it was characteristic of guides to assimilate the manner of the sports they worked for—becoming quite high-nosed, like butlers and chauffeurs. Guides' fishing equipment escalated accordingly, and they spent large chunks of their pay for tackle like the sports'—English reels, for example, and bamboo rods. Hartman's mentor was an old guide named Myron Smart, from Milo, and Hartman remembered his saying, "Out in the woods, you live different, and you do different. You know, I've been in the woods all my life, and I think I get more enjoyment out of the trips than the sports."

In a bogan near the campsite, we stopped to pick fiddleheads—enough for all ten of us for supper. A bogan is a pocket of still water projecting from a river. In other parts of New England, the term is "logan." A fiddlehead is the new leaf of certain ferns—ostrich ferns, cinnamon ferns, hay-scented ferns, evergreen wood ferns. When the leaf first develops, it is coiled like the head of a violin, and, in this young state, is crunchy in texture, sweet in flavor, bland, and succulent—incredibly delicious. We drew up the canoe and loped through the woods, excited by the colonies of ferns. The fern tops are fiddleheads for several days. It is a maxim of the woods that blackflies do not appear and trout are reluctant to bite until the fiddleheads are gone. We have seen damned few trout and no blackflies. When blackflies hatch, said Hartman, he repels them with fly dope—a mixture of citronella, pennyroyal, and tar. It makes him smell like a new driveway. Sometimes, fighting blackflies or mosquitoes, Hartman builds a fire in a bucket, throws green grass into it, and sets the bucket upwind. And no-see-ums, the all but invisible insects that mass on the skin and eat it as if they were acid—what does he do about them?

"I use Vicks Vaporub," he said. "It's the only thing that works."

We saw two beaver swimming in the bogan, cutting long wakes across the still water. On shore, we found the scat of fox and bear.

It rained all night at Seven Islands—heavily and steadily— but tapered in the early morning to drizzle and mist. Hartman was up at four-thirty, in the first light, in a sleeveless under- shirt, beneath a balsam, shaving. The air temperature was forty-eight degrees. In the low light and mists of that early morning, Seven Islands was even more beautiful than it had been the afternoon and evening before. The bottoms of clouds were touching the plains of grass. I thought of all the water that had fallen in the night, and of the engineered flood that would stop the river. Seven Islands, not far from the head of Lake Dickey, would at times be under fifteen feet of water. At other times, as the dam made its electricity and coped with the river's irregular contributions of water, the surface of the lake would go down as much as forty vertical feet, and Seven Is- lands would then emerge, like the engulfed cathedral, coated with mud.

After a breakfast of trout and fresh hot raisin bread, we moved on downstream to Priestly Bridge, a loggers' crossing —part bridge, part gravel causeway. Barringer and Hartman had to leave the river there, as they had planned, although they would have liked to stay—would have liked to go with us through the Big Black Rapid. Barringer explained that Maine is "a banana republic" and they had to hurry back to Augusta to see if their bureau was still there.

The spring ice had not been kind to the causeway. The big floes had plowed into it and carried hundreds of tons of it some distance downriver. A bulldozer had been hauled in on the logging road to reclaim the gravel from the river, and the bulldozer was there now, downstream, gathering the gravel spillage and slowly hunkering it upstream. Back and forth the dozer grunted. The dozer belched, coughed, and wheezed. In what was now approaching a hundred miles of the St. John, the only inhabited cabin we had seen was a warden's near Baker Lake, and the only person we had seen (other than travellers in canoes) was a man in a bulldozer in the middle of the river.

SIX MILES BELOW the Big Black Rapid, we stop for the night on a grassy ledge that was once a logging road—cut into a steep hillside, twenty feet above the river. Down the hillside we tumble rocks and build a fireplace. Building the fire itself takes longer, in part because the rain has returned and—for dinnertime—is inconveniently heavy, and in part because I do a hurried and slovenly job of putting the fire together. With added shavings, added bark, and a lot of blowing, I eventually have a blaze that can shrug off the falling water. The Byrds and Mike Moody set up a rig of flying tarps—wide sheets of blue nylon held high with saplings and rope. Moody departs for the mouth of a brook. A year out of Nasson College, in Springvale, Maine, he apparently got his degree in fly-fishing, for he stays at it six, seven hours a day. The fireplace, hissing away, is just outside the shelter of the tarps, and we are now clustered inside—six of us, anyway—variously sipping gin, rum, and bourbon, and watching Saltonstall boil water. In all the mail-order catalogues in Saltonstall's collection, there is nothing approaching rum in the rain. Certainly, gin has good loft and weather repellence. But this rum—a hundred and fifty-one proof—is watertight.

The St. John, framed in spruce, with big rock ledges protruding, bends from view a mile down, and Saltonstall—never too wet to sell the river—says the scene reminds him of anchorages on the Maine coast, of fjordlike bays that penetrate the islands there. He says, "Don't you think so, Tom?"

Tom Cabot—who is a connoisseur of maritime islands and has many Maine ones in his private collection, who has slept in hundreds of Maine anchorages in his yawl, Avelinda—does not seem to be under the illusion that he is looking out from the shelter of the blue tarpaulins through the smoke of our fire at a piece of Penobscot Bay. He nods agreement, though, and smiles, and toasts the river with a gesture of his cup.

In the morning, big rips of blue appear in the eastbound clouds. On the river again, Tom is with me, and we are bound for Chimenticook Stream. A bend or two, and Sam Warren sees a yearling moose. He gets out of his canoe and goes after it, on a dead run up the riverbank. He learns that he is slower than the moose. He wanted to ride it. We have seen otters, ospreys, black ducks, mergansers, loons. No bears. There is ice this morning in the river—small chunks from big pieces on the bank, near trees with shredded bark. It is sixty hours to June.

"How many chains now, Sam?"

"Oh, fifteen, at least, I'd guess."

A thousand feet. Wide enough, surely, for four canoes. But gradually we string out in a long tandem—out of earshot, and even out of sight. Tom tells me about March, 1923, when he was twenty-five years old and shipped three canoes (wood-and-canvas) to the Quaboag River, in central Massachusetts. With five others, he planned to go eighty miles in a day and a half—down the Quaboag to the Chicopee and down the Chicopee to the Connecticut and down the Connecticut to Hartford. The water seemed fast enough to make that possible. Perhaps it was, but Tom and his friends would never know. In the first twenty miles, they totalled the three canoes. One broke completely in half. The two others came through irreparable, while Cabot and company, hanging on to the gunwales, washed down among cakes of ice. Somehow, all this inspired Cabot's affection, and he wrote an article for the journal of the Appalachian Mountain Club on the joys of white-water canoeing. It helped build interest in the nascent sport, and it led as well to Tom's collaboration (with John Phillips) on *Quick Water and Smooth*, the first guidebook to New England canoeing. Because northern Maine was the professionals' exclusive terrain, northern Maine was not included. This is Tom's first look at the St. John River.

Tom is about five feet ten, a trim and athletic man, with dark eyebrows, weathery skin, and a prominent nose in a somewhat narrow face. He wears black rubber nautical boots; an old, thin down jacket; a perky white hat with a blue-and-yellow band. His rucksack, stencilled "T. D. CABOT," must be fifty years old. His paddle is maple and is dark and scarred. He strokes steadily and smoothly as he talks, telling one story after another, and, conserving himself, he does not dig up the river. Statistically, he is old and decrepit. He's seventy-eight, and he has had several operations for abdominal cancer. But he looks sixty and acts forty, and to the question "How could an old man like that go down a wild river anytime, let alone when ice is still on the ground?" the answer seems to be that

Tom's infirmities may have crossed his body but may never cross his mind.

With Julius Caesar and Chief Crazy Horse, Tom is one of few people whose names have appeared in the line index to Bartlett's *Familiar Quotations*. The familiar quotation, of course, is what John Bossidy sardonically said in giving a toast, in Boston, at the 1910 midwinter dinner for the alumni of the College of the Holy Cross. He said:

> And this is good old Boston,
> The home of the bean and the cod,
> Where the Lowells talk only to Cabots
> And the Cabots talk only to God.

Bossidy was paraphrasing. Five years earlier, on an analogous occasion, a member of the Harvard Class of 1880 had said:

> Here's to old Massachusetts,
> The home of the sacred cod,
> Where the Adamses vote for Douglas,
> And the Cabots walk with God.

Tom Cabot, who has been everything from a Harvard Overseer to Director of International Security Affairs in the Department of State, will walk and talk with anybody. Especially talk. Listening to him is like listening to a ballgame on the radio, and in the canoe he makes the hours fly. He tells of an expedition he once led to the Sierra Nevada de Santa Marta, in Colombia, the highest coastal mountain mass in the world, and of a day in 1927 when he climbed Mt. Katahdin on skis. He was the first person (and possibly the last) ever to do that. He often mentions Harvard and his wife, Virginia, to each of whom he has been married for more than fifty years.

Qualified to be at least a dozen kinds of snob, he appears to be only one kind: in the way that English people refer to "red-brick" and "glass" universities, he talks about "freshwater colleges" in the U.S.A. He was once, briefly and unhappily, president of the United Fruit Company. (Saltonstall says that Tom "refused to bribe the Costa Ricans, and the bananas never got out on time.") But primarily he worked in his family's business, the making of carbon black. He is an engineer, and aggressive, and he developed and internationalized the company so that it became the world's foremost in its field. Made from aromatic petroleum residuals, carbon black is used to color things black, including printer's ink, but mainly it goes into rubber tires. Carbon black is about a third, by weight, of every tire that rolls on the roads.

"So why are you telling *me* all this, Tom? You're a Cabot. You're supposed to talk only to God."

Tom grins, and tells me what his father, Godfrey Lowell Cabot, used to say when asked that question. A look of shock and horror would come over old Cabot's face, and, backing away, he would say, "But I thought you *were* God."

We stop for the day near the mouth of Chimenticook Stream, setting up our tents on the edge of what was once a logging camp. A few clearings are all that remain, and some big logs that form a kind of sitting-frame around our fireplace. This was the settlement of the Castonian lumberjacks, reputed to have been the toughest, wildest, unruliest on the river, their axes, their crosscuts, and even their cabins long since obviated by the chain saw, the truck, the skidder. Chimenticook Stream is wide and fast—is in itself a river—and is white with high turbulence from bank to bank, pouring down from the west and into the St. John. I wade out into the mouth to fish, and in five minutes have a trout on the line. Fifteen minutes later, I have another, and tomorrow's breakfast is gaining weight. Unfortunately, though, my legs are numb, and I can no longer feel the river bottom through my shoes. I drop a thermometer into Chimenticook—forty-three degrees. It is apparently not too cold for these remarkable trout, but it's too cold for me, and I retreat to the campfire.

The air grows colder, too, falling into the thirties, and we build up the fire. We'll be shooting the Big Rapid tomorrow, and the thought of it comes to mind from time to time. The person who died there twelve days ago was an airman from Loring Air Force Base, which is in Limestone, Maine, about eighty miles east of the river. He was twenty-one years old and happened to be a native of Maine. With three other airmen, he rented a twenty-foot Grumman canoe, and all four —two too many for safety—were in it on the river. They had no life jackets (which are required by state law). When the canoe turned over, near the head of the Big Rapid, all four left it and tried to swim to safety—a literally fatal error. There is almost no reason to leave a canoe when it overturns, and there are any number of reasons to stay with it, the first of which is that it floats. It's a life raft. If it is pointed downstream—as it should be, so it has a more favorable mean free path through the boulders—the swimmers should place themselves on either side of the upstream end and wash on down to calm water. If the canoe is across the current and resists being turned around, then the swimmers should cling to the upstream side—a terribly important matter to remember, because when a canoe happens to press a person into a rock and pin a person there, it does so with a force of some ten thousand pounds.

John Kauffmann, knocking his pipe on one of the big logs,

pulls his field jacket up closer about his neck. He is disturbed by the death in the river, and dismayed by the foolishness that caused it. If four people get into a canoe and break every rule of sense and practice, and one of them dies, canoeing in general takes a loss. Some people think that anyone who goes down a white river is a suicidal fool—even if the rapids, as here, are far between. Kauffmann is not a white-water competitor—a wild-water or slalom racer. He is a canoe traveller —analogous to a cross-country skier—but he knows what the racers do and how they do it, and to learn their techniques he has been to school. "What we're trying to do with the white water on this trip is to get through it," he says. "A rapid is a problem, and we solve it. But we are not really involved with the white water. If you want to understand it, you have to get in there and wrestle with it, deal with it on its own terms, literally immerse yourself in it, as the racers do. That is the best training for this kind of tripping, because if you have it you know what white water is. The person who can most peacefully walk down the streets of New York is someone who has a black belt in karate. Under wilderness conditions, you just don't shoot a rapid unless you are certain of success. The primary rule in wilderness is: When in doubt, carry. Sometimes you misjudge. There's an eye for white water—like the eye in any other sport—and if you are away from rivers for a time you can lose your eye. From shore, standing waves can look smaller than they actually are. After a few rapids, you warm up, and your eye comes back. In the first place, though, you have to know what you're looking at. You must know what an eddy is. There is one below every ledge and behind every rock—with water flowing gently upstream—but look out for souse holes. I just don't understand the hydraulics of

(166)

the souse hole. You must know how to make an eddy turn. It's easy to do, but you have to learn it. The eddy is your emergency landing field. You spin into it—through the eddy wall. If the bowman turns too soon and leans upstream, you dump. You can also go into the eddy with a back ferry. Once you're in the eddy, the canoe just nuzzles up to the rock and sits there, as still as if it were on a pond. Another major rule is: Never lean upstream. You lean upstream and the gunwale lowers, and then the rapid gets its paws on the upstream gunwale and pulls it down. Skiers learn to lean away from the mountain. In standard, open canoes like ours, you have to hit an adroit compromise between paddling too hard and not paddling hard enough. If you paddle too soft, the standing waves will rock you and may roll you over. If you paddle too hard, you may take in a lot of water. Remember: there is a critical limit to the amount of water you can take in. You have to stop and bail or dump the water. Or you'll just eat the river. So drive—but don't drive in too deeply. Talk a lot to each other. It helps things go right. Sometimes the deepest water, the main chance, is too damned rough. Say you've got heavy water. You've got big waves in there. You've got buddhas. You back-ferry. Face forty-five degrees off the direction of the current and paddle backward. You move sideways, across the current, like a ferry, and you avoid that vacuum pull that tends to drag you into the heaviest water. These skills should be practiced and practiced, like shooting baskets. Every one of these skills is applicable to saving your canoe and your cargo and getting through with a whole skin. You don't have to be a slalom racer, but if you immerse yourself for a while in the white-water sport you get to know some hydraulics and you get to know what the river can do not only against you but for you. Those white-water people really know what they are doing."

Tom Cabot says he thinks he'll go through the Big Rapid with John Kauffmann. He has the dibs, and rightly so. He doesn't know that John Kauffmann owns an old aluminum canoe that looks like foil in which a turkey has been roasted.

TOWARD FIVE IN THE MORNING, there is a veil of mist from sky to river and in it hangs the moon. Half gone now, gradually eclipsing itself, it tells us how long we have travelled. Half a moon.

Breakfast at six. Strong tea. "Sheep dip" was what the lumberjacks called their tea. We need it. The air is just above the freeze point. We do not eat light. Trout. Fried potatoes. Sourdough pancakes. Big red boiled "logging berries"—the lumberjacks' term for beans.

Tom Cabot returns from a walk in the woods. "I just saw a cow moose," he says. "I looked up, and there was the ass of a moose."

By nine, the sky is blue around big clouds. The day looks good on the river. Easing through the morning, we drop ten miles—Schoolhouse Rapid, Fox Brook Rapid, Poplar Island Rapid—and hunt around for a place to have lunch. For Saltonstall, as guide, any old sandspit will not do. He looks over a brook mouth fringed with alders, crinkles his nose, and keeps paddling.

"Why didn't we stop there?"

"He didn't think it was aesthetic enough, and, being an aesthete, he thought we had better move on," Cabot explains.

Tom is part aesthete, part Wall Street, and he can take his scenic settings or leave them alone. He knows both sides of the wilderness argument, and he is not always with nature in its debate with man. He has seen Lake Powell in Utah, the result of the dam in Glen Canyon, and while he knows what was lost in Glen Canyon, he is (for reasons of public recreation) not sorry the lake exists. Glen Canyon is sometimes brought into discussions about the St. John, because Glen Canyon was remote and few people knew it was there until it wasn't there anymore.

Saltonstall finally picks a luncheon site under three big white pines—symbols of Maine, the Pine Tree State. There were far-reaching stands of them here once, throughout the north Maine woods. They were cut for the masts of navies. These above us are among the few left. Old-growth eastern white pine, they're up there a hundred feet—their kind the tallest trees in Eastern America. If the lake fills over this point in the riverbed, these pines will reach up like masts from a shipwreck, and even their skysail branches will be twenty-five fathoms down.

The Big Rapid is three miles below. We move toward it—all crews the same as for the Big Black Rapid—with everything trebly lashed. Moody and I have the eighteen-foot Grumman, and have again been designated by the guide to go first. If we find trouble, our problem will suggest alternatives to the others. We are the refectory slaves, testing the food of kings.

The four canoes stop on the left bank, and we study the rapid. It does not look forbidding or, for the most part, fierce. It will not be like crossing a turnpike on foot. It is a garden of good choices. Overwhelmingly, it is a spectacular stretch of river—big and white for a full mile before, continuing white, it bends from view. The river narrows here by about a third, pressed between banks of rock, but it is still hundreds of feet wide—big boulders, big submarine ledges, big holes, big pillows, big waves, big chutes, big eddies. Big Rapid. About two-thirds of a mile down, on the left shore, a lone birch leans crazily toward the river. Below the birch, there appears to be a bankside eddy. Shouting above the sound of the rapid, we form our plan. Moody and I are to get into that eddy, and bail, and wait there for everybody else.

"Are you ready?"

"What did you say?"

"All set?"

"Yes, it's lovely here. Possibly we could stop here for another lunch."

"Get going, you sarcastic bastard."

"See you there."

And so we're in it. We make choices, and so does the river. We shout a lot, above the roar. Words coordinate the canoe. My eye is certainly off the mark. I underestimated the haystacks. They are about as ponderous as, for this loaded canoe, they can safely be. I look steeply down at Moody in the bottoms of the troughs. But the route we picked—generally to the left, with some moves toward the center, skirting ledges—is, as Kauffmann would say, solving the problem. We are not playing with the Big Rapid. We are tiptoeing in and hoping it won't wake up. Under the slanting birch, we swing into the eddy and stop. Two. Three. Four. Everybody home, and we bail many quarts.

The river now bends almost ninety degrees to the right, and we can see around the bend to another anchorage, under an isolated maple with an ovate crown.

The run this time is more difficult—the bow kicking high into the air and returning to the surface in awkward slaps. We dig for momentum, sidestep rocks, but not nimbly, for the canoe is sluggish with shipped water. Anxious to get into the calm below the maple, I try a chute that is just about as wide as the beam of the canoe. It's a stupid and almost unsuccessful move, and I get out of the canoe and climb up on a boulder to wave the others around the chute.

We bail a few gallons. Everybody is dry. We relax and joke and look down the rest of the rapid. Less than a mile below we can see flat, and much wider, water. We're so full of ourselves now it's as if we were already there. We do and do not want to be there, for after the end of the rapid the run is smooth and short to Allagash and the end of the wilderness river. The St. John after that is another river—a borderland, farmland, potatoland river—and then a Canadian, developed river, and not what we think of when we think of the St. John. So we look back upstream, at the whiteness of the river here in big display, coming out of a hundred miles of forest.

A canoe appears, bouncing in the waves. Half a mile above us, it rolls over and begins to wash down. Tom Cabot grabs a rope and runs up the bank, jumping from ledge to boulder, boulder to ledge. Everybody follows, but as we get nearer to the capsized canoe we realize there is nothing we can do. It is near the middle of the rapid. We can't throw a rope two hundred feet. The two paddlers are afloat and are hanging on, but the canoe—a fifteen-foot Grumman—is broadside to the current and they are on the downstream side. They are missing rocks, fortunately, but they are apparently oblivious of the danger of being caught between a rock and the canoe. We shout at the top of our lungs, "Get on the other side! Get on the upstream side!" But they don't look around. They can't hear us.

We watch them helplessly, and we return to our canoes. Because the water in the river is little more than ten degrees above freezing, the two in the river could have a greater problem with cold than with rock. When they reach our level, Kauffmann and Cabot move into the rapid in their canoe, Moody and I in ours. Cabot throws them a rope. One of them appears to be shaking but assures us that he is all right. Back-paddling, we wash along with them until the force of the rapid begins to decline, and then we haul in tandem and bring them and their canoe ashore.

One is tall, bearded, and, so it seems, physically unaffected. Relief is the last thing he is about to feel. It has apparently not crossed his mind that the river could have kept him. Instead, he shows fury, frustration, disappointment—like an athlete who has had his big chance and blown it. All the way to the north woods he has come, and has paddled a hundred miles downriver to dump in the Big Rapid, and, kneeling by his canoe, he pounds fist into palm in disgust, saying, "Damn! Damn! Oh, God damn!"

The other paddler is short and thin, and is shaking deeply from cold. He minimizes it, tries to be nonchalant, but does not seem disappointed to be standing on the bank. His T-shirt is dark gray, and above the left breast are small black letters—"YALE."

Tom Cabot questions him about the shirt, asking if it means that he's a student there.

"Yes. I'm there now."

"And how far along are you?"

"I'm '78."

Over Tom's face comes a small-world smile, and he says, "How about that! I'm seventy-eight, too."

WE MOVE DOWN the wide, placid, but still powerfully flowing river, and around a big island to Dickey. Looked at from our point of view, it is the beginning of the constructed world; approached the other way—to the end of U.S. 1 and then to the end of Maine 161—it is the utter end of the line. It's a hamlet, miscellaneously spread up the river slopes: frame houses, house trailers, overturned automobiles, general store, a single gas pump (Shell), over which hangs a giant rack of antlers—bull moose. Under wet laundry strung on someone's porch sits a snowmobile. There's a skidder on a lawn. The river draws us downstream, and Dickey recedes from view.

With low ground on the right and steep-rising forest to the left, we go down the final corridor, three miles or so of straightness, and come to the many-islanded mouth of the Allagash River. The Allagash rushes into the St. John, chopping the current, dumping nutrients into the big river, like all the other feeder streams. On the largest island—Gardner—we end our trip. Allagash, Maine, even smaller than Dickey, is across the way. We pitch our tents on high ground, facing back upriver —a view through the channels among the islands and on up the long wooded passage we have just come through. The river is framed in hills, the one on the right rising steeply some eight hundred feet above the St. John, the one on the left set back a mile from the river across the low, marshy ground at the end of the Allagash. The scene is a big one, but nothing of the size of what the imagination now superimposes on it. Outlined in the air between the hills and above the rivers is the crestline of Dickey Dam. It is more than three hundred feet above us, and it reaches from hill to hill. The dam is two miles wide. It plugs the St. John. It seals the Allagash marshland. Smaller than Oroville, bigger than Aswan, it is the twelfth-largest dam on earth. It contains what were once Aroostook mountains (Township Fifteen, Range Nine), blasted to shards and reassembled here. Its long downstream slope—the classic profile of the earth-fill dam—moves up before us to the crest. If we could put our canoes on our backs and portage up that slope, we'd see fifteen miles of whitecaps in the wind—a surging sea, but just a bay of Lake Dickey, whose main body, bending around a point to the left, reaches fifty-seven miles over the improved St. John. Paddles dipping, we fly the Big Rapid at three hundred feet, and, where the native trout have departed, we fish—thirty-five fathoms above Chimenticook Stream—for stocked Confederate bass. Chimenticook Bay is a five-mile reach, and Big Black Bay is thirty. In all, the lake bottom includes some ninety thousand acres of stumps, and, because Lake Dickey is one to three miles wide and no bridge is contemplated or economically feasible, two hundred thousand acres of standing timber are isolated from the rest of Maine. The lake fills up in spring, and the water is mined for power during the rest of the year, gradually revealing—along three hundred and fifty miles of shore—thirty thousand acres of mud. From the dam, and through the St. John-Allagash north Maine woods, runs a transmission line, continuing for four hundred and fifty miles, to southern New England, and carrying seven hundred and twenty-five megawatts of electricity for two and a half hours a day. That's all. That is the purpose of the Dickey dam. It is a soupçon, but anything more would drain the lake.

Many decades ago, the United States and Canada considered developing a tidal electric power source in Passamaquoddy Bay. It seemed a pretty good idea—pump-storage, with the tide as pump—but its daily output would be so erratic that another source would be needed to smooth out the curve of power. A conventional dam could do this, on the upper St. John. The Passamaquoddy project was eventually abandoned, but it had put the St. John dam in the book of public works, and dams are not recorded there in delible ink. For some years, though, few people were much interested in spending hundreds of millions of dollars for so small an amount of electricity—for a "peaking power" dam that could supply its power only during roughly a third of each day's peaking time. With the oil embargo of 1973, the situation changed, and the so-called Dickey and Lincoln School Lakes Multiple Purpose Project came back into the conversation. (To even out the flow from the big dam's irregular releases, a small dam would have to be built as well, a few miles downstream, at a place called Lincoln School.) New England power is largely derived from oil—seventy million barrels a year—and the dam at Dickey would save a million and a half barrels each year. Never mind that it would give New England roughly one per cent of its electricity. Never mind that it would almost surely cost, in the end, a billion dollars. It would provide pollution-free, Arab-free, indigenous New England power. The Corps of Engineers came through with a handsome benefit-to-cost ratio, indicating the shrewd Yankee good sense of building the dam, with computations based on a three-and-a-quarter-percent interest rate and zero future inflation. Additional cogent arguments were conjured as well—including flood control for villages downriver (dikes, built for a small fraction of the cost of the dam, would do), an upwelling of employment in the

depressed environs of Dickey (never mind that the employment would be gone in a few years, when the construction
jobs had vanished and a few people with clipboards had come
from somewhere else to run the dam). It was felt, finally, that
Maine, a state of two thousand lakes, needed a new one for
summer recreation, and in the benefit-to-cost computations
the recreational value of Lake Dickey was set at one million
two hundred and fifty thousand dollars, while, on the other
side of the ledger, the St. John River in its natural state was
assigned no value at all.

Panic about the Arabs brought all this on, but deeper than
the panic is an apparent belief that it is the right of people to
have all the electric power they can afford to buy, with the
subsidiary right of squandering it when and how they please
and of buying it at the same rate at any time of day. We throw
away more power than a Dickey Dam could ever give us, by
ten times ten times ten. We throw it away in kilowatt-years.
And anyone who would do that would throw away a river.

John Kauffmann, packing up his gear, winces in the direction of the damsite and says of Lake Dickey that it would be
"like an artificial mountain in the Rockies." He says that he
thinks there are plenty of technical arguments sufficient to
prove the foolishness of the building of the dam but that in this
case one point is really enough: "It would be a sin to murder
that beautiful river." Tom Cabot, in his carbon-black boots,
says he sees no benefit that would justify the cost.

Each year, of late, when the public-works-appropriations bill
has rolled out on the floor of Congress, Congress has taken a
vote on the St. John. Before the energy crisis, when the environmental movement was still going forward, the vote went
against the dam, but since then the vote has gone the other

way, getting up a few hundred thousand dollars here, a million there, to move the Corps through its studies toward the days of construction. The vote on construction funds—the vote to settle it all—looks to be in the offing for the nineteen-eighties. The St. John, it is said, was traded for the Allagash, at the time that the Allagash was preserved in legislation. If so, it was an uneven trade. When the guides of the Allagash take their vacations, they load their canoes and go down the St. John.

BRIGADE
DE CUISINE

THE FIFTH-BEST MEAL I have ever sat down to was at a sort of farmhouse-inn that is neither farm nor inn, in the region of New York City. The fourth-best was at the same place—on a winter evening when the Eiswein afterward was good by the fire and the snow had not stopped falling for the day. The third-best meal I've ever had was centered upon some smoked whiting and pale mustard sauce followed by a saltimbocca, at the same place, on a night when the air of summer was oppressive with humidity but the interior of the old building was cool and musty under a slowly turning paddle fan. When things come up so well, culinary superlatives are hard to resist, and the best and second-best meals I have ever had anywhere (including the starry citadels of rural and metropolitan France) were also under that roof—emanations of flavor expressed in pork and coriander, hazelnut breadings, smoked-roe mousses, and aïoli. The list of occasions could go deeper, and if it were complete enough it might number twenty or thirty before the scene would shift—perhaps to the fields of Les Baux or the streets of Lyons. The cook who has been responsible for such pleasure on this side of the Atlantic was trained on the other side, in kitchens in various places on the Continent, notably in Switzerland, and including Spain, where he grew up in a lavish and celebrated Andalusian hotel that was managed by his father. His father was Austrian, but his mother was English, and so, from the age of eight, he was sent to be educated in Great Britain. As a result, he is in manner, speech, and appearance irremediably English. He has an Oxbridge accent and a Debrettian flourish of names—not one of which he will allow me to divulge. His customers tend to become his friends, and I had been a friend of his for something like five years before I thought to ask him if I could sit in his kitchen and take notes. He said it would be all right, but with the condition that I not—in any piece of writing—use the name of the restaurant, or his name, or the nickname of his wife, Anne, who is not known as Anne and is always called by her nickname. We further agreed that I would not even mention the state in which they live and work, or describe in much detail the land- and waterscapes around them, let alone record what is written over the door of the nearest post office, which is, as it happens, more than five miles and less than a hundred from the triangle formed by La Grenouille, Lutèce, and Le Cygne.

The man's right knee is callused from kneeling before his stove. He would like to see his work described. He would like to be known for what he does, but in this time, in this country, his position is awkward, for he prefers being a person to becoming a personality; his wish to be acknowledged is exceeded by his wish not to be celebrated, and he could savor recognition only if he could have it without publicity. He works alone, with Anne (who makes desserts and serves as hostess, bartender, *sommelière*). In a great restaurant of Europe, the team in the kitchen will be led by the *gros bonnet*, and under him a *saucier*, an *entremettier*, a *potagiste*, a *rôtisseur*, a *grillardin*, a *friturier*, a *garde-manger*, and any number of *commis* running around with important missions, urgent things to do. Here—with Anne excepted, as *la pâtissière-en-chef*—this one man is in himself the entire *brigade de cuisine*. It is his nature not just to prefer but to need to work alone, and he knows that if his property were invaded and his doors were crowded up with people who had read of him in some enamelled magazine he could not properly feed them all. "There is no way to get qualified help," he explains. "You'd have to import kids from Switzerland. If you did, you'd lose control. The quality would go down the drain." In the *haute cuisine* restaurants of New York, kitchens are often small, and, typically, "five ill-educated people will be working there under extreme pressure, and they don't get along," he says. "Working alone, you don't have interaction with other people. This is a form of luxury."

Sometimes, at the height of an evening there are two customers in his dining room. His capacity is fifty-five, and he draws that number from time to time, but more often he will cook for less than forty. His work is never static. Shopping locally to see what is available today, reading, testing, adding to or subtracting from a basic repertory of roughly six hundred appetizers and entrées, he waits until three in the afternoon to write out what he will offer at night—three because he needs a little time to run to the store for whatever he may have forgotten. He has never stuffed a mushroom the same way twice. Like a pot-au-feu, his salad dressing alters slightly from day to day. There is a couple who have routinely come to his dining room twice a week for many years—they have spent more than fifteen thousand dollars there—and in all that time he has never failed to have on his menu at least one dish they have not been offered before. "I don't know if they're aware of this," he has told me. "We owe it to them, because of the frequency of their visits. They keep us on our toes."

In the evening, when his dining room is filling and he is busy in the rhythm of his work, he will (apparently unconsciously) say aloud over the food, and repeat, the names of the people for whom he is cooking. A bridge-toll collector. A plumber. A city schoolteacher. A state senator—who comes from another state. With light-edged contempt, he refers to his neighborhood as *Daily News* country. There are two or three mobsters among his clientele. They are fat, he reports, and they order their vegetables "family style." There is a couple who regularly drive a hundred and twenty miles for dinner and drive home again the same night. There is a nurse from Bellevue who goes berserk in the presence of Anne's meringue tortes and ultra-chocolate steamed mousse cakes, orders every dessert available, and has to be carted back to Bellevue. There is an international tennis star who parks his car so close against the front door that everyone else has to sidle around it. Inside, only the proprietors seem to know who the tennis star is. The center of attention, and the subject of a good deal of table talk, is the unseen man in the kitchen.

"Usually when you go out to dinner, the social event revolves around the people you are eating with and not the people who prepared the food. Soon after we started going there, he appeared by our table and wanted to know how something was—a shrimp al pesto he was trying for the first time. We have been there about once a month for nine years and he has never disappointed us."

(1 8 4)

"He's better than any restaurant I've eaten in in New York."

"He's a shy, compulsive, neurotic artist."

"He could never expand. He is a legitimate perfectionist who would find anyone else's work inferior to his own. No one would meet his standards. *He* doesn't meet his standards. Sometimes when I try to compliment him he refuses the compliment."

"I see him as one of the last of the great individualists, very happy in his kitchen, with his illegal plants out back. If he were to become prominent, his individualism would be damaged, and he knows that."

In part, the philosophy of this kitchen rests on deep resources of eggs, cream, and butter, shinbone marrow, boiled pig skins, and polysaturated pâtés of rich country meat. "Deny yourself nothing!" is the motto of one of the regulars of the dining room, who is trim and fit and—although he is executive vice-president in charge of public information at one of the modern giants of the so-called media—regards his relationship with the chef as a deep and sacred secret. "The place is not chic," he goes on. "It is no Southampton-type oasis. The people there are nondescript. In fact, that place is the only realizable fantasy I have ever had. The fantasy is that there exists a small restaurant in the sticks, with marvellous food, run by civilized, funny, delightful people who have read every book and seen every movie and become your good friends—and almost no one else knows about them. I used to fantasize such people. Now I know them. They exist. And the last thing in the world they would want is fame that is associated with hype and overpublicity. They are educated, sensitive, intelligent. Their art is what comes out of the kitchen. I'm sure he wants his work appreciated, but he doesn't want visitors coming to his hideaway for purposes of seeing the freak—the guy out in the woods who is making three-star meals. He would like to be appreciated for the right reasons—like an author who wants to be writing instead of going on TV talk shows. He is delighted when someone finds him, but wary, too. I think one proof of his sincerity is that he could raise his prices but he doesn't. He could advertise, but he doesn't. Somehow, that would be making too much of a commercial venture out of his work. It is inconceivable to imagine how his business could be run to make less money."

The chef is an athletically proportioned man of middle height—a swimmer, a spear fisherman. One day when he was thirteen he was picking apples in a tree between North Oxford and St. Giles and he fell out of the tree onto a bamboo garden stake. It impaled his cheek at the left corner of his mouth. His good looks are enhanced, if anything, by the scar that remains from this accident. He has dark hair, quick brown eyes, and a swiftly rising laugh. Anne is tall, finely featured, attractive, and blond. Each has eaten a little too well, but neither is falling-down fat. They work too hard. She works in a long ponytail, a cotton plaid shirt, unfaded dungarees, he in old shirts with the sleeves rolled up, rips and holes across the chest. His trousers are generally worn through at the knees. There are patches, sutures of heavy thread. His Herman boots are old and furred and breaking down. He pulls out a handkerchief and it is full of holes. "I don't mind spending money on something that is going to be eventually refundable," he explains. "A house, for example. But not a handkerchief." Most of the time, he cooks under a blue terry-cloth sailor hat, the brim of which is drawn down, like his hair, over his ears.

He was working with a Fulton Market octopus one morning, removing its beak, when he happened to remark on his affection for the name Otto.

"I like Otto," he said. "I think Otto is a sensational name. It's a name you would have to live up to, a challenging name. It suggests aloneness. It suggests bullheaded, Prussian, inflexible pomposity. Someone called Otto would be at least slightly pompous. Intolerant. Impatient. Otto."

Anne said, "He has written his autobiography in that name."

"I like Otto," he said again. "Why don't you call me Otto?"

I said, "Fine, Otto. I'll call you Otto."

Otto stepped outdoors, where he set the unbeaked octopus on a wide wooden plank. "Otto," he repeated, with savor. And he picked up an apple bough, a heavy stick about as long as his arm, and began to club the flesh of the octopus. "Otto," he said again, moving from one tentacle to the next. "I like that very much." Smash. "You do this to break down the fibres." Steadily, he pounded on. In time, he said, "Max is a good name, too—a sort of no-nonsense, straightforward name. Otto sounds humorless, and I don't think I'm humorless."

"Fine, Max. I'll call you Max."

"I like the way Max looks," he said. "It looks wonderful written on paper. You have the imagery of 'maximum,' too. And all the Maximilians." He struck the octopus another blow with the apple bough. "However," he went on, "I prefer Otto. Otto is autocratic. One word leads to another."

He carried the octopus inside. He said he has a cousin in the Florida Keys who puts octopuses in his driveway and then drives over them. "It's just to break down the fibres. I don't know what happens. I just know that it works." He went into the restaurant bar and took down from a wall an August Sander photograph of an anonymous German chef, a heavy man in a white coat of laboratory length over pin-striped trousers and highly polished shoes. The subject's ears were small, the head a large and almost perfect sphere. On the upper lip, an aggressive mustache was concentrated like a grenade. The man was almost browless, his neck was too thick to permit a double chin, and his tiny black eyes—perhaps by the impertinence of the photographer—were opened wide. In his hammy hands were a bowl and a wooden-handled whip. "This pig-faced guy is a real Otto," said the chef. "When our customers ask who that is in the picture we say he is our founder."

As we returned to the kitchen, I thought about the chef's actual name, which, like the man's demeanor, like the man himself in nearly all his moods, is gentle and unaggressive—an all but dulcet name, ameliorative and smooth, a name like Randal or Malcolm or Neal or Duncan or Hugh or Alan or John. For all that, if he wished to call himself Otto, Otto he would be.

Anne said, "He is less pompous than when I met him."

"Never let it boil," said Otto, lowering the octopus into a pot. "It mustn't boil. It should just simmer."

Nine o'clock in a spring morning and with a big square-headed mallet he is pounding a loin of pork. He has been up for three hours and has made school lunches for the two of his children who are still at home, boned some chicken, peeled potatoes, peeled onions, chopped shallots, shucked mussels, made coffee, swept the kitchen, made stock with the head of a twenty-pound grouper, and emptied outside a pail of scraps for the geese. His way of making coffee is to line a colander with a linen napkin and drip the coffee through the napkin. He ate a breakfast of leftovers—gâteau Saint-Honoré, Nesselrode cream-rum-chestnut mousse. He said, "I always eat dessert for breakfast. That's the only time I like it. For the rest of the day, if I'm working, I don't eat. It's wonderful not to eat if you're in a hurry. It speeds you up."

Anne works late and sleeps late. Otto goes to bed when his cooking is done and is up, much of the year, before dawn. Even at 6 A.M., he is so pressed with things to do that he often feels there is no time to shave. Into the school lunches today went small pork cutlets. He said, "I really don't believe in letting children eat the food served at school. Hot dogs. Baloney. Filth like that." His children carry roast chicken, veal, various forms of fish instead. At home, at the inn, they cook their own meals and eat more or less at random. The family business being what it is, the family almost never sits down at a table together. Sometimes the children, with friends, have dinner in the restaurant. Otto says, "They dress as if they're going to a disco, contemptibly wearing their collars outside their jackets, which is worse than wearing a blazer patch." He charges them half price.

The pork loin flattens, becomes like a crêpe. He dips the mallet in water. "All the cookbooks tell you to pound meat between pieces of waxed paper," he remarks. "And that is sheer nonsense." He is preparing a dish he recently invented, involving a mutation of a favored marinade. Long ago he learned to soak boned chicken breasts in yogurt and lemon juice with green peppercorns, salt, garlic, and the seeds and leaves of coriander, all of which led to a flavor so appealing to him that what he calls chicken coriander settled deep into his repertory. In a general way, he has what he describes as "a predilection for stuffing, for things with surprises inside," and so, eventually, he found himself wondering, "Maybe you could translate a marinade into a stuffing. You could pound a pork loin thin and fold it like an envelope over a mixture of cream cheese, fresh coriander leaves, lemon juice, and green peppercorns. Then you'd chill it, and set it, and later bread it. Sauté it a bit, then bake it. It should have a beguiling taste."

Picking up a knife now, he extends his fingers beyond the handle to pinch the blade. He rocks his wrist, and condenses a pile of parsley. There are calluses on his fingers where they pinch the blade. "The great thing is the *mise en place*," he says. "You get your things together. You get ready to cook. You chop your parsley, peel your onions, do shallots, make the hollandaise, make demi-glace sauce, and so forth." He does most of this in the center of the room, a step from the stove, at a long, narrow table that sags like a hammock. He works on two slabs of butcher block, and around them accumulate small tubs, bowls, and jars full of herbs and herb butters, stocks and sauces, grated cheeses. A bottle of apple-jack stands nearby for use in pâtés, and a No. 10 can full of kosher salt, which he dips into all day and tosses about by hand. Everything he measures he measures only with his eyes. How does he know how much to use? "I just know what is going to make things taste good," he says.

"Even with garlic, for example?"

"In garlicky dishes, you can hardly use too much—as long as you don't burn it."

He nibbles some parsley, wipes the block. On his shoulder is a hand towel, and with it he polishes his working surfaces as if he were polishing cars. He wipes the edge of the stove. He wipes the lips of pots. After he sautés something, he wipes out the interior of the pan. All day long the cloth keeps coming off the shoulder—or out of a rear pocket when it has migrated there—and as it grows foul it is frequently replaced. Like a quarterback, a golfer, a dentist, he would be unnerved without his towel.

When he finishes a patch of work—stops pounding loin of pork, completes a forcemeat for quenelles—he neatly puts the product away. Moving on to some new material, he carries it to a working surface, and cuts or separates or pours out just what he needs, and then returns the matrix—to the refrigerator, or wherever it came from—*before* he begins the new preparation. If he did not do this, he would risk chaos. His day will grow in frenzy and may eventually come a bit unstuck, but even in the whirl of the height of the evening he never fails to replace a source before he works on the substance.

He has a Vulcan gas stove with two ovens, a broiler, and six burners. Every time he turns it on he has to use a match. He keeps matches in a McDonald's French-fry packet nailed to a post. He saves the wooden sticks to use again as tapers. "We're really cheap," he confesses. "We wash our Reynolds Wrap and use it again."

His evolving salad dressing is stored in whiskey bottles and is topped up a few times a week with oil, egg yolk, wine, tarragon, marjoram, chervil, salt, pepper, chives, garlic, parsley, onions, scallion tops, vinegar, mustard seed—and almost anything but sugar. The thought of sugar in salad dressing disgusts him, although he knows it will sell salad dressing. He blends in some lightly boiled potatoes. They homogenize the dressing, he says, emulsify it, hold it together.

There is no top on the blender. Otto and Anne cover it with their hands—sometimes with a napkin. The blender is old and bandaged with tape. They have an electric mixer. "It's the worst-engineered thing I've ever seen. It spits ingredients into the air." To facilitate their preparations they have no other appliances. There is not even an electric dishwasher, just a three-tub stainless deep sink where Anne washes dishes in the dead of night, except on weekends, when a high-school student comes in to help. Three plugs stop the sink. A sign on the wall above says, "HANG PLUGS HERE. THIS IS A PROPHYLAXIS AGAINST DEMENTIA NERVOSA. PLEASE!" No rotisserie. No microwave. No Cuisinart in any form. "We're not anti-technology. We're just anti-junk," said Otto one morning. "There's no reason to be anti all 'labor-saving' things—just from sheer perversity to be against them—but, as it happens, there is nothing a Cuisinart can do that I can't do as quickly. And after using a Cuisinart I would have to clean it. Steak tartare cut with a knife has a better texture than it does if it comes out of a Cuisinart. The Germans call it Schabefleisch. For that matter, it is easier to cut hamburger meat than to make it in any kind of machine. If you grind it, you then have to clean the grinder." I asked him to make me a hamburger. He removed from the refrigerator the hundredth part of a ton of beef, sliced off a portion, put the rest of the meat back in the cooler, and returned to his working block, where his wrist began to flutter heavily, and in thirty seconds he had disassembled the chunk of beef and rearranged it as an oval patty. He ate some of the meat as he worked. Fast as it all happened, the cutting was done in three phases. He began with a one-handed rocking motion, and then held down the point of the knife with his left hand while pumping the handle with his right. He ended with a chopping motion, as if the knife were a hatchet. As he made the patty, he did not compact it crudely in his hands like a snowball. He tapped it together with the flat of the knife. The knife was Swiss (*hachoir* size), the blade vanadium stainless steel. "It's a lot of bull not to use stainless," he said. "If you know how to sharpen a knife, you can sharpen a stainless knife. You can't use a carbon knife to cut anything that has acid in it. If you cut anything acid with a carbon knife, it develops big black splotches. The splotches flavor the food." From under the stove he pulled a damaged iron skillet. Something that looked like a large bite was missing from the rim. He cooked the hamburger, turning it, touching it, turning it again and again, using the knife as a spatula. One morning he made fresh pork sausage for me the same way—mixing into the patty the salt, thyme, pepper, and coriander that are the essences of the flavor of sausage. The awakening aroma was vigorous and new. He tasted the raw pork as he went along. He said sausagemakers do that routinely. He observed that if one does need to make use of a meat grinder it is a good idea to put chunks of the meat into a freezer for twenty minutes beforehand. This in some way—he has no idea why—greatly reduces the stringiness that will often clog a grinder.

The kitchen has the dimensions of a fair-sized living room, and the refrigerator is a multi-doored affair that fills one end from wall to wall. The kitchen at a New York frog pond would not be half as large. (A frog pond, in Otto's vernacular, is any French restaurant, but particularly the finest and Frenchest of the supraduodenal boutiques.) Otto much admires André Soltner, chef of Lutèce, for removing (after he took over the ownership of the restaurant) some of his dining space in order to expand the kitchen. In Otto's kitchen, there is room for an old brass-studded leather Spanish chair. There is a television set, a big Grundig Majestic radio. On spacious high shelves are the chef's unending agents of flavor—his angelica seeds, his sorrel jam, his twenty-seven-dollar pelures de truffes, his valerian root, his Ann Page filberts, his Sun-Maid currants, and a thousand other things. Holding a deep, half-filled pan below my nose, he says, "This is rendered beef fat. We render all our pork and beef fat. It is extraordinarily unhealthy, but smell it. It smells of roast beef. Cooked in this, French-fried potatoes taste nutty and have a thick crust. The Belgians do all their *frites* like that. You can burn yourself badly, of course. I wouldn't want a large deep-fat fryer here. I'm too accident-prone. I burn myself all the time. The awful thing about burning is that you always burn yourself on a useful part of the hand." On a windowsill in the kitchen he grows *Aloe vera,* and tends it with affection, a handsome plant with its lanceolate, serrate, basal leaves. When he burns himself, he takes a leaf of aloe and slices it from the side, as if he were filleting a small green fish. He presses the leaf's interior against the burn, and holds it there with a bandage. "That takes the burn right away."

Outside, in his kitchen garden, Otto grows asparagus, egg-plant, chili peppers, bell peppers, tomatoes, cucumbers, pota-toes, spinach, zucchini, and chard. He also grows chervil, fennel, parsley, horseradish, basil, chives, marjoram, arugula, and tarragon, among other herbs. He freezes his herbs, he dries his herbs, and he aspirates the "h." He knows how to pronounce "Hertford," "Hereford," "Hampshire," and "herbs." He went to school in Oxford. Chervil, he says, is as potent to smoke as marijuana. "Black agaric is growing by the house, but I have not yet plucked up the courage to eat it. I grow my own garlic because the aroma is so much stronger when fresh. Garlic, fresh, throws a long cast through the kitchen."

(194)

The garden is not much affected by the shade of a condemned elm, where morels grow. Seashells in deep profusion —clam shells, oyster shells, conch shells, mussel shells—make tabby of the surrounding ground. Hold a conch to your ear. You can almost hear the sea. There are dogwoods, maples, white and Scotch pines, junipers, and dying apple trees beside the long drive that leads to the front door. The building is tall and proportional, not offensively ungainly, three stories, white, with many windows and a red tin roof. It glows at night at the end of its lane, and in daylight stands aloof in a field of tall grass, which is silvery brown after an autumn frost—fox grass. The place was a commune once, a boarding house, a summer hotel. There were two red barns. The communists burned up one for firewood. Otto's geese nest in the other. When Otto and I went in there once, he said, "It's a myth that geese are so dangerous. They don't bite hard." Wanting to show me some eggs in an embankment of down, he shoved aside a nesting goose. She struck, ineffectively, at the tough skin of his hand. I thought I'd like to see what that felt like, so I extended a hand of my own toward the head of the goose. She struck and struck again. She savaged my hand. She raised a pulpy red welt. Otto's geese patrol the grounds. Sixteen of them march up and down the driveway. "Geese once protected the Roman capitol," he says. "If something alarms these, they will make a commotion. But not during working hours." He used to kill and serve his domestic geese, but the flock has grown too old. He raised ducks and chickens, too. "Eating grubs and insects, the odd bit of corn, they tasted infinitely better." But he gave that up in surrender to the pressures on his time. He cautions you to beware the dog. Oh, no, not Zulu—not the shaggy black fun-loving Tibetan mastiff.

Beware Fofa, the bitter little brown-and-white spaniel with beagley undertones—Fofa, half cocked, with the soprano bark and the heavy bite.

Behind the inn are a can-and-bottle dump, rusting fragments of dead machinery, lengths of snow fencing, an automobile radiator, used lumber, two iron bathtubs, three mattresses, a rubble of used cinder blocks. There is little time to tidy what the dark paints out. The chef, who is not always ebullient, does not seem to care much anyway. "One of my great disadvantages is that I grew up in Spain in a luxury hotel with lots of servants," he will say. "I'll never be able to live as well as that, no matter how much money I make. It sort of crushes one's ambitions." He lives where sewer lines run up against winter wheatland and arms of forest interrupt the march of towns. There are heavy concentrations of wild deer. A man up the road sells mutton to hunters to take home as venison. On Otto's property, a clear stream flows into a good-sized pond. Water falls over its dam. He makes quenelles sometimes with pickerel from the pond. He makes quenelles, too, with whiting and other ocean fish and with a combination of shrimp and veal. "The veal binds them together and makes them very fluffy. My quenelles are much better than any quenelles you actually get anywhere. I don't know why. My quenelles have spring." To drink the pond or to share with the geese the scraps of Otto's profession, raccoons appear, and skunks, opossums—every creature of the woods, including one whose name would blow all this away. Otto will kill such creatures only to eat them. He has a Havahart trap in which he catches skunks. He takes the trap down the road to where some "perfectly contemptible" neighbors live, and releases the skunks there. He and Anne pick blueberries and wild grapes.

They gather dandelions for salads, and blackberries for cobblers and pies. He has cooked, and served to customers, stinging nettles and the fiddleheads of ferns. He gathers sheep sorrel for soups and salads. He once served creamed cardoons. In a lake not far away, he dives for crayfish, collecting them from under boulders and ledges. "The sauces you can make with their heads are unbelievable." He has shot and served rabbits and squirrels (Brunswick stew). He shot a raccoon and attempted a sort of coon au vin but considered the dish a failure. Sometimes there are wood ducks and wild geese in the pond. Over the land at dusk, woodcocks swoop and plummet, sometimes into the oven. Otto eats thrushes and blackbirds ("Delicious") but does not serve them. He would like to raise and serve kid, but he could not bring himself to kill one. He feels it would be "like killing a kitten." And, for all his youth in Spanish kitchens, he says he could not bring himself to take the life of a suckling pig. When, however, the odd pheasant happens through his fields of grass, he is not the least bit reluctant to go through the steps necessary to roast it for twenty minutes and then flame it with cognac and put out the fire with madeira. Disjointed, the pheasant next enters a heavy clay crock and is covered over with slices of goose liver and peelings of truffle. "Then I nap it with a fairly strong game gravy, really a demi-glace of game, made with rabbits. I hang them a bit, let them get a little high." He adds more sliced goose liver and truffles; then he covers the crock with its heavy lid and glues it down tight with a dough of egg white, water, and flour. He sets the pot in a bain-marie, and puts the whole rig into a very hot oven—for less than half an hour. The contents are ready when the dough turns brown. Pheasant Souvaroff. It was in the *Spezialrezepte der Französische Küche,* one of his textbooks when he was in Basel.

OTTO ROUTINELY DUSTS meat with white pepper "to lock in the freshness." Its taste seems unaffected. "It loses nothing," he says. "Bacteria don't like to eat their way through pepper any more than you would." Since he told me that, I have gone off on canoe trips with the meat in my pack basket dusted with pepper. The meat lasts for days. Otto doesn't camp. He once came down with pneumonia after sleeping a night on the ground.

When he makes béarnaise, he uses green peppercorns, preferring the stronger taste. When he makes bordelaise, he uses pork rinds, boiled until tender, in preference to marrow. He does almost everything, as he phrases it, *"à ma façon."* As a result of a tale often told by English friends of his parents, he is a particular admirer of a parvenu member of the peerage whose eccentric and umbrageous reputation had caused his applications to be rejected by any number of London and provincial clubs. At the helm of a yacht, he appeared one year at the Royal Regatta flying a pennant lettered "MOBYC," which, he was by no means reluctant to explain, was the simple heraldry of My Own Bloody Yacht Club. "I do things MOBW—my own bloody way," says Otto. "I should write that —or *'à ma façon'*—on the menu after every dish."

The unfortunate peer. He may never have tasted English marrowbones roasted after being sealed with flour. "A very clubby thing they are, marrowbones, done that way," says Otto. "The ends are closed hermetically, with dough. When the bone is roasted, you remove the crust and eat the marrow with a spoon. They serve that at the best clubs—of which I also am not a member."

In his affection for marrowbones, he collects veal shanks— slowly, one at a time as they arrest his eye—and they pile up like cordwood in the freezer for about three months. He pan-fries them in butter and olive oil. He sautés his bouquet garni. He then braises the lot in stock, tomato purée, herbs, and wine. And when he has the sauce in place and the bones on plates and ready to serve, he dusts them with fine-chopped lemon peel, parsley, and garlic. "It's called gremolata," he says, "and that is what makes the osso bucco explode." Not absolutely everything is, or needs to be, *à ma façon*. That one, unaltered, is from the *Joy of Cooking*.

In a roasting pan with hickory chips he is smoking shad roe. He will make a shad-roe mousse. "But it's not really a mousse. It's more like a butter. A form of pâté." He is struggling to name it because he has not made it before. He buys his hickory chips at the sporting-goods store—three dollars a pound— if he is pressed. He knows a carpenter, some distance away, who gives them to him for nothing. He smokes shrimp, trout, turkey breasts, and whiting, and turns pork loin into Canadian bacon. After twenty minutes with the chips, seven fresh rainbow trout will come out of the pan at what he considers acceptable (and I find remarkable) levels of taste and texture. He prefers the trout he smokes outside. He has a semi-dugout igloo made of earth and block, full of tunnels and traps, in which he cold-smokes trout for twenty-four hours. The wood is from his dying apple trees. He gets up to tend the smoker two or three times in the night. The principal difference between the twenty minutes inside and the twenty-four hours outside is that the resulting flesh is not opaque, it is translucent. When he smokes salmon out there, it takes thirty-six hours. He sometimes gives ducks a little outdoor smoke before he roasts them in the oven. "If I ever perfect cold-smoking," he says, "I'm going to smoke swordfish. It is fantastic. It turns pink, like a rose."

He rocks a knife through some scallions, hauls a grouper out of storage and begins to reduce it to fillets. He eats some scallions and, slipping a hand into the refrigerator, pops a couple of shrimp and two or three fresh scallops. "Fresh scallops stink like boiling cabbage for a while," he remarks. "These no longer stink. They breathe. They freshen themselves and come clean. Here are some I put away last night in lime juice with pepper flakes and red onion. Try one. Beautiful, isn't it? Seviche. I just make stuff and keep making stuff through the day until I've got enough. Then I sit down and write it out."

Anne enters the room, her first appearance of the morning —hunting shirt, dungarees, long hair akimbo. "Every spring I go mad. I am subject to the same swirling forces that pull the crocuses out of the ground," she reveals. "It is because I retain fluids."

Her husband seems to agree. He says, "She is subject to the same forces that govern the tides."

The forces have spread her hair to form a spectacular golden Afro, beaming outward from a physiognomic sun. She removes Otto's hat. It has become too grubby for her to look at in this part of the morning. He makes no struggle, but he is not completely assembled without his terry-cloth hat. He never eats aspirin. If he has a headache, he fills a plastic Baggie with ice, places it on his head, and pulls down around his temples the brim of his terry-cloth hat. Anne has much to do. She will make a mocha meringue. Then a gâteau victoire au chocolat. But for the moment she is only holding her head. She says, "I can't do anything until my head is clear."

I ask how long that might be, and she says, "It's almost clear."

Anne is Latvian and was six when she left the country. Her American-accented English contains no trace of those six years (that I, at any rate, can discern). Her predominant memories of Riga are of food—wide bowls full of caviar, mountained platters of crayfish, smoked lampreys served under crystal chandeliers at banquets in her home. In an album is a photograph of Anne's mother all in white satin among sprays of lilies and roses bending attentively toward a bunting-covered drape-folded canopied bassinet—the day of the christening of Anna Rozmarja. Anna Rozmarja Grauds.

Otto sums it up. "They were rich," he says. "I mean, they were rich rich."

"When I was a little girl, I was swathed in ermine and mink. I don't have a need for it now. It's been done."

"Her family had flocks of money, many ships. It was one of the First Families of Latvia, which is like being one of the First Families of Scranton."

"When the Germans took over the house, they allowed us to live on the top floor."

Words rise quickly in Anne's mind, but in speaking them she often hesitates and stumbles, and most of what she says comes slowly. "When the Russians were after us, we had to hide in the country. I remember the cows and the river and the food. Latvia is rich in milk and cheese and eggs. Even in the war no one was hungry. When we were escaping, we stayed at a farm where there were hams and wheels of cheese and things."

"Was that far from Riga?"

"In LLLatvia, nnnnnnothing is far from Riga."

Tilsit was not far from Riga, and Tilsit was not even in Latvia. Otto's grandfather was an architect in Tilsit. One day, the architect saw an advertisement in a newspaper in which sums of money were mentioned in connection with the connubial availability of a young woman in Salzburg. "Her brother placed the ad, and this chap came down from Tilsit and married her," Otto recounts. "It was the only way she could attract a man. She was quite plain."

"She was a handsome woman," Anne informs him.

Otto says, "She was about as handsome as Eleanor Roosevelt. She was a violent Nazi, that grandmother."

Her husband, at any rate, was excoriated by his family for "promiscuous marrying into the proletariat." Her son, Otto's father, went to *Gymnasium* in Salzburg and was later trained in hotels in Berlin and Munich. By 1936, when he was asked to be manager of the Reina Cristina, in Algeciras, he had been married, in England. The Mediterranean and Iberian Hotels Company, Ltd., an English concern, wanted someone they could trust who could also get on with the Germans. Otto's father carried a German passport during the Second World War.

Otto was born in Buckinghamshire, in July, 1938, and was taken home on a Japanese ship. Food was scarce in Spain for many years thereafter—to the ends of, and beyond, two wars. Gypsies, near starving, came to the hotel, asked for food, performed circus stunts as a way of paying, and then ate less than they were given. Asked why they would ignore food set before them, they said that if they ate a great deal they would soon be hungrier than they would be if they ate little. When Otto was nine, he discovered a boy in a persimmon tree on the hotel grounds stealing fruit. Otto happened to be carrying an air rifle. Pointing it, he ordered the boy to descend. On the ground, the boy "broke for it," and began to climb a garden wall. Otto threw a brick and knocked him down. Proudly, he reported the achievement to his parents. His father cracked him over the head. Otto saw the boy as a thief; his father saw the boy as someone so hungry that he had to steal—and therefore it was proper to let him steal.

"You must remember," Anne will say of her husband, "that he learned early what food really is. He knows what it is to be without it. He has a grasp of the sanctity of food. That is his base. He finds delight just in seeing his ingredients. He goes on to luxury after that. Remember, too, that he ate awful meals endlessly—for years. He was in school in England after the war."

Tutored from the age of three, Otto was sent to Britain a year after the German surrender—to Tre-Arddur House School, on Tre-Arddur Bay, in North Wales, a place that, according to him, "specialized in ridding industrialists' sons of their accents, boys from Yorkshire and Lancashire." Otto spoke Spanish, French, and German, and virtually no English, so he had several accents that were targeted for destruction, too. He was called Dago or Greaser, because he came from "Franco Spain." When he was caught in this or that misdemeanor, the headmaster, gnashing craggily, told him not to "use your Spanish tricks" at Tre-Arddur. "My character was deformed there." Otto's tone is more factual than bitter. "I was a happy kid before then, and I became a morose loner.

Eventually, when I was invited to join things, I realized I no longer needed to join." The headmaster whipped the boy for his miserable handwriting. On the rugger field, the headmaster caned anyone who funked a tackle. "We won a lot of rugger matches. I was a hooker—in, you know, the center of the scrum." The Tre-Arddur year had its fine moments. The assistant headmaster fished in Scotland and brought back enough salmon to feed everyone in school.

Otto lived for the long vacs in Spain, for the big sardines on sticks over beach fires, the limpets, the wild asparagus, the fishing, and the catch of red mullet baked on fig leaves and tile. The Reina Cristina was lush beyond thought with its fountains and pools under bougainvillea, its date palms and tangerines, its Islamic arcades and English gardens. "You would have to be a Saudi sheikh to live that life again." English colonials, Andalusians, Murcians, titled and rich, "the whole of the south of Spain knew each other very well, they were very cliquey, and when they came to Gibraltar to clothe their women in English finery they stayed at the Reina Cristina." Above them all stood Otto's father, six feet five inches, thin and regal, actually a dominant figure among the sherry people and the rest of his distinguished guests. Guy Williams (Williams & Humbert), the Gonzalezes, the Palominos, the Osbornes, the Domecqs. "My father was, you know, *amigo íntimo* with all of them." Having four hundred employees, he was as well a figure of first importance in back-street Algeciras. He and a cork company were the principal employers in the town. He had his standards. He never hired a former altar boy. He felt that altar boys were contaminated by priests. He was scrupulously sensitive to the needs and natures of his staff. When Otto called the chef's son a *mariquita azúcar*, his father made him write a calligraphically perfect note of apology. On a tour of countries to the north, the family went out of its way to stop in Lourdes, because the Reina Cristina's housekeeper had mentioned that she would like some holy water with which to cure her black dog, which had come down with terminal mange. Approaching home through dry hundred-degree heat on the brown plains of the Iberian plateau, Otto and his younger brother suffered so with thirst that they drank the holy water. Their father filled the bottle from a tap, gave it to the housekeeper, and the dog was cured. The boys were thrashed about once a week—their mother's riding crop, their father's hand. There was no cruelty in it, merely custom. Otto calls his parents "permissive," and cites his father's reaction to his experiments with hash. Otto had an underwater-diving companion named Pepe el Moro who would sniff kif before diving in order to clear his sinuses and increase the depth of the dives. Otto sniffed, too. When his father learned that his son was using narcotics, he said only, "Stop that. It's unhealthy." When the *cuadrillas* were in town, the great matadors stayed at the Reina Cristina. Otto as a child knew Belmonte, and later Litri, Ordoñez, Miguelín. Their craft so appealed to him that he knew every moment of their ritual, from the praying in the chapel to the profiling over the sword. In the album is a snapshot of Otto with Ernest Hemingway on the veranda outside the Cristina's bar. Otto marvels at "the incredible patience" Hemingway displayed toward "a callow youth" in his teens. Otto's family had a farm in the mountains with an irrigation system that he still thinks of as nothing less than lyrical—its pools and rivulets descending among terraced beds of kitchen plants. His father also managed the Hotel Reina Victoria, in Ronda. Otto would go there on horseback, the more to be involved in the beautiful country—the Serranía de Ronda—and he paid for all his needs with Chesterfield cigarettes. He went slowly when he went back to school.

His mother's parents lived in Oxford, and he moved on from Tre-Arddur to St. Edward's because St. Edward's was there. It was a distinguished public school, distinguished for having been repugnant to young Laurence Olivier some decades before. Otto was hungry there, not caring for the food. With his air rifle, he killed sparrows and thrushes in his grandparents' garden and roasted them on spits over open fires. In his form, he won the St. Edward's general-knowledge prize in all the years he was there. He was very fond of his grandparents. His grandfather was J. O. Boving, an engineer known for a proposal to harness the Severn bore. He gave his grandson a copy of the Boving family tree, which is fruited, for the most part, with farmers. Its mighty trunk, emerging from the soil, has cracked to pieces a Corinthian temple, thus implying the family's durability relative to the artifacts of the earth. Anne, absorbed, now looks up from the picture. She says, "Most of my family should hang from a tree."

She pours cream from a cup into a bowl, and the cream is so thick that it clings to the cupside like mayonnaise. In bottles, it will not pour at all. To have such cream, she drives many miles each week to a farm in another state. Between layers of pecan cake, she is about to establish three concentric circles of royale chocolate and whipped cream. She has turned to this project after finishing another, in which a layer of meringued hazelnut was covered with a second story of hazelnut Bavarian cream that was in turn covered, top and sides, by a half-inch layer of chocolate cake that had been formed upon an overturned pie plate. Atop this structure was a penthouse confected of chocolate, butter, egg yolks, and brandy. "It looks simple, but it takes so bloody long," she said as she finished. "To admit you eat something like that, these days, is almost like confessing to incest. I was a size twelve before I met Otto. Now I'm size eighteen." Her height saves her. One might well say that she is grand, but she could not be described as fat. Her husband, for his part, works sixteen hours a day, is in constant motion, professes to eat almost nothing, and should be quite slim. By his account, "a couple of cucumbers" is about all he consumes in a day. Somehow, though, he has acquired at least twenty-five pounds that he would like to do without.

Now and again, he will stop to hold a pastry sleeve for her or hammer a dented cake pan back into form, but in the main they work separately, and rapidly, at spaced stations of the table, he slicing some salmon, completing a brioche to enclose it, she making puff paste, or a cake from yogurt cheese. (It takes a couple of days to drip, through cloth, the whey out of a gallon of yogurt. The yield is a quart of cheese.) She makes two, three, four, even five new desserts in a day. A light almond dacquoise is—as much as anything—the standard, the set piece, from which her work takes off on its travels through the stars. The dacquoise resembles cake and puts up a slight crunchy resistance before it effects a melting disappearance between tongue and palate and a swift transduction through the bloodstream to alight in the brain as a poem.

OTTO LICKS SHAD-ROE PÂTÉ from a rubber scraper, wipes clean his working surfaces, and carries to the refrigerator a sour-cream aggregate of curried Moroccan lentils, tasting a spoonful as he puts them away. He leaves the kitchen. Time to drive who knows how many miles for supermarket shopping. Behind the wheel and rolling north, he says, "Supermarkets occasionally have fresher stuff than you can buy anywhere else." He is more or less forced to shop retail anyway. He feeds two hundred people a week, not enough to warrant wholesale buying if he is going to offer a virtually different menu every night—if he is going to shop, as he does, opportunistically, and "just make things," willy-nilly, through a free-lance working day. If he happens to see scallops the size of filets mignons, he will take them home, grill them, and serve them under sauce béarnaise. He knows a certain ShopRite that is "wonderful for brains, sweetbreads, and chicken," and the Grand Unions of his region are supplied now and then with amazingly fine beef. He reads the ads. He makes his rounds. He walks through a supermarket, sees some good shell steaks on display, and tosses fifty pounds of them in small packages into his cart. He drives eighty miles for Westphalian ham. He drives an upper-middle-aged eight-cylinder Dodge, a car so overpowered it is no good on ice. The family call it their "off-the-road vehicle." They had a Volkswagen bus once. Otto is a competent driver but easily bored and tending toward sleep. One day, with him snoozing and safely belted, the bus rolled over three times and spilled green crawling lobsters onto the road. To avoid the irritation of a summons, Otto gave the lobsters to the cops. On the dashboard of the Dodge now are two plastic packets of malt vinegar from Arthur Treacher's Fish & Chips. "I like junk food," Otto declares. "Treacher's chips are awful. They don't seem real. They seem to be made of mashed potatoes. But the fish is good. Actually, it is great."

"Define 'great.'"

"Specifically, the batter is delicious and the fish is acceptable. The fish is white and moist. It has no flaw. The batter is very clever. Water, flour, baking powder, a bit of cornmeal—we think it's like a churro batter. The texture is just wonderful—crunchy and crisp. You don't concentrate on taste but on texture. What a horrible thing to say about food! They have plastic packets of sauce tartare there, too. You suck it out. It's degenerate." He will go big distances for a McDonald's Egg McMuffin. "It's a triumph," he explains. "It's inspired. With melted cheese instead of hollandaise, it is eggs Benedict for the masses. I don't know why it wasn't thought of long ago." If you ask for a doggie bag in Otto's dining room, your pheasant Souvaroff or your grilled squid rings in aïoli sauce are returned to the table in a polystyrene container that first held an Egg McMuffin. (Otto is generous to a fault, and the unwary amateur can eat his way into a stupor.) His professed affection for junk food is pretty much used up on Arthur Treacher and the Egg McMuffin. Other examples are few and faint. "I've had a Big Mac. Over the years, I've had a Big Mac four times. Once, when I was quite hungry, it was good." He enjoys the sort of anisette Italian sausages that are sold in hard rolls from old white vans. He has never crossed the threshold of a Colonel Sanders. Fried chicken is one of his favorite things on earth. He soaks lean chicken overnight in milk, and fries it in pure raging lard.

Soft drinks?

He shakes his head, but reconsiders. "Oh," he says, "I'll drink a Tab if I have a headache."

Coffee?

"No. Very little. Six or seven cups a day, no more. And twenty cups of tea." He also guzzles vichy by the quart.

Beer?

"Only on Saturday night. A six-pack, after work."

Wine?

"When we go out. Not often at home."

Booze?

"I've been known to drink four or five pink gins. Gin and Angostura. If it weren't for my work, I could drink all the time. You simply can't cook and drink. You cut yourself and burn yourself. You lose your edge. You can't do it and drink. Impossible."

"Faulkner drank. One of his relatives is supposed to have asked him, 'Bill, are you drunk when you write those stories?' And Faulkner said, 'Not always.' "

"Oh," says Otto, "Evelyn Waugh has a very good line on drinking. One evening during the war, his commanding general said to him, 'Waugh, you're making a spectacle of yourself. I must ask you to stop.' And Waugh—he was the rich man's John O'Hara—he said, 'Surely, sir, you can't expect me to change the habits of a lifetime to accommodate your whim.' "

Once, when we were out on the road like this, Otto said he often wished he could keep on going—to destinations more exotic than the Grand Union. He was not altogether content with this region. He had dreams of San Antonio. He thought about Key West. He said he felt a need for "new momentum," felt "imprisoned in the economics" of the present inn. Waitresses had netted as much from the business as he and Anne combined. In a year, several thousand dollars were going for heat alone, and even more to insure the ungainly wooden building. After he had paid the oil company and the insurance company, what was left was less than he could earn by doing unskilled labor. He said that in Algeciras there was one fire engine and it performed two functions. It put out fires in the cork factory and it watered the ring at corridas. Homes and restaurants did not burn. They were made of fieldstone and mortar. Otto would like to construct a new building half underground, heated and powered by the sun, and with such a high percentage of masonry in its materials that it would be virtually fireproof—a restaurant where heating bills and fire insurance are covered by hors d'oeuvres.

At an A. & P. he picks up bibb and ruby lettuce, at the ShopRite potatoes and brains. "The A. & P. have wonderful produce. Sometimes. And they always have bibb lettuce." The next stop is in a mall parking lot, between a Rite Aid Pharmacy and a K Mart, in the shadow of a Great American. "The fruit in here is terrible," says Otto as he picks out the Great American's six best pears. Moving his cart along, he collects five pounds of bean curd, some bean sprouts, and a couple of dozen Japanese midget eggplants. "Bean curd is the cow of the Orient," he says. "It has many of the same nutrients as milk. Look there. Eggroll wrappers. When you can buy bean curd and eggroll wrappers in a supermarket in a town like this there's some sort of quiet revolution going on." He sees and excitedly handles five packages of lovely big leeks. "Hey, I'm glad I came! I'll make leeks vinaigrette, certainly, and leek soup. When the Welsh come to play rugger at Twickenham, they have leeks in their lapels. If you cut off the roots of leeks and plant them, they grow. That will appeal to your Scottish sense of thrift." Scallions. Onions. Outsize artichokes. Endive. Escarole: "It's slippery. It's meaty. It's got everything!" Parsley root: "Hey, great! Here, eat one. I put it in with parsley for flavoring, but mainly I just eat it raw, eat it all myself. It's too good for the customers." A parsley root in its appearance suggests a stunted and misshapen albino carrot. It has the texture of an apple and the taste of parsley. "It's good sliced in soup. Or grated in a salad." He takes a bottle of ReaLemon from a shelf, saying, "Ever smelled this? It smells like skunk." By a forest of bottles of Frothee creamy head for cocktails, he stops, picks one up, and reads the label, finding there a form of glycol that he identifies as a substance used in brake fluids. Two pounds of bacon. Thirteen and a half pounds of fresh ham. Seven and a half pounds of veal. Veal kidneys. Veal hearts. Eleven half pound packages of sweetbreads go into the cart. There is a gap in the tilting mirrors behind the meat, and a butcher's startled face is framed there. "That's all the sweet-breads we have," he says. "That's all there is."

That may be all there is in this tank town. It hardly bothers Otto. For all his rampant eclecticism—and the wide demands of his French-based, Continentally expanded, and sometimes Asian varietal fare—he knows where the resources of his trade are virtually unlimited. Mondays, when the inn is dark, he leaves his Herman boots in his bedroom—his terry-cloth hat, his seam-split dungarees—and in a dark-blue suit like a Barclays banker he heads for New York City. "In a few square blocks of this town are more consumer goods than in the whole of Soviet Russia," he remarked one time as he walked up Ninth Avenue and into the Salumeria Manganaro, where he bought a pound of taleggio ("It's like a soft fontina") and was pleased to find white truffles. "They're from Piedmont. Grate them on pasta and they make it explode." At Fresh Fish (498 Ninth), he bought river shrimp from Bangladesh weighing up to a quarter of a pound each. He bought sausage flavored with provolone and parsley at Giovanni Esposito (500), and at Bosco Brothers (520) he stopped to admire but not to purchase a pyramid of pigs' testicles, which he said were delicious in salad. "Texas strawberries, you know. They're wonderful. They're every bit as good as sweetbreads. Boil them tender. Dry them. Dredge them in flour. Pan-fry them." At Simitsis International Groceries & Meat (529), he bought a big hunk of citron in a room full of open bins of loose pasta, of big bags and buckets full of nuts and peppers, of great open cannisters of spices and sacks full of cornmeal, hominy grits, new pink beans, pigeon peas, split peas, red lentils, semolina, fava beans, buckwheat kasha, pearl barley, Roman beans, mung beans. "This place is fabulous. If I had a restaurant in New York—oh, boy! New York has everything you could possibly want in food. If you look hard enough, you'll find it all." At Citarella (2135 Broadway, at Seventy-fifth), he admired but did not buy a twenty-pound skate. He had walked the thirty-five blocks from Simitsis to Citarella. He prefers to walk when he's in town. I have seen him on the street with a full side of smoked salmon, wrapped in a towel, tied to a suitcase like a tennis racquet. If Anne is with him, he rides. "You poach skate and serve it with capers and black butter," he said. "It's a wonderful fish, completely underrated. I shot a big electric one in the Caymans." Citarella had flounder roe for eighty-five cents a pound. "You pay four dollars a pound for shad roe," said Otto. "Flounder roe is every bit as good. Shad roe has the name." He stopped for tea, ordering two cups, which he drank simultaneously. At Zabar's (Eightieth and Broadway), he bought thin slices of white-and-burgundy Volpi ham. "It's from St. Louis and it's as good as the best jamón serrano." At Japanese Food Land (Ninety-ninth and Broadway), he bought a couple of pounds of bean threads and four ounces of black fungus. On the sidewalks and having a snack, he ate twelve dried bananas. "That's, actually, nothing," he remarked. "I once et thirty-six sparrows in a bar in Spain. Gorriones, you know—spitted and roasted."

He tried to prove to himself not long ago that with United States ingredients he could duplicate the taste of chorizo, a hard Spanish sausage. He had to throw a good part of it away, because he failed to pack it tight enough and "fur grew inside." Casa Moneo, on Fourteenth Street between Seventh and Eighth, "is the best place for chorizos," he says. "They're made in Newark. They're as good as you can get in Spain."

He also buys chorizos at La Marqueta—a series of concession stalls housed below the railroad tracks on Park Avenue in Spanish Harlem. Chorizos. Jamón serrano. Giant green bananas—four for a dollar. Dried Irish moss. Linseed. Custard apples. "When they're very ripe they get slightly fermented. Mmm." He will buy a couple of pounds of ginger, a bunch of fresh coriander, a couple of pounds of unbleached, unpolished rice—letting go the dried crayfish and the green peanuts, the Congo oil and the pots of rue, letting go the various essences, which are in bottles labelled in Spanish: Essence of Disinvolvement, Essence of Envy and Hate. Breadfruit. Loin goat chops. "OHIO STATE UNIVERSITY" shopping bags. "Goat is milk-white when it's young. I don't want to get into an argument with these people, but that is not kid, it's lamb." Seeing a tray of pigs' tongues, he calls them "beautiful." And high-piled pigs' ears: "You slice them thin."

He drops in at the Bridge Kitchenware Corporation, 212 East Fifty-second Street, nods at Fred Bridge, and says, "I'm looking for a whip for crème fouettée. I have never seen one in America that's any good." Bridge hasn't either. Bridge has

(214)

overcome the problem, however, by having a supply of stainless ones made for him in France. Otto looks over several as if he were choosing a new squash racquet. "Perfect," he says, eventually, to Bridge. "Very beautiful. Flexible." He buys a quenelle scoop. Rummaging in the back of the store, he picks up a tin sieve. A clerk frankly tells him not to take it because it is no good. "That's why I want it," he says. "I've never seen one that was any good. The best of them won't last six months." He asks for parchment paper. To "make stuff *en papillote*," he sometimes uses, instead of parchment, narrow bags from liquor stores. "Tied at each end and oiled, they are perfect *en papillote* bags, as long as the paper has not been recycled. You can't make things *en papillote* in recycled paper because of the chemicals involved. Some restaurants use aluminum foil for *en papillote*. Contemptible."

He has lieutenants—certain fish merchants from his general neighborhood—who shop for him at the Fulton Market. But often enough he goes there himself, his body, at 4 A.M., feeling what he calls the *resaca*—"when the tide goes out and leaves the dry sand." He loves this world of rubber boots and bonfires, wet pavement and cracked ice, and just to enter it—to catch the bright eye of a fresh red snapper—is enough to cause his tides to rise. "There is no soul behind that eye," he says. "That is why shooting fish is such fun." Under the great illuminated sheds he checks everything (every aisle, bin, and stall), moving among the hills of porgies and the swordfish laid out like logs of copper beech, the sudden liveliness in his own eyes tempered only by the contrast he feels between the nonchalance of this New York scene and the careful constructions of the Algeciras wholesale fish market, where "they display the food with a lot more love."

"You never know what is going to be good. You have to look at everything," he says, and he looks at bushels of mussels, a ton of squid, bay scallops still in their shells. "Make sure they're not Maine mussels," he remarks, almost to himself. "If they are, forget it. Maine mussels are very clean, but they're small and awfully tough. You just want the big squid. The New Jersey squid." He looks at a crate of lobsters. They are dragons—up into their salad years—and three of them fill the crate, their heads seeming to rest on claws the size of pillows. "People think they're dragons because they look like dragons, but they're called that because they are caught in dragnets," he says, picking one up and turning it over, then the second, and the third. The third lobster has many hundreds of green pellets clinging like burrs to its ventral plates. "Eggs. They're better than caviar," says Otto. "They're so crunchy and so fresh-tasting—with lemon juice, and just enough bland vegetable oil to make them shine. You remove them from the lobster with a comb."

Baskets of urchins disappoint him. "See all the white spots? The freckles? See how the spines are flat? If the spines are standing, the creature is very much alive." For many months, he and his legates have been on the watch for urchins that are up to his standards. They must be very much alive because their roe, which is what he wants, is so rich and fragile that it soon goes bad.

He views with equal scorn a table of thin fresh herrings. He serves herring fillets in February, and this is not February. "That's the only time of year when we can get big fat herrings. They're sensational then, maybe a day or two out of the sea. You have et bottled herring, have you? Awful. Herring, or salmon, in sour cream. They don't use crème fraîche. They

(2 1 6)

use a sauce with dubious taste but with better keeping quali-
ties." Otto never prepares herring the same way twice, but his
goal is the same if his ingredients are not. He uses, say, vinegar and dill with peppercorns and onions, and his goal is to
give the herring "a taste so clean it's lovely."

He feels the slender flanks of sand lances, and he says,
"You dredge them with flour, drop them into deep fat, and
eat them like French fries." He presses the columnar flank
of a swordfish, pleased to have it back in the market. He
quotes Ted Williams. It is Williams' opinion that the surest
way to save the Atlantic salmon is to declare the species full of
mercury and spread the false word. "Swordfish is a bummer in
the freezer," Otto says. "But there are all sorts of fish you *can*
freeze. Shrimp are better frozen properly on a ship than carried for days to market unfrozen. In properly frozen shrimp
there's never a hint of ammonia. Scallops freeze well, too—
and crabmeat, octopus, striped bass, flounder, conch, tilefish,
grouper. Red snapper frozen is no good. It gets watery, water-
logged. A soft-fleshed fish like a sea trout is no good frozen.
Freezing tuna or bluefish precipitates the oily taste. No frozen
fish is better than fresh, but well-frozen fish is better than fish a
week old."

Groupers—weighing thirty, forty pounds—face him in a
row, like used cars. "You can split those big heads," he says.
"Dredge them in flour and pan-fry them. Then you just pick at
them—take the cheeks, the tongue."

There are conger eels the size of big Southern rattlesnakes.
"With those I make jellied eel, cooked first with parsley, white
wine, and onions. Almost no one orders it. I eat it myself."

As he quits the market, he ritually buys a pile of smoked
chub, their skins loose and golden. "Smoked chub are so

good," he says. "They just melt like butter. You can eat half a dozen quite happily on the way home in the car."

LUNCHTIME IN THE KITCHEN AND OTTO, who never eats a meal when working, offers me an artichoke and some veal with wild mushrooms and Portuguese sauce. "The best veal is not young but nearest to beef," he says, malleting and dusting the slice before him. "Heavy veal—older veal—is easier to work with, and it looks healthier. Do you know what Provimi is? It's an artificial milk feeding that more or less bleaches veal on the hoof. Keeps it from turning pink. Ugh." He has been trimming romaine and chicory, and he puts the trimmings into a pot and steams them until they collapse. With a sprinkling of parmesan, they whet the palate. "I never throw anything away," he says, "unless it's been paid for." He picks up a handful of hot greens and shoves them into his mouth.

"English people are less conscious of utensils than Americans are," says Anne.

He replies, "That is because you can't buy your hands."

" 'Eating food with a knife and fork is like making love through an interpreter,' " she goes on. "Somebody wrote that. I can't remember who."

Lunches have been good in the kitchen—Otto's fast foods, in his fashion, selected not to slow up his routine.

Veal and Westphalian ham dusted with marjoram and wrapped around big fried croutons. He pan-fries them on a skewer and deglazes the juices with wine to make a full-bodied, gelatinous gravy.

Sautéed squares of lemon sole, with Swiss chard and anchovies which he tosses in a frying pan, holding the handle with both hands as he flings the chard and anchovies into the air.

Smoked whiting, seviche, cucumbers, and Vouvray.

Octopus al amarillo, with saffron, onions, potato, parsley, garlic, and wine—a peasant Spanish dish he has been eating all his life. "It's the sort of thing the maids would make at home for me after I'd been clamming, or caught an octopus or an eel or any fish with firm flesh."

Fried bread with tomato, garlic, and oil. "It's working-class food. The Spanish servants made that for me, too. It was comparable to a white child's being fed by slaves in the South. I learned from the Spaniards to stay away from expensive oil. It is said that the finest olive oil has the lightest color, and that is as great a myth as the maple-syrup myth. Dark, Grade B maple syrup has more flavor than Grade A. This is good green oil. Expensive oil is jejune and very pale."

He made a crêpe one day, filling it with spinach and shrimp. "You can put anything in a crêpe and sell it," he confided.

I asked if he had eaten at La Crêpe.

"Once," he said.

"And how was it?"

"We liked the cider."

One noon he handed me a very large bean curd grilled like a steak and standing in a soy-based sauce with ginger, vinegar, and scallions; another noon, shad roe. Cooks vulcanize shad roe. This, however, was light and springy and all but underdone. "Why not undercook everything?" Otto said. "That way, if you need to you can cook it some more."

Directly from the sea I brought some mackerel one day, and we built an applewood fire outside. For the occasion, he quickly assembled a small cinder-block fireplace, and at the finish he kicked the hot blocks apart so he could get the mackerel right down on the fire and "burn" it, giving it what he called "a good Spanish smell"—the smell of wood smoke in broiled flesh.

Alex comes into the kitchen now, home from school under a tumble of hair—amazingly tall for an eighth-grader and as mature in manner as appearance. He moves lightly through the room on big feet, amusement indelible in the corners of his mouth. "Jesus saves," he remarks. His father's look suggests approaching aircraft. His father is preparing leeks. Alex circles the kitchen, and, as he goes out, says, "Moses invests." Anne was divorced. The three older children are hers. Alex is theirs. For his most recent birthday he was given raw fish and a Roman coin—mackerel sushi, octopus sushi, fluke sushi, shrimp sushi, and salmon sushi, followed by a boiled lobster. "Lobster is delicious raw but not for a little boy," says Otto. Two boys and two (college) girls—they work for their parents from time to time as waiters. When Alex was learning to take orders, a customer—an old family friend—asked him for a chocolate-covered frog. Intently, the grandson of the late distinguished manager of the Reina Cristina of Andalusia wrote down, "1 chocolate frog." He thought it was a drink.

Otto puts away his marinating leeks, makes some wine-butter-cream-and-parsley sauce, tastes the sauce, and tosses a lump of crabmeat to the cat. Alex returns to the kitchen and pours himself some milk. His father, putting the sauce away, tells him, "If Moses had brains, he would have landed in Saudi Arabia."

Fish man calls—one of the emissaries to the Fulton Market —giving news that electrifies Otto. Anne is in another room.

After putting down the phone, he shouts exultantly to her, "I've got sea urchins from Maine! Greg says they're perfect. We'll eat them raw." It would appear that the urchins are too good for the customers. "If they're truly fresh, they should be eaten raw," he goes on. "On the other hand, I could make a fish ragout with urchin-roe sauce. I've never tried that. The roe is pungent stuff, but a little of it would make the ragout sauce subtle—with cream, butter, fish fumet, and reduced white wine." His mind keeps turning, pausing over this or that possibility, and in his generosity he is obviously expanding his thoughts to include the clientele. "Perhaps I'll take some urchin egg and spread it on fish and broil it. It gives a lobster taste. Yes. Also, I'll make an urchin mayonnaise." He has not seen the creatures yet. He may be forging ahead of himself. While he stands here and plans and dreams, what if their spines are falling like pick-up-sticks? He answers the question with a rattling-fast trip in the Dodge, and when he comes back he is carrying a basket of *Strongylocentrotus drobachiensis* in the flush of life, spotless, glistening, their spines erect—tiny little porcupines frightened green. Anne and Otto begin to crack them open and remove with spoons the golden-orange ovaries and testes collectively known as roe. The open urchins are passed like cups of wine. The roe looks and tastes something like scrambled egg, but no comparison with another food can really suggest the flavor. It is the flavor of sea-urchin roe, light and pleasantly aromatic, with the freshness of a whitecap on the sea. Anne, removing it, says, "This is a religious experience." And, since one does not gorge on urchin roe, they turn soon from feeding themselves to filling a jar for use with dinner.

From a high shelf at one end of the kitchen, where cookbooks and culled magazines run fifteen feet from wall to wall, Otto pulls his copy of the *Joy of Cooking*. He looks in it to see what it has to say about sea-urchin roe, and is surprised to find no recipe. So he turns to Elizabeth David, there being no culinary writer for whom he has more respect, and also to A. J. McClane's *Encyclopedia of Fish Cookery*. The *Joy of Cooking* is rumpled, swollen, split, bent, frayed, and bandaged, its evident employment matched on the bookshelf only by Auguste Escoffier's *Le Guide Culinaire*, which belonged to Otto's father and in appearance is even more exhausted. "You cannot live without the *Joy of Cooking*," Anne remarks. "It is not great and complex, but it is diverse and basic. It is a book that will translate other books. We have fifty books and more, but if we have a problem we go to the *Joy of Cooking*."

"There is nothing fake or pretentious in it," her husband says.

"It is America's touchstone."

"It tells you how to skin a squirrel."

"Beyond the basic information, basic recipes, you might be surprised how much it includes. It tells you everything from how to poach eggs to how to prepare a raccoon."

"It is very good on bread, and even has a breakdown on grains."

"It tells you how to make a Sacher torte."

"It tells you how to do live snails, how to build a smoker, how to cook octopus, how to prepare a possum, how to make rouille sauce. Put rouille sauce in bouillabaisse and it explodes. Rouille sauce is not in Larousse. But you'll find it in the *Joy of Cooking*."

Otto reaches for his Pellaprat—Henri-Paul Pellaprat, *Modern French Culinary Art*—and it comes off the shelf in half volumes. During a marital-professional fracas, Anne once took hold of the Pellaprat and Otto did, too, and each tugged in a warlike direction. The Pellaprat, in its photographic and textual elegance, deals with the roe of the sturgeon and the roe of the shad but not with the roe of the urchin. Otto flips randomly at the book and lays it open to page 291, where there is a color photograph of Russian coulibiac of salmon, incorporating sturgeon marrow with egg and salmon, en brioche—a sort of czarist eggroll, this one pictured with generous slices off the loaf, latticed trimmings crusty brown. "Mine does not look as good as that, but it tastes better," he says. One of the books that have been with him since his days as a cook-apprentice is Gringoire and Saulnier's *Le Répertoire de la Cuisine,* which is a work analogous to the *World Bibliography of Bibliographies.* It is, in effect, a menu of menus—listing, for example, three hundred ways to do sole. Humbling even to someone with a continually changing repertory of six hundred dishes, it is a catalogue of everything that God's personal chef might be expected to know.

After St. Edward's, Otto went to hotel schools in Germany and Switzerland and worked for a time in Madrid. He says his father had brainwashed him into wanting to become a hotel manager, but after a brief education in accounting and reception, and even briefer experiences with electricians and plumbers, he could see that his interests were wholly in the kitchen. In the kitchen of the Euler, in Basel, he was systematically taught every aspect of cooking in a basic procedure that lasted a year. Given two kilos of butter, twenty-four egg yolks, and "a wire whisk the size of a ball bat," he attempted to create a pond of hollandaise. It curdled. Conversely, he was told to make eighty omelettes one at a time. In that way, he would learn. Augean jobs were deliberately assigned to him, tasks of almost unbearable tedium—immense bales of spinach to trim alone—in the expectation that he would muster a chef's endurance or quit. He went to school in Lausanne as well, and worked at Vittel, in the Vosges, and at the Ritz in Madrid, where he was used most often as a bartender because he was multilingual. In the restaurants there, he developed a sense that staff should dine well. "The help should always eat what the guests eat. If they don't, they'll steal off the plates. When I worked in Madrid, we were always stealing off the plates. What was meant to be four slices was two when it got to the table." Subsequently, he cooked at the Reina Cristina and also worked as a waiter at the Rock Hotel, in Gibraltar. He was fired from that job after the headwaiter, responding to a bell for ice, found him enjoying a drink with Margaret Leighton and Laurence Harvey. Otto may wash his aluminum foil, but he has a prodigal's sense of the highest, best uses of money. At a ship chandler's in Gibraltar, he would buy a couple of pounds of caviar—at thirty dollars a pound—and go off with friends and "just eat it."

His father was dying, and Otto was helping him with his last project, the development of a small restaurant overlooking the Bay of Gibraltar. After the funeral, in 1959, he went to England. He had received a call-up notice, and he cooked for a time at a Wimpy Bar in Oxford before reporting to Perth, in Scotland, for training with the Black Watch. He became a commissioned officer in counterintelligence, functioning mainly from Berlin. "I wouldn't have minded staying in the Army, to tell you the truth. I had a wonderful time in the Army. I liked the power of leadership. I found it intoxicating."

"Then why did you come out?"

(224)

"I didn't have an independent income."

Finca el Bornizo, his family's place in the mountains, had been remodelled as a small resort that could handle twenty guests. Otto cooked for them. In winter, the only vegetables available to him were chard, carrots, and celery. He had to serve chard, carrots, and celery twice a day and be extremely inventive. For a short time, he sold real estate on the east coast near Valencia, and there developed his knowledge of paella and his regard for parellada, for huge roasted scallions, for toasted-hazelnut sauce. His love of mussels dates from that experience, too—an affection that has been enriched in the United States by the high cost of clams. Returning to Andalusia, he met a Latvian named Gunars J. Grauds, who had spent enough time in America to imagine the vast fortune that might come to the developer of a chain of Spanish motels. His loss leader was the Rio Grande, at Kilometre 116 on the road from Algeciras to Málaga, and Otto cooked for him there. Otto thought that Gunars' wife bore an extremely close resemblance to Rita Hayworth—and that, specifically, is why he took the job. When Gunars' sister appeared in the country, Otto forgot Rita Hayworth.

Set into the wall above the fireplace in their American farmhouse-inn is an enamelled Spanish tile on which appears St. Paul's cryptic advice "*Mejor es casarse que abrasarse*" ("It is better to marry than to burn"). The fireplace is in the room where the customers sit and have their apéritifs while they wait for a message from the kitchen that it is time to go to table for dinner. I remember from the first moment I walked into it the compact and offhand rural European character and feeling of that room. With its nonchalant miscellany of detail, it was beyond the margins of formal design, but it was too pleasurable merely to have been flung together and too thematic not to imply a tale. There was a pair of bullfight prints—one called "La Lidia" and the other a depiction of a *desencajonamiento*—and protruding sharp-horned from the wall between these pictures was the head of a fighting bull. The animal had been raised on the *dehesa* of Pepe Alvarez and killed in the ring with a sword. Crossed Spanish swords had been hung above the fire. All around the room were wrought-iron Spanish sconces with small amber bulbs. There was a three-hundred-year-old map of the Danube, a two-hundred-year-old map of "Magna Britannia." There were hand-carved cabinets. There were tall wicker chairs, Queen Anne chairs, and Spanish brass-studded leather chairs in groups on a red tile floor. I eventually learned that many of these things had come down through the chef's family—to America from England via Spain. There were heavy red curtains on brass rods. The ceiling slanted upward in the mansard manner, with boards of tongue and groove. The silent paddle fan hung down between exposed checked beams. Staring back at the bull were the small glass eyes of a taxidermal fox—just its head and neck, on a plaque—and near it were photographs made in Alaska of dog foxes and vixens. A poster in one corner said "Extinct is forever" and presented line drawings of vanishing and vanished creatures—Cape lion (1860), quagga (1883), Labrador duck (1875), solenodon, snow leopard, northern kit fox.

Summoned to dinner, one moved through a dark drafty hall decorated with a cigarette machine, coat hooks, two water-colors of foxes by Ralph Thompson, and plaster-cast reproductions of six Manhattan gargoyles. The dining room, curtained red, suggested a small loft held up by hand-hewn posts and beams, and was lined with starburst sconces around heavy tables of Spanish walnut, with woven placemats and fresh flowers. The floor sloped remarkably enough to tip one's sober balance, and the direction in which it sloped was toward the kitchen. A glass of wine needed to be chocked or it would slide off a table and crash. At one end of the room was a Flemish oak chest seven feet tall with insets of ebony. On its top were an empty magnum of Château Margaux, a copper cask that had once held the chef's father's preferred sherries, and (a taxidermal masterpiece) a whole red fox. The great chest, like so much else in these rooms which had come down from forebears, helped produce a sense of generations, a deep familial atmosphere. Yet there was nothing, of course, nothing whatsoever, that had come from Latvia.

Anne's father, owner of ships, was also the captain of a ship, and when he was ordered to leave his country he stayed on his ship. Russians boarded the ship and took him away. The family heard later that he had died in a Soviet hospital. Anne says, though, that "people from Latvia who died in Russia did not die in hospitals." As a child, hidden in the countryside, she was told never to say her name to anyone. "Don't say your name or they'll come and get you." She was not to play with other children. If anyone were to ask if her family owned property, she must remember to say no. To this day, she recoils inwardly when someone asks her name. When she goes to town to shop, there are implications of poverty in her clothes. "It's because they'll come and get me," she says, and then adds, "I don't really believe that. Things are not quite that bad. I'm odd, but I'm not crazy. Nothing bad ever happened to me. I was just a normal refugee. But as a result of it all you know forever that everything that is peaceful and beautiful and runs on time isn't there. What is there—just lurking there—is disorder."

By November, 1944, the Germans had been driven into the

west of the country and the Russians were assuming control. It was a time for attempting to escape. Against a red night sky, an ambulance moved Anne, her mother, her grandmother, and others from one farm to another and to the coast. A dory took some twenty people to a fishing boat. Anne wore a green taffeta dress. Gold coins had been stitched into her underwear. The family had more to their name than a few gold coins—if they could get to it. They had funds in a bank in England, a ship or two in America. A German submarine surfaced in the night and approached the fishing boat. In their panic, the party heaved chests of silver into the Baltic. The Germans let them go. Off Gotland, a man went ashore in a barrel and arranged for the group to stay in the refugee center there. They spent Christmas in Gotland, and what Anne remembers primarily is the smell of ginger cookies. "All my life, I've been obsessed with food." After Christmas, they crossed to the Swedish mainland. They spent a year there, in "this fairyland of food, of open sandwiches and the smell of baking in the air." Age seven, she moved to England. Postwar England. "Watered-down oatmeal. Baked beans and spaghetti on toast. I threw up. There was one egg a week. I lived on Ovaltine." For all the drama of her escape from Latvia, the war did not make its deepest impression on her until it was over and she was in England, where she saw, for example, pictures of a bombed-out school, walls half gone, hallways in rubble, coatracks "with all the little coats hanging there." She lived in the Dominions Hotel looking out on Hyde Park, and watched from her window "English ladies walking their Pekinese" when she was not "chained to a little desk," learning English from a tutor. She could read and write Latvian. She was forced to learn English in one year. "I was taught English mercilessly. A child is not a person in England. 'You will learn English,' they said. 'You *will* learn English.' " She learned. She learned to stammer.

Like so many people with similar obstructions, she has a beautifully textured sense of language. She is not just at home in English. She is in vigorous charge of the language that stops her tongue. She will have difficulty trusting a recipe that says that something should be "thinly sliced" or "coarsely chopped" or that egg whites should be "stiffly beaten."

There was a family ship that had sought asylum in the West and had been in the service of the United States government when it was torpedoed and sunk by the Germans. Insurance money came out of it like bubbles. That money made it possible for Anne and her mother to move to America. She had two older brothers. In the war, Gunars had been in the Wehrmacht and Vilnis in the United States Army. Anne was educated in New York, Pennsylvania, and Switzerland, and grew to be a tall and arrestingly attractive woman. In 1956, she married a career officer in the American paratroops. Separating from him in the nineteen-sixties, she moved with her children to Spain. Gunars was there, building a sort of Andalusian Howard Johnson's at Kilometre 116 on the road from Algeciras to Málaga. She was a more than able cook, and as a gesture of affection soon after she arrived she began making Latvian borscht for her brother. The *gros bonnet* of the motel came walking into the kitchen. He grasped at once what was happening and began to offer what she recalls as "cryptic criticisms." He was English, and polished, and not unpleasantly arrogant, a Harrovian sort of Lady Margaret Boat Club chap with a lyrical sense of flavor, a man with a dulcet name and a generally analogous manner who wished he had been christened Otto. He said, "You're using beef and you should be using duck bones. That's not proper at all."

"We began arguing," Anne says, finishing the story. "We began arguing, and have been arguing ever since."

He, at the moment, is assembling the *mise en place* for his paella and she is making trifle—slices of génoise with fresh peaches, fresh sliced strawberries, sherry, blackberry brandy, apple wine, and custard cream. They came to live in the United States, she says, because she chose it as the country where her children should be educated.

Otto says, "I think that was a mistake."

He had motives of his own. He was prepared to leave Spain, in no small part because he felt that anything he might accomplish would be done with his father's reputation behind him. His affection for his father notwithstanding, he had no desire to become that sort of alloy. New Mexico seemed the obvious place to go, and they went there, and took an extensive look, and found it "ugly" and "not remotely Spanish—it would take five years to get to love it." So they settled in *Daily News* country and became professional partners, with the understanding that he is *el mandamás*—he who gives orders.

"I can cook every bit as well as he can, but I couldn't make so many meals under pressure," she says. "I can make elaborate seafood mousses and sauces, but I complete one item in four hours. His ability to juggle things in his head in the course of an evening is amazing, and that is the difference between a chef and a cook. He makes appetizers, entrées, more appetizers—overlapping in time—and he keeps it all in order for as many as fifty-five people, and brings it all off by himself. You have to have that before everything else. Being a good chef is functionally less aesthetic than mechanical. You either have the aesthetic or you don't. Then, you have to have the timing—the actual feeling of what needs more cooking and what needs less cooking, varying times for each type of fish, and so forth. If he is cooking eight different things, and each takes a different amount of time, he has all that, always, ordered in his head."

"Women do not make good chefs because you have to juggle too much in your head," Otto adds. Anne abruptly looks up from her work and regards him as if he had just sprinkled powdered cloves over a pike mousse. "A person who is easily rattled can't do it," he goes on. "You've got to be unflappable."

I nibble some smoked whiting and return my gaze from Otto to Anne.

"Careful," she tells him. "You're on dangerous ground."

To accommodate the paella, he lifts from a shelf a huge iron skillet, diameter of a manhole cover, and says, "Women are not cooks for the same reason they're not backhoe operators. Imagine a woman trying to lift this. On a Saturday night I lose five pounds."

"Careful!" Anne repeats. "You don't know what you're saying."

"Certainly I know what I'm saying. A third reason women aren't chefs is that kitchen workers, by and large, are Nazis. Super rednecks. They were taken out of school at fourteen. They have no ethical sense or standards. They're the sort of people who would not tolerate working for a woman."

"We are both extremely opinionated," Anne says.

Otto may be el mandamás, but their relationship is complicated by marriage, and, as he describes it, "in her role as wife she does not give unquestioning obedience." When their opinions collide, she has been known to pick up a wine glass, hold its stem between two fingers high above the tile floor, and open the fingers. She has picked up water glasses and sent them smashing into the kitchen wall. He once threw a shot glass that hit her toe. It has been my inadvertent role, in my visits over the past year, to suppress to some extent these customary events. Thus I have altered, in however minor a measure, the routines I have come to observe. As his usual day accelerates toward dinnertime, the chef's working rhythms become increasingly intense, increasingly kinetic, and finally all but automatic. His experience becomes his action. He just cruises, functioning by conditioned response. "You cook unconsciously," he says. "You know what you're going to do and you do it. When problems come along, your brain spits out the answer." With a working, eating journalist sitting on a stool not far from the stove—pecking facts, pecking bits of salmon cured in salt and saltpetre with dill and sour cream—the chef is more or less obliged to think and to answer questions, with the result that he stops to consider what he is doing, and this makes the doing all the more difficult, as if he were a surgeon on television tying knots with one hand. His volatility is inhibited, too. On days when I am here, I am some sort of weather front that holds back the buildup of his afternoon storm. At least that is what Anne tells me. And he nods, and grins. It's true. In the presence of the media he throws fewer bottles and glasses. The sin, stink, and brimstone go out of his language. I have not once seen him crack an egg over Anne's head, as he confesses to doing from time to time. Nor have I seen *her* heaving duck scraps on the floor. "Duck scraps" is their term for the garbage they save for the geese. In crescendo situations, she will dump duck scraps on the kitchen floor, then clean them up, feeling better. "Communication, relation-

(2 3 2)

ships, interaction, baloney," Anne says. "You only live with yourself. You are only in your own head. You *govern* your reactions to others. Throwing things, breaking things, you are keeping your own house in order."

Occasionally the storms of the kitchen roll on into the evening. Once, in a real line squall, Anne shouted into Otto's face: "Will . . . you . . . calm . . . down! The . . . customers . . . will . . . hear . . . you!"

Otto thundered back: "I don't give a bloody damn *what* the customers hear!"

The door to the kitchen swung open. "I heard that," said a customer, poking his head a short way into the room.

Anne's mother lived with them for a time. One day she was present when they were fighting in the kitchen. Anne told her to leave. She refused, saying, "I want to watch the divorce." Anne filled a pitcher with water and advised her mother that she would pour it all over her if she did not go to her room. Mother stayed put. Anne upended the pitcher.

There is nothing Anne and Otto will agree about more readily than that the tensions of the kitchen are mere blips in their routine—unavoidable, and possibly important. More than once they have ended up together on the kitchen floor, hugging their Tibetan mastiff. Take hold of his paw and he moans.

NAP TIME and, before retiring, Otto runs down to the nearest Grand Union for his last-minute shopping, saying, as the electric eyes recognize him, "This is a terrifically expensive store. You only buy the minimum." With a list in his hand, he buys lemons, strawberries, apples, walnuts, romaine, parmesan, chocolate, and chicory. As he hurries past the meat, his eye is stopped by twelve pounds of irresistible rib-eye beef, and he puts that in his cart, too. "It's on the menu for those wretched people who live in developments up the road," he says. "I'll make a bordelaise."

Otto the Neighbor contributes his share of covered dishes to the suppers of churches he does not attend, but he sees very little of the people who live around him, in part because he prefers it that way and in part because he works so much that he has no time to repair his rail fences let alone put his foot up and talk. Neighbors for the most part ignore him and he ignores them, except when young Almquist from up the road comes through on his snowmobile and Otto outshouts the thing for making shrapnel of his nap. After working nine hours or so, he needs serenity and rest to get himself ready for the payoff zone of his day. Often he doesn't sleep but just reads for two hours in bed—books somewhat more than periodicals, fiction more than fact. (He reads after work each night until he falls asleep.) His other diversions are few, and are analogously solo. When he skin-dives, he likes to go alone. He describes squash as "a good game—you can play it alone." But he seldom plays games. His two primary diversions are reading and restaurants. "He eats as well as he cooks," Anne says. "I love to eat out with him." Anyone would. Anyone who could recognize him on a city sidewalk—with his Savile Row look and his carelessly flying hair—would do well to drop all other plans and shadow him whither he goes. Say he happens to be walking along Madison Avenue in the general purlieu of Altman's. Stay back. Be polite. Respect his treasured privacy. Stay across the street if possible, but by all means keep him in sight. Stand by as he browses windows and goes into wet-suit stores. When he comes out, and crosses Thirty-fourth Street, make the light. If he goes into, say, Salta in Bocca, linger two minutes outside. Now go in, too. With luck, you will be seated at a table near him. Listen. Watch. At any rate, contrive to learn what he orders. He orders spiedino. You order spiedino—slivers of prosciutto cotto and mozzarella with capers and anchovy sauce in a casing of sautéed fragrant bread. He orders a bottle of Verdicchio. You order a bottle of Verdicchio. He orders paglia e fieno, a green-and-white straw-and-hay pasta in a silky butter-cream-and-parmesan sauce. Precisely what you wanted for lunch.

Otto, on such occasions, picks up ideas. He duplicates at home what he eats in town. Coming upon a dish he has never seen, he pulls it apart and looks it over. "Sometimes you say, 'Ah, I can duplicate that.' Other times you know you'd never be able to do it. There are flavors that are hard to decipher. It's easier, of course, to tell what's in something raw than in something cooked. I cribbed pork hocks from the Veau d'Or —you know, pieds de porc. Pieds de porc are usually in vinaigrette sauce, but these were slightly crisp on top and saturated with a gravy that made your lips stick together. It was a strong gravy. It had a good sharp mustardy taste—a very rich demi-glace sauce with a lot of good French mustard in it. We serve that every so often."

"What do you call it on your menu?"

"Braised pigs' knuckles."

At Kitcho, on Forty-sixth Street, he first ate soba—cold green Japanese buckwheat noodles dipped in sauce. He went home, got out his buckwheat, and made soba. Many years ago, after a visit to Charley O's, on Forty-eighth Street, he

Xeroxed their soused shrimp—cooking shrimp in pickling spice and then making a marinade of the sauce they were cooked in, adding onion, garlic, and sherry. He likes to go to The Siamese Garden, on Fifty-third Street, where he regards the clientele as "seedy State Department types—you half expect a hand grenade to come rolling your way." He once tried a shrimp roll there that created effects he found agreeable and novel, so he pulled the thing apart, went home, and made something almost identical, using Chinese cabbage, ginger, onion, Alaska midget shrimp, lemon grass, and fermented-fishhead sauce. Impressed by a chef at Peng's, on Forty-fourth Street, who turned chopped shrimp into spheres of flavor and air, Otto bought a basket of quahogs at the Fulton Market, took them home, ground them up, combined them with flour and beaten egg white, a touch of hot sauce, vinegar, onion powder, salt, and pepper, and dropped the mixture by the spoonful into hot olive oil. The spoonfuls bloomed. He serves them as "clam puffs." Otto's appreciation of Japanese food is enhanced in the American milieu, because in a general way he thinks that our Japanese restaurants are "straightforward—their materials are obviously fresh," and he cannot say as much for the commercial conveyance of some other national cuisines. To illustrate, he flips open *Chef* magazine and quickly finds an ad for Trufflettes. "The unique artificial truffle with real truffle flavor keeps indefinitely under refrigeration," says the text. "Perfect for decoration. Won't melt even if boiled. Perfect black inside and out." Tossing aside the magazine, Otto says, "That's what almost the whole food industry is—what can be got away with rather than what can be done. That's why we go to Japanese restaurants."

Otto is the wave of the past. This is the age of the microwave and the mass-produced entrée, and while he is working at his daily preparations the chefs of other inns are watching the clock in their morning classes in college. Under the stately shade of credit cards, freezer-bodied "reefer" trucks pull up at country inns with chicken Kiev, veal cordon bleu, crêpes à la reine, and rock-frozen "Cornish" hens stuffed with a mixture of wild rice and mushrooms soaked in cognac. Such deliveries, of course, are made in cities, too—clams Casino by the case, crab imperial, coquilles Saint-Jacques, crêpes de la mer, crêpes cannelloni, quiche Lorraine, filets of beef Wellington. Otto has often heard that the best maker of instant entrées is Idle Wild Farm, of Pomfret Center, Connecticut, a division of Idle Wild Foods, of Worcester, Massachusetts. Driving through northeastern Connecticut one time, I stopped in at Idle Wild Farm to watch its cooks at work. There was no identifying sign, no proclamation of the marvel of the presence of such an operation in the oak-and-maple countryside thirty miles west of Providence. Set back from a narrow tertiary road was a ranch house that had been converted to an office, and attached to it was a spread-out mustard-colored building—not Gulden's yellow, it should be said, but Dijon gold. The kitchen inside was vast and immaculate, windowless, brightly illuminated in close approximation to daylight. Cooks, assemblers—two hundred in all—were working there. Down the center of the room ran a broad conveyor belt on which completed products—chicken breasts cordon bleu, shrimp-lobster-and-crabmeat Newburg—moved slowly toward, and ultimately disappeared within, a horizontal stainless-steel cylinder that was aswirl in cold fog and resembled an Atlas missile. This was Cryotransfer 36 II. In the course of a day, it takes in some five to ten thousand appetizers and entrées, sprays them with liquid nitrogen at three hundred and twenty degrees below zero, and, seven minutes later, emits from its far end food so frozen it could scratch granite. A succession of living goldfish once went into Cryotransfer 36 II. They came out resembling jewelry. Only the big ones died. When a fishbowl filled with water restored them to room temperature, the little ones swam as before. Coming in from either side to the central conveyor were twenty-five tributary conveyors, each attended by a team in blue, preparing a different item. There was a manicotti conveyor, a chicken-breast-cordon-bleu conveyor, a beef-Wellington conveyor. The cooking teams were under instructions to stop and wash their hands every hour. The room had been disinfected with chlorine. There was food for hospitals and airlines as well as for couples in candlelight, and beside one of the tributary conveyors sat a young woman making omelettes. With an ice-cream scoop she reached into a large steel tub that contained thawed whole eggs that had been mixed with carrageenan to become a bright-yellow custard. The carrageenan would help the omelettes stand up. After lifting a scoopful of the egg mixture some twelve to fourteen inches above the moving conveyor belt, the young woman rolled her wrist. Splat, the yellow custard landed on the belt and spread out much like a flapjack, its dimensions programmed exactly by the height of the free fall, the density of the egg custard, and the volume of the scoop. Metronomically the cook repeated the process, and in rows of three the yellow discs moved away from her and into an infrared oven. She smiled. There is no cafeteria at Idle Wild Farm. The cooks eat lunch from vending machines, or they bring brown bags. Emerging from the oven, the omelettes were not permitted to go on to the central conveyor. Cryotransfer 36 II would shat-

(238)

ter them like glass. With other delicate products—crêpes cannelloni, crêpes de la mer—they went to a room where air was
gently circulating at twenty below zero.

Beside another tributary conveyor, a woman held a pair of
scissors in one hand while she weighed breasts of chicken with
the other. The breasts were boned, skinned, and glistening—
material clean enough and fresh enough to be eaten raw—and
they weighed more or less five ounces apiece. More or less was
not the way of this kitchen. The chicken in an Idle Wild Farm
chicken breast cordon bleu must weigh precisely five ounces.
The scissors took care of that. Add a little, snip a little, from
chicken to chicken. Add pre-portioned ham and cheese. There
was a separate cook for each addition, and an automatic
shower of egg batter, and a machine to coat the product with
breading. Another scale weighed the assembled breast—seven
ounces.

This was the farm where a retired promoter named Jacques
Makowsky crossed Cornish gamecocks with Plymouth Rock
chickens to develop what he decided to call the Rock Cornish
Game Hen. Makowsky is gone and so are the chickens. The
farm buys them from Maine to Delmarva and in upstate New
York. The old "kill line" is now the Formula Room, where
spices and sauces are mixed in tubs, but the senior entrée on
Idle Wild's list is still the Rock Cornish hen stuffed with wild
rice. The general manager now is Dieter H. Buehler, Cheva-
lier du Tastevin, who, in the thirteen years before he came to
Connecticut, fed a hundred and fifty million meals to the pas-
sengers of Trans World Airlines, as its dining director. His
degree is from Cornell. His memberships include the Beefeater
Club and the Chaîne des Rôtisseurs. Tall and polished, amiable, verbal, in a pin-striped shirt and a striped tie, he walked

through the kitchen like an executive seraph walking on a cloud, for he was knee-deep in drifting mists of nitrogen as he said that by 1982 the typical American family would be eating fifty per cent of its meals in restaurants of one type or another, and cooks were simply not going to exist to handle this demand. It was the mission of Idle Wild Farm to usher the world appropriately into the era of "the kitchenless kitchen."

I had told him something about Otto. "For how many years will that sort of person be around?" he said. "With changing life styles, who wants to spend his life in a kitchen? Who wants to work in a kitchen fifteen hours a day and seven days a week? We are filling a need. We are here to improve the quality of the existence of people like your friend, to help them not to have to work fifteen hours a day but still maintain a high standard in their operations, with food they are proud to serve."

After such advances in the art, the French could not be far behind. And, indeed, there is a new shop in Paris called the Comptoir Gourmand, where the celebrated chef Michel Guérard—who has earned three Michelin stars at his restaurant in Gascony—sells frozen entrées for six or eight dollars a brick: trout-with-mushrooms poached and frozen, fish terrine with watercress sauce, cryogenic calf's-tongue pot-au-feu.

"At Idle Wild Farm, we do things in small batches, with a lot of love and care and special handling," Buehler went on. "In the more modern restaurants, there are minimal kitchen facilities. Menus are limited. They run a broiler and they roast prime ribs, but the staff is basically unskilled. The staff is college kids. Don't ask a college kid to do a cordon bleu. We help the operator to better utilize his time, and with our appetizers and entrées there is never a disaster on a chef's bad night."

The big reefers that go out from Idle Wild Farm are headed for regional distributors, such as Berkshire Frosted Foods, in Pittsfield, Massachusetts; Pocono Produce, in Stroudsburg, Pennsylvania; Smith, Richardson & Conroy, in Miami; and A. Peltz & Sons, in New York City. From the distributors, restaurants order Kievs for their customers and lasagna to feed the help. One can buy Idle Wild products retail at Hammacher Schlemmer, on Fifty-seventh Street, thickly packed in dry ice. The instructions are abecedarian. Anyone who knows how to tell time can turn out veal cordon bleu or crêpes à la reine. There is no "slack." The product goes directly from the freezer to the oven—so many minutes at four hundred degrees. There are adjusted instructions for conventional ovens, convection ovens, microwave ovens, infrared ovens, deep fryers. "One thing that holds us apart from other people is that we can make anything at all on a custom-processed basis," Buehler said. "There's a fifty-case minimum—two thousand pieces. That's a production run."

We were joined by Jacques Noé, Idle Wild's executive chef, who spends most of his time working out new dishes. Noé was born in Asnières, one bend down the river from Paris, and he worked in Parisian restaurants and was trained in kitchens in France and Switzerland. He has been in America more than twenty years, mainly in Boston, working in restaurants and as a teacher in a cooking school. Handsome and blue-eyed, with a light-brown mustache, he spoke with the sort of suave French voice that, in English, seems to be emerging from a purring cat. That morning, as it happened, he had been working on a coulibiac of ocean bass, which was not a true coulibiac, he explained, because the recipe called for phyllo dough instead of a brioche. In fact, he was testing the recipe with scrod. He had a sample ready for submission to a customer. With few exceptions, he hastened to say, the dishes prepared at Idle Wild Farm do not deviate from the descriptions one can read of those dishes in *Larousse Gastronomique*. We stopped to observe a team assembling individual filets of beef Wellington. The puff pastry was in squares like handkerchiefs. In tall racks beside the conveyor were thick slices of filet mignon charred and appetizing as a result of a trip through the "automatic searer." Actually, they were raw within and frozen solid. Freezing the meat beforehand prevents blood from leaking out during the assembly process. In *Larousse* you would hardly expect to find something called Wellington, and indeed you do not, but, Noé explained, it is orthodox to accompany the meat either with some liver pâté or with duxelles ("a kind of mushroom hash"). "Liver pâté in this country is not very well accepted," he said, and therefore an ounce of duxelles was being placed on each filet. To absorb moisture during thaw, bread crumbs were sprinkled on the meat, too, and then it was turned over while the puff pastry was folded around it in a manner known as butcher wrap. So that steam would escape during cooking, it was one woman's job to poke a hole in the pastry with her pinky. Next came a wash of egg and milk in vital proportions, for the egg and milk would help the puff pastry become a rich and ceramic brown. If the proportions were awry, the crust could go black before the beef inside had thawed. "We save labor, save time in the kitchen," said the chef. "What we make for restaurants we send out of here raw and ready for people to put in the oven. We don't save a lot of time if we cook it for them." The act of removing a frozen entrée from a freezer and putting it into an oven is known as "restoration."

(242)

"Do you miss working in restaurants?" I asked him.

"Oh, yes. Yes."

"Why?"

"I miss the excitement. I don't miss the six days a week and the long hours and the holidays. They were not my holidays. But I miss . . . In a restaurant, you never know what to expect. I miss the pressure, the challenge. I love a big crisis."

When I described to Otto that visit in Connecticut, he said, "Those people are pandering to chefless kitchens. Eventually, American restaurants will buy almost all of their materials that way, and they will be limited to a set number of dishes. On the other hand, a frozen entrée, well made, gives people a hint of what could be possible. It's something like what Maurice Girodias, of the Olympia Press, said about pornography: 'It gets people to read who otherwise wouldn't read.' "

He paused. His thought shifted. "The chefs at the big frog ponds have more than enough pride not to use something they haven't had a hand in," he continued. "They want their signature on the dish. But they're not above compromise. They're not above using frozen turbot and frozen Dover sole. Dover sole comes into this country frozen, and anyone who says it isn't frozen is a liar. The frog ponds always have it." His expressions of apparent contempt for this ethnic group should not be misinterpreted as distaste for French cuisine. It is, rather, distaste for the manner in which French cuisine is sometimes derived in America. He is not shy to spend his minimum wages in the ne-plus-expense-account restaurants of the city, and when he is in one his nostrils filter out the scent of money. The prices don't ruin his dinner. Nor do prices create in him, as they seem to in some people, a favorable prejudice. Milieus, for the most part, don't interest him, either. His concentration is on the table. Waiters are contemptible until they prove that they are not. "The less the waiter can afford the meal, the more hostile he's going to be." Otto once tried to correct a captain's pronunciation of "Montrachet." He said, "Both 't's are silent."

The captain said, "No. One pronounces the first 't.' "

"Are you French-Canadian?" said Otto.

He regards restaurant owners generally as "a shabby lot." They overcook their country inns in order to collect fire insurance—that sort of shabbiness—and, in the city, "if Jackie Onassis is coming they bump you." He calls that "shameful," and says, "A reservation is a contract." He admires The Four Seasons—the splendiferous show aside—because he thinks The Four Seasons does things well "and in an enlightened, honest fashion." With his shoes off under the table there, he is clearly relaxed and happy, addressing his pike-and-salmon pâté, his sweetbreads-and-spinach, his asparagus maltaise. In Lutèce, he keeps his shoes on, out of respect, perhaps, for the proprietor-chef but scarcely for the elegance of the clientele and least of all for the funereal snobs with pencils and pads who carry the food from the kitchen. There is a man seated at the next table in bulging dungarees. Otto likes very much the mousseline de brochet et écrevisses. "It's hard work," he says. "Hard to keep hot. Hard to serve. The pike has to be boned. Then it's thrown in with eggs and cream and condiments and bread panada in a Robot Coupe—a commercial Cuisinart." He tastes from other plates on his table—a bit of pâté en croûte et terrines ("it's O.K.—just O.K."), and pèlerines à la méridionale ("Very good, not overcooked—*al dente*"). He is not awed by André Soltner, in the kitchen—at least not to the extent that he has been awed by Japanese. "The turbot is delicious, very fresh, perfectly cooked," he says of another of Soltner's entrées—turbot de Dieppe poché, hollandaise. "My guess is it was frozen,* which is the only kind you can buy, unless it is flown over. It's probably Holland turbot— three dollars a pound with the head on, and the head is a third of the fish. No doubt it swam past Dieppe. Turbot is easy to cook. You can't make much of a mistake." Lutèce's sole farcie Elzévir, on the other hand, does not seem to him very fresh. "It isn't pristine," he says. "It has a fishy taste. Oh, yes, it's Dover sole. It has the firm texture. You can do things with it you can't do with American flounder. Stuff it. Roll it. Make paupiettes. Dover sole is crunchy. It has a bite to it." He examines Lutèce's coquelet à la crème aux morilles. "It's juicy and good," he says. "It isn't squab. It's Cornish hen, you know—Frank Perdue. There has been a certain sacrifice here of quality for volume. Prices are higher. Rents are higher. I mean, the guy's a businessman." And what man of business would not have on his menu ris de veau financière? Sampling, Otto finds its pastry light and crisp but the sauce too reduced and not distinguished. "If you et it, your beard and your mustache would congeal together," he says to me. "The sweetbreads themselves are white. No fibre. Delicious. There should be truffles in the financière garnish. Financière means money, riches. We could do without the olives. A financière garnish has ground mushrooms, kidneys, cockscombs, and small chicken-forcemeat quenelles. Do you see any cockscombs? If you can make something better than the correct way—I mean, objectively better—then go ahead and do it. But be careful if you're a French restaurant in New York and are

---

* Otto guessed wrong.

charging a fortune. If you're supposed to have truffles or morels or cockscombs and you cheat—that's reprehensible. We'll let him off on the cockscombs, but he could have gone to a kosher butcher. His prices are not chicken feed. When he is asking two or three hundred dollars to give four people their dinner, he should go by the book. Right?"

THE CUSTOMERS ARE UNAWARE of Otto's bell. It rings in the kitchen when they step on a mat in the vestibule, and it produces in him a sense of dimming houselights, a conditioned adrenal twitch. Just by the way they trip the bell, they sometimes tell him who they are. The tennis star is on the list tonight (a long-footed, insistent ring) and the bridge-toll collector (brief and unassuming) and the couple who come here twice a week (a mixed staccato). "We'll have forty people— some nice people, quite a few decent people," Otto says. He reserves his compliments for less than half his clientele. "Many people who eat here seem to appreciate it," he continues. "They're thankful. And they are what has kept me going. Thirty per cent are excellent eaters. Ten per cent are fun to talk to. Five per cent know about food and really enjoy it. To them we can sell pretty much anything, because there is some trust. I've served cod-roe salad with roundels of roe. The people who tried it loved it, but in general it didn't go. It was just too unfamiliar. Remember, however, what P. Lorillard said: 'The quickest way to failure is to try to please everybody.' "

He is cooking a steak for Anne. She battles anemia—and prepares for her evenings—with thick shells of sirloin. He has trimmed off a slice or two for himself, raw, and another for

Mercedes, the cat. "All I've had to eat today is some tea and a bit of cucumber," he claims. "It's wonderful not to eat if you're in a hurry. It speeds you up." His way of not eating comes to roughly eight thousand calories a day. The steak is searing in a ribbed iron skillet. How can he tell, without cutting in, just when the colors are what he wants inside?

"Just by touching it," he says. "You can tell exactly." He quarters some scallops and splits the long legs of Alaskan crabs—last-minute preparations. "The customers are sometimes afraid to order steak because they think they should have something fancier," he goes on. "So I tart it up with bordelaise. Or béarnaise. That way, it's got a bit of sophistication. If they want it 'well done,' I'm pretty uncompromising. I just don't do it 'well done.' To cook it that way is such a shame."

The ovens are set at four hundred degrees, where they will stay unless he becomes unusually busy, in which case he needs four-fifty. Anne, dressed for business, wears a white-and-black polka-dot jacket over a floor-length black dress. Her hair is swept back and knotted in a bun. She says of her husband, "He is safe in here doing the work he loves, here in the purity of his little inner sanctum. To me it is a different operation. I'm up front with the people. I have to listen to urologists and bulldozer operators telling me things about food. After eleven years, your opinion of the public is low. I used to think anyone eating reasonably well-prepared food will know he's eating it, but I move through the dining room sometimes and it's depressing. For some people, we could just as well open a can. They are so used to artificial flavors that when you give them actual food they don't know what it is. They look at fresh whipped cream with suspicion."

Otto says, "The only kind they've seen has come out of an aerosol can. To show them what it actually is, I go into the dining room and whip the cream there."

People ask for ketchup, and they put it on fillet of sole Florentine, on scallops in garlic butter.

"They ask, 'What's fresh this evening?' or 'Are these good?'"

"If it wasn't good, we wouldn't serve it. They complain that veal chops are tough, because they've never had good, firm veal. They want to know if the wines are good. We chose them."

"A great many people think anyone who owns a restaurant is crooked. So their attitude is that we are dishonest and are trying to put something over on them and they have to be very swift in order to catch us. They've read somewhere that manta rays are cut up and sold as scallops. So they ask us if our scallops are ray."

A woman once asked for Chivas on the rocks. Anne went into the pantry and poured Chivas on the rocks, and when time came to ask about another, the woman said, "Not here."

"Why?"

"That was not Chivas."

"Oh, but it was. We don't do that sort of thing."

"A restaurant can't stay in business if it doesn't cheat."

"You get out of here!" Anne screamed. "You get out of here and you *never* come back!"

The woman ran for her car. "I was shaking," Anne recalls. "I shook for a couple of days. I have a rule of thumb. Never trust anyone who drives a Cadillac."

There is a printed menu—a short list of items that do not require long preparation, are always on hand, and "don't scare people," such as grilled rib-eye steak, grilled lamb kidneys and sausage, shrimp in ajillo sauce, and émincé of veal zurichois—sautéed veal strips with wine, cream, and scallions. There are three soups, home-smoked trout, snails, marinated mushrooms. "People want a menu in their hands," Otto says. "They want to eat boring things. They actually want to eat stodgy stuff. Marinated mushrooms, you know, are for nowhere people. I serve baked potatoes so often because I'm tired of people saying I'm too cheap to serve them. They bitch if you give them something else." He makes Swedish-fried potatoes, which are cut in ganglion strings and cooked in very hot fat, where they enmesh in a filament mass that comes up golden and crisp. Yet the nurdier clients want foil. They don't want golden-brown Brillo pads. "They want potatoes cooked in an oven in foil," Otto says. "If the potatoes are in foil, that's gourmet."

"When did you last serve a potato in aluminum foil?"

"Never."

"Why not?"

"They're not baked potatoes. They're steamed. Mind you, if the customers were uniformly objectionable there would be no joy at all. Many of our customers are open-minded people. We have served octopus and snails successfully since the day we started. There is, in fact, less Mickey Mouse about Americans than anyone else I've ever dealt with—French, German, Spanish, English. Basically, the Americans are more secure."

Tina, his waitress, arrives—trim, dark-haired, petite. She studies Otto's written list of extras and asks him to explain what she doesn't understand—as does Cam, his waiter, young and Filmland handsome, with a cadet's vertical spine, and bright-blond hair. Cam is in high school and is Anne's son.

The bell sounds, long in the foot, and sounds soon again, sporadic and sharp. Otto's working surfaces are as clean and prepared as athletic fields, surrounded by the *mise en place*. He takes his towel from his shoulder and nervously wipes them cleaner. He has regained his blue terry-cloth hat. It sits on the back of his head. His sleeves are rolled. Tina goes out with the list.

Half a dozen customers are waiting in the wicker chairs under the head of the fighting bull and the chart of the endangered species. Some are looking at the printed menu. Some have not picked it up. She greets the first group and reads the list. "These are tonight's extras," she says. "For appetizers:

RUSSIAN COULIBIAC OF SALMON

SMOKED SHAD-ROE PÂTÉ MOUSSE

QUENELLES OF VEAL AND SHRIMPS

STUFFED CLAMS

LEEKS VINAIGRETTE

MUSSELS À LA POULETTE

OCTOPUS SALAD.

And the entrees:

BREADED PORK LOIN CORIANDER

PAELLA À LA MARINERA

OSSO BUCCO

SAUTÉED SCALLOPS AL PESTO

SAUTÉED CHICKEN BREASTS WITH
   APPLE-CIDER SAUCE

BROILED FILLET OF GROUPER
   OURSINADE."

Someone in the party says, "Imagine all that out here in the sticks!"

The host, an old customer from the Upper West Side, says, "This is not the sticks. This is the apex of the civilized world."

Tina, in response to questions, explains "oursinade," "coulibiac," and "à la poulette," and reads out the list again. Otto has learned never to write "marjoram" on his extras list. People hear it as "margarine." Oleomarjoram. When he made sweetbreads with veal-forcemeat quenelles, various customers said the horsemeat was very good, and Otto has never used the word "forcemeat" on his extras list again.

Tina returns to the kitchen. "One clam, one coulibiac, one octopus, one mousse, two pork loins, one osso, one grouper," she says, presenting the order also in writing.

More footsteps on the bell. From my stool near the stove, I say to the chef, "Good luck."

He says, "I'll go into the chapel and pray."

He has dripped melted butter through a hole in the roof of the golden-brown coulibiac. Now he cuts an inch-thick slice. The interior is white and yellow and reddish-orange. "I'll make a lot of money out of this one," he says. "The materials, per serving, are not expensive. The more work you do, the more money you make. There's no profit in a shrimp cocktail."

Moving rapidly from worktable to stove to refrigerator, he shelves the coulibiac, shoves clams into an oven, and fetches a bowl of octopus. He eats some octopus. "Crunchy," he says. "That's how it should be. If you cook octopus until it's tender, all the buds come off. I've never made it this way before. This is based on a picadillo salad, which is as *andaluz* as gazpacho. You see? Here is a completely new dish, and they go along with it." He serves it on a bed of romaine with a light tartar sauce, which he made when he got up from his nap.

The stuffed clams are not ground up, as stuffed clams almost always are. Nor are they served in shells. They are whole, and collected in a ramekin, and submerged in a matrix consisting of onions, bread crumbs, garlic, marjoram, olive oil, butter, a drop of hot sauce, and some chopped curly lettuce, "which is very stringy, gives it consistency, puts some weave into it." He started cooking clams in this fashion as a way of using up old bread. His bread contains a thirteen-to-one ratio of unbleached flour to rye, and when it is old it is durable. It makes what he calls "good tough bread crumbs that hold up." When it is fresh, its aroma alone would melt butter. He does not make it every day because he and Anne eat so much of it they endanger their health. Other days, they give their customers commercial French bread they themselves scarcely touch.

He removes from the oven a ramekin of clams, gouges one out with a finger, and offers it to me. It is light and springy and aburst with flavor. "I think they're the best stuffed clams around," he says, sculpting over the cavity he has made in the dish and putting it back in the oven so the heat will erase his theft. With reference to the people who are waiting for the clams, he says to Tina, "They can go in now," and she goes out to shepherd them to their seats. He builds on a plate a buttery mound of shad-roe pâté mousse, garnishes it with a bit of cress, and puts it on a tray with the octopus, the salmon, and the clams, saying, "I think that people should eat at my convenience, not that I should cook at their convenience. *Pour savoir manger, il faut savoir attendre.* If people have any common sense, they will subordinate themselves to the cook's wishes. In any event, here, they go into the dining room when I am ready." The four appetizers on the tray are as attractive to the eye as they are to the nose and will be to the palate.

They are informal, a little offhand, arranged with enough artistry to imply care but not so much as to suggest that the care was squandered on cosmetics. A year or so ago, on the first evening I spent with Otto in his kitchen, he turned to me at this moment and said, "I want to make a point. There is something that happens to food when it goes from the kitchen to the dining room. It looks better in there, because it is in a dining room. A metamorphosis takes place."

The second order has come in, and the assembly of its appetizers will coincide with the timing of the first entrées. The bell rings. The pattern of the night compounds. Grouper fillet, in a skin of flour, is searing in a skillet. He flips it, flips it back. He turns things in skillets not once but many times. He is using a knife as a spatula. He is not contemptuous of spatulas. A knife is more often in his hand. He lacks time to switch instruments. He is a chef, not a dentist. He removes the skillet from the flame. He brushes the grouper with a purée of urchin roe, oil, and fish fumet, and he sets the pan in the oven.

"How long are you going to leave that in there?"

"I don't know. I have no idea. Until it's cooked. Five minutes probably. More or less."

Tina enters, saying, "Octopus, mussels, onion soup." Anne is behind her, saying, "The Siegels are ready when you are." She has a small silver frog in her hand, a gift from a customer. There are other presents as well—a bottle of Château Haut-Brion, a tin of caviar, an authentic Habana cigar. Otto rolls the cigar in Saran Wrap and stores it in the cooler. He will smoke anything. There are customers who have brought him joints. The presents tonight have such loft because his people have discovered what many of them feared—that Otto is selling the inn. In a short time, he and Anne will be gone. After

(2 5 3)

eleven years, they have sought and found release from the heating-oil company they have in effect been working for, the insurance company that has collected their rewards. Their buyer and successor is an experienced New York waiter.

Seven-fifteen, and before the chef now are five sets of orders. Seventeen appetizers. Seventeen entrées. The Vulcan seems to be functioning on its own. Below the high blue flames of six surface burners, there is a shutting and opening, opening and shutting, slamming percussion of doors, with sudden veils of escaping steam and puffs of brown cloud. "It's the pork loin. It's got to be a little burnt to taste right." Of some grouper in the other oven the reverse is true—in its fragile urchin purée. He pulls it out and looks it over, touches it, smells it. "Delicate," he says. "It almost smells like egg." The surface of the fish is mustard brown. He has opened the door a dozen times to watch that color develop. We sample the grouper before letting it go to the customer. The sea-urchin flavor seems to me to be the sort that is so modest you have to chase after it. Otto has his own vocabulary. With apparent pleasure, he compares the flavor to iodine.

He continuously touches and tastes the food. He pinches it. He taps it. He licks and nibbles it. He tastes every part of every dish as he puts it together and the whole when it is done. He wipes and wipes again the front edge of the stove, wipes his block surfaces, washes his hands. He moves about his kitchen with athletic stamina. When the pressure is highest, he runs. "It's like having a hobby that pays you," he says. "I actually enjoy this, thank God."

"Two quenelles, one seviche, conch chowder, two paellas, two ossos."

A quarter to eight, and the china is rattling. Pot lids are

spinning on the floor. The oven is up to four-fifty. Otto is moving so fast his work has become a collage of itself, as—all in a minute—he pours out lime juice, eats a handful of seviche, tosses veal into a skillet, and hunts through wild mushrooms for deposits of grit. Chaos cannot get at him in the depths of composition. Those are finished compositions going out through the door—the mottled brown envelopes of pork loin, the drape-fold saucing of the poached quenelles. He is not only cooking. He works on all the levels of the kitchen. He sections the bread. He cuts and apportions desserts. He slices open the baked potatoes. "See. They are nice and floury," he says. "Conservatives order baked potatoes. Liberals ask for rice." He smacks his forehead. "Oh, Christ Almighty, I forgot the rice." Moving to correct one error, he makes another. He nicks a mocha meringue. Anne, passing through, stops to help. She shaves chocolate above the meringue, and the dark concealing snow drifts over the field of beige. "The most important thing to learn is how to rescue," she says.

"The most important thing to learn is to go slowly," says Otto. "There is a wonderful Spanish expression: 'Dress slowly. We're in a hurry.' If you remember that, you slow up, and you make less mistakes."

"Do you serve mistakes?"

"I'm not going to eat my errors, not if they taste good. An error that tastes good is a 'classic mistake.' A 'classic mistake' is a discovery. That's how I learned to put sapsago cheese into al-pesto sauce. I put it in by mistake." Sapsago is a green Swiss that smells like a farm. It is good for grating, "for flavoring anything," he says. "Quiche. Vegetable soup."

"Where do you get it?"

"Macy's."

Unless someone specifically asks for vegetables, he serves none with entrées. "I generally have, if nothing else, carrots, celery, Brussels sprouts, and artichoke hearts around, and I often have ratatouille as an appetizer, but I'm damned if I'm going to give away vegetables when people just leave them on the table. If they want vegetables, all they have to do is order them."

Someone asks for sour cream, and, as it happens, there is none in the house. Otto somehow feels he should have it, and so, for a single customer, he takes time to pour fresh thick cream into a bowl and whip it with a whisk, adding salt and vinegar. As the mixture stiffens, it takes on with remarkable exactness the texture of sour cream. He cuts up a scallion, mixes it in, and serves this patrician substitute to the unsuspecting stranger.

He licks his thumbs. "Wild mushrooms give veal sauce a meaty flavor," he says, finishing an osso bucco. He walks to the sink with an iron skillet, eating the remainder of the sauce. The predominant color of the osso bucco is cordovan, and it is pearled with shining marrow.

He cuts raw pork and eats some, too. He tosses a piece to Mercedes. "This cat eats more in a day than the average Indian eats in a year," he says. The cat nonetheless is skinny and sour. Otto himself eats so much meat that he occasionally turns vegetarian to give himself a cure. He doesn't work in June, and just by taking it easy he loses thirty pounds.

Otto's broiler has at times failed him, and on these occasions, to help finish certain dishes, he has used a propane torch. Crossing the ocean long ago on the S.S. Constitution, he saw baked Alaska beautifully browned, and he wondered how that was done. He went to the galley, where a chef was

(2 5 6)

"baking" the meringue by playing over its surface the flame of a portable torch. "That was my first acquaintance with American know-how, which seems to be declining," he remarks, tossing pork-cutlet gravy in a big iron skillet with such vigor that it spills into a surface burner and flames leap two feet high. "Ever see a gas-stove repairman? They have no eyebrows."

Eight-twenty-five, and six are waiting, in the thirteenth hour of his working day. He puts herb butter into godets with mussels, and, arranging two plates of scallops al pesto, eats a generous fraction of the scallops. "O.K. O.K. Small and springy."

Anne enters. "Mr. Almquist says we have been good neighbors and wants us to know he will miss us," she tells him.

"I wish I could return the compliment," says Otto.

He bites one end of a huge boiled leek. Its center shoots out the other end. He drops a little saffron in the blender, adds water, and lets the mixture churn for many minutes as the color changes, grows, from flax to jonquil to canary to high lemon chrome. He mixes it with chicken stock and undercooked rice. A purist would do a whole paella at once, but Otto thinks rice comes up too crunchy that way and the *puristas* can go back to La Costa Brava. In a big iron skillet in sizzling oil, he half cooks scallops, mussels, shrimps, and floured grouper. In a pot with stock, he has tomatoes, bell peppers, peas, and bites of crab. Bringing the pot to a boil, he empties it into the skillet, and puts the skillet in the oven. Five minutes go by. "I forgot garlic!" he cries out, and rapidly dices a dozen fresh buds that throw a long cast through the room. "This you can do something about," he says, opening the oven and tossing in the garlic. "What's awful is when you forget to put sugar in the caramel custard." The chef is not inherently impressed with paellas, retaining in his prejudice an Andalusian coolness to this triumph of Valencian peasants. So he overcompensates. Arranging the mussels like symmetrical black petals against a field that is pink, red, yellow, and orange, he achieves a paella that is beautiful to see. "Kitchens in New York are so small they could not possibly cook to order many things on a busy night," he remarks, eating what is left of the rice in the pan.

Anne comes in again. "The Hubers are ready when you are," she says, also informing him that to keep herself going she will need some mashed potatoes. He mashes her potatoes. She takes away with her as well a ball of butter that is equal in volume to an Acushnet Titleist. Otto glances significantly at the butter. Retreating toward the pantry, she says over her shoulder, "I weigh less than two hundred pounds."

Searing grouper, he brushes it with urchin roe while ambidextrously reaching into an adjacent skillet to turn over a steak without the help of a utensil. He presses the steak with his fingers. He kicks the mastiff out of the kitchen. A third iron skillet stands empty over high blue flame. To see where the heat is, he places the palm of his hand flat on the bottom of the pan. He is in no great hurry to pull the hand away. "You never know where the hot areas are," he says. "They're never in the same place. They move around the pan." After melting butter, he sets a floured breast of chicken in the hot part of the pan.

Tina requests rice, which is being finished in the broiler. Otto reaches in and rests a hand on the rice. He says it is almost ready. Some years ago, he had a waitress who regularly wore miniskirts. He would ask her to stand on high stools to reach for out-of-the-way spice. "It's O.K. now," he tells Tina. "Take the Hubers in."

Tripping over a pan that he left on the floor, he spills a large quantity of al-pesto sauce (butter, basil, olive oil, parmesan, sapsago, and hazelnuts), and as he cleans it up he synopsizes aloud the plot of a novel in which a pet dog becomes a woman's lover and later causes an accident fatal to her husband.

Tina comes back to the kitchen, saying, "The Hubers would like to take a minute longer."

Otto gives this some thought, and he consents.

OTTO IS ASLEEP NOW. He drank some beer and made his bows and smoked his gift cigar, and then he took his leave, soon after work. With many of his customers, his appearance at their table at the end of their meal has become routine to the point of obligation. He seems not to mind. In all other ways he may avoid the light, but in these moments he seeks—and he says it in so many words—evidence that he has made people happy. Those customers he looks upon with favor he thinks of also as friends, and he will even invite them to "come around on Sunday" for lunch when the restaurant is dark. He is confident that he can go almost anywhere in the region and the sort of business he wants will follow. "And why wouldn't it?" he says. "All my friends will know where I am." He seems equally secure in his chosen anonymity, feeling certain that— far from being likely to betray him—his friends will see themselves as his cabal.

He accepted the compliments of the tennis star tonight

(smoked shad-roe pâté mousse, paella à la marinera). The tennis star brought him poinsettias. In 1973, the tennis star bet Otto a bottle of Dom Pérignon that Bobby Riggs would "beat the ass off that broad." When Billie Jean King was gelding Riggs, she was winning champagne for Otto. He talked Roman coins tonight with a man who comes regularly from a town seventy miles to the west (quenelles of veal and shrimps, breaded pork loin coriander). Otto advised him to read Robert Graves' translation of Suetonius. The customer had the book in his car. There was an Austrian—a stranger to the inn—who fought with the British at Tobruk (Russian coulibiac of salmon, osso bucco). Grateful for his praise, Otto joked with him in German.

Now the inn is quiet, Anne up and working while her family sleeps. She says she believes in guardian angels. She says her good luck is so pervasive that she pulls into gas stations and has flat tires there. She had luck today. When the sea urchins came, she had made enough trifle and baked enough cake to cover her desserts. She works on urchins now—cracking, scooping, separating out the roe. The column of gold is rising in the jar. She says of their move to another place that they are not going far, not far from New York, no telling where. "He has to feel comfortable. I trust in his paranoia to tell us where to go. What is certain is that we'll be between nowhere and no place, and things will be the same. For all those people who want flames and white gloves, there will be no flames or white gloves. What we have is simple food. Simple food if it is good is great. If you understand that, you understand him."

Her hair has come out of its knot, and a long strand crosses one eye. She puts down her work, dries her hands, and runs them backward from her temples. She speaks on, slowly. "You may have grasped this, but I don't know him very well. If you're close to a screen you can't see through it. He doesn't know me, either. We're just together. People are unknowable. They show you what they want you to see. He is a very honest person. Basically. In his bones. And that is what the food is all about. He is so good with flavor because he looks for arrows to point to the essence of the material. His tastes are very fresh and bouncy. He has honor, idealism, a lack of guile. I don't know how he puts them together. I don't know his likes and dislikes. I can't even buy him a birthday present. He has intelligence. He has education. He has character. He has integrity. He applies all these to this manual task. His hands follow what he is."